URI GELLER'S
life
SIGNS

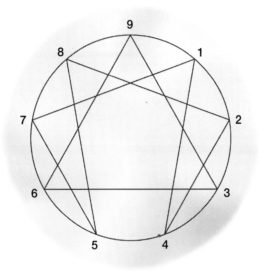

URI GELLER'S
life
SIGNS

Transform Your Life By Understanding Your Personality Type

Reader's
Digest

The Reader's Digest Association, Inc.
Pleasantville, New York • Montreal

First published in Great Britain in 2002 by Marshall Editions Ltd.
Copyright © 2002 Marshall Editions Developments Limited

MARSHALL EDITIONS STAFF
Project Editor   Theresa Lane Bebbington
Editor   Nicola Munro
Managing Art Editor   Helen Spencer
Art Editors   Jane Tetzlaff
Design Assistant   Ella Butler
Picture Editor   Sarah Stewart-Richardson
Production   Nikki Ingram
Editorial Coordinator   Gillian Thompson
Contributor   Christopher Stevens

READER'S DIGEST PROJECT STAFF
Project Editor   Nancy Shuker
Project Designer   Judith Carmel

READER'S DIGEST ILLUSTRATED REFERENCE BOOKS
Editor-in-Chief   Christopher Cavanaugh
Executive Editor, Trade Publishing   Dolores York
Senior Design Director, Trade   Elizabeth Tunnicliffe
Director, Trade Publishing   Christopher T. Reggio

Library of Congress Cataloging-in-Publication Data
Geller, Uri, 1946-
  Uri Geller's life signs : transform your life by understanding
your personality type / [as told to] Christopher Stevens.
    p. cm.
  Includes index.
  ISBN 0-7621-0353-1
  1. Parapsychology. 2. Personality. I. Title: Life signs. II. Stevens,
  Christopher. III Title

BF1031 .G355 2002
158.1--dc21
                    2001048634

Address any comments about URI GELLER'S LIFE SIGNS to:
        The Reader's Digest Association, Inc.
        Adult Trade Publishing
        Reader's Digest Road
        Pleasantville, NY 10570-7000

Printed and bound in Portugal by Printer Portuguesa
Originated in Singapore by Master Image

1 3 5 7 9 10 8 6 4 2

A Reader's Digest Book
Conceived, edited, and designed by
Marshall Editions Ltd
74 Shepherd's Bush Green,
London W12 8QE

Uri dedicates this book to the wholehearted efforts of each and every person around the globe to bring peace to our troubled Earth. With abundant healing thoughts and prayers for the children and adults of every continent, may we, at long last, achieve unity and harmony forever more.

The information in this book should not be substituted for, or used to alter, medical therapy without your doctor's advice. For a specific health problem, consult your physician for guidance.

If you would like to find out more about Uri Geller, email
urigeller@compuserve.com

and if you are interested in his life and work visit his website
www.urigeller.com

Front cover photographs:
left: Uri Geller, center & right: Digital Vision

Back cover photographs:
clockwise from bottom left: 1, 2 & 3: Digital Vision,
4: Randy Faris/CORBIS, 5 & 6: Digital Vision,
7: William James Warren/CORBIS, 8 & 9: Digital Vision

Back flap cover photographs:
Portrait of Uri Geller provided by Carlton TV

Foreword

I met Uri Geller a few years ago and was completely taken by his charming personality and also by his intuition and creativity and his heightened sense of awareness. Uri's extraordinary abilities are the expressions of a very sensitive soul who has, through the evolution of his consciousness, developed extraordinary cognitive and perceptual abilities.

Many times what we call the paranormal is the normal to a person in an expanded state of consciousness. As a physician, I was brought up to believe in a scientific world view, which says that everything has an explanation. When we do not understand the explanation of a phenomenon, we refer to it as a miracle. When we do understand it, we refer to it as science. I have always intuitively understood that, although each of us has an individual personality and that no two souls are alike any more than two faces or two fingerprints are alike, it is possible to have a scientific understanding of how and why people behave the way they do.

Uri Geller's Life Signs is a very useful theoretical framework developed from an ancient system that allows us to understand all the human traits of personality. Uri explains how this knowledge can be used to understand our basic archetypes and, from there, he proceeds to give extraordinarily useful information on self-development, relationships, coping with stress, improving self-confidence, enhancing performance, and becoming more fulfilled and empowered.

I hope you will read this book but, more important, that you will incorporate this knowledge into your life so that you too can create magic in your life as Uri has so successfully done.

Deepak Chopra
Author of *Grow Younger, Live Longer*

Contents

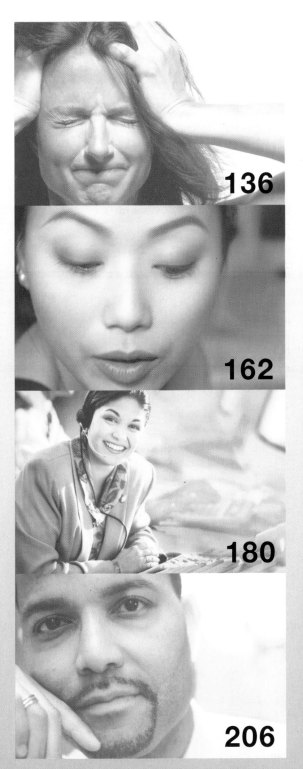

136

162

180

206

Introduction

I became aware of a system that defined nine basic personality types when I began writing novels in earnest, about five years ago. As I probed the motives of my characters, I realized that most human drama occurs because the protagonists cannot understand each other.

The protagonists speak the same language and may live closely with one another for years, yet their perceptions of themselves, their relationships, and the world may be radically different. In real life, many people are ignorant of how different the viewpoints of others can be. It is much more than an issue of self-interest—it is something that begins at the core and affects every particle of mind, body, and spirit.

As I was developing the central characters in my novel *Ella,* I wanted to create a family similar to the one I remembered from my own childhood. This included a dominant father, a protective mother, and an adolescent puzzled by psychic powers that science could not explain and that no one—neither friends, nor family, nor teachers—trusted.

I captured the atmosphere of my childhood, but the characters seemed to walk into my mind out of another life. Ella herself was everything I was not—timid, withdrawn, introspective, and fearful, without the self-confidence to articulate what was in her heart. Was this really the child at the center of my being? I am outgoing, often brash, brimming with chutzpah, always the extrovert, never short of words. So who was Ella? This question led me to do some research into personalities.

I began reading about George Gurdjieff, the mystic who at the turn of the 20th century wandered the East in search of ancient wisdom. Around the time of World War I, he began teaching about the enneagram, a system based on nine points around a wheel, intersected by lines, which formed a star with an open base. All the characters described by the enneagram were instantly recognizable, yet surely, I thought, there were more than nine types of personality?

In fact, as I soon realized, there were infinite possibilities for individual personalities, but all could be grouped into those nine categories. The categories were like spectrums that ranged from the best aspects of human behavior to the worst.

I continued to read all I could about enneagrams but was touched by growing doubts. Several of the writers seemed to be hemmed in by rules they had established themselves—that all personality types have a "wing," a secondary personality that sits next to their primary personality on the wheel, and that every type has one way of improving and one way of falling apart. This seemed counter to everything I had seen and felt.

I also sensed that no one had yet begun to map the full range of every spectrum. I, myself, have not succeeded in doing that either—to study your fellow man is a lifetime's work and much more than that—but I believe I have arrived at a more complete map of common traits than has ever been achieved before.

This unique system had no name. The word enneagram really refers to a mystic pattern, not the nine personality types. As a long-time student of astrology, or star signs, I had noticed that the parallels with this system were many—so I have chosen to name my system "Life Signs."

My purpose in studying the Life Signs is not only to help you understand and fulfill your own potential, but also to help you realize how the patterns of your character connect you to other types of personalities and to empower you to uncover new facets to your own mind and soul. I hope this book will be your guide to a more positive way of life.

Much energy,

CHAPTER ONE

Introducing the Life Signs

Life is a journey of discovery within ourselves; as we grow and develop, we gain new insight into our personalities. The questionnaire in this section is designed to boost your self-knowledge. When you have completed it, you will know which of the nine Life Signs is yours. Understanding your Life Sign will provide you with powerful tools for discovering your own essential personality type.

History of the Life Signs

The Life Signs have been developed from the ancient wisdom of the enneagram, which encapsulates all human personality traits.

The nine Muses play music in this 16th-century painting by Jacopo Tintoretto.

From the heart

For a newcomer, the history of the Life Signs could begin now. This is how I felt when I was introduced to the enneagram and began to shape it into a tool that could help me to understand myself and others around me. You don't need to know the ancient connections to begin working with the unique tools provided by Life Signs.

The enneagram is depicted by a nine-pointed star enclosed in a circle (see pp. 68–69); each point represents a personality. Where this wisdom was first discovered, no one really knows. The name suggests it could predate the Roman Empire, and some scholars believe it was known by civilizations 10,000 years ago, long before the development of writing. The nine personalities are symbolic in many civilizations.

Links with the Kaballah

Many of the insights you will discover in this book were woven into the secret lore of Jewish mystics, the writings called the Kaballah. These were begun shortly after the dawn of Christianity and reached their peak in Provence and northern Spain during the 12th and 13th centuries.

At the heart of the Kaballah are the sephiroth, the forms of intelligence that flow from God. The first sephiroth is a crown, from which come nine human virtues: wisdom, intellect, love, justice, beauty, firmness, splendor, foundation, and kingdom. These nine virtues correspond to the nine Life Signs: the Magician possesses wisdom; the Intellectual has a fine mind; the Mother Hen epitomizes love; the Reformer loves justice; the Artist values beauty; the Busy Bee has firmness of purpose; the Actor possesses splendor; the Believer puts life on the best foundation; and the Boss creates a kingdom.

The Greek and Egyptian connections

Enneagram is a word created from two Greek words: *ennea,* meaning nine, and *gram,* meaning symbol. In Greek mythology the nine daughters of Zeus and Mnemosyne made up an ennead, called the Muses. Calliope was the goddess of epic poetry; Clio, the goddess of history; Erato, the goddess of love poetry; Euterpe, the goddess of lyric poetry and flute music; Melpomene, the goddess of tragedy; Polyhymnia, the goddess of songs; Terpischore, the goddess of dance; Thalia, the goddess of comedy and pastoral poetry; and Urania, the goddess of astronomy.

The nine chief gods of Ancient Egypt were called the Great Ennead: Atum was the creator, Shu the god of air, and his twin sister Tefnut the goddess of moisture; their children were Geb, the masculine earth and Nut, the feminine sky. Osiris was god of the dead and Isis his wife, goddess of love; her sister Nephthys brought Osiris back to life and opposed Seth, the god of war.

The Islamic and Christian background

Islamic scholars speak of the connections between the enneagram and the 1,400-year-old teachings of the Sufi Muslims. The Christian theologian Saint Thomas Aquinas, writing in the 13th century, believed that nine orders of Angels had perfect knowledge of their own natures: Guardian Angels gave guidance to humans; Archangels guided leaders; Principalities guided nations; Powers bestowed judgment; Virtues executed commands; Dominations offered leadership; Thrones supported the natural order; Cherubim were God's living chariot; and Seraphim purified humans with fire.

Each of these civilizations followed beliefs that developed around nine distinct personalities or traits. Like human nature itself, the history of the Life Signs is steeped in mysteries that, when unfolded, simply reveal deeper mysteries.

For your information

Recent history

The rediscovery of the enneagram is attributed to Georgei Ivanovitch Gurdjieff, the mystic who at the end of the 19th century searched Tibet, India, and Arabia for esoteric truths. His disciple, the Russian journalist Peter Demianovitch Ouspensky, published Gurdjieff's teachings. Ouspensky believed Gurdjieff had uncovered an oral tradition that unlocked the nine essential personality types.

By 1956 the Bolivian Oscar Ichazo, founder of the Arica Institute, made his contribution toward the enneagram by forming a theory of psychoanalysis that centered on "ego fixations," or personality types. It was developed by his student Claudio Naranjo, a Chilean psychologist, who worked with the Jesuit priest Robert Ochs.

It was as a Jesuit seminarian in Toronto that Don Richard Riso first encountered the enneagram in 1973. Seeing the tradition in a Western light and knowing the works of Freud and Jung, he formulated the oral wisdom into written questionnaires, which was the beginning of the use of enneagrams in personality tests.

Nine Signs, three groups

All people are different. Of the 6 billion souls who are living on this planet, each one has an individual personality. No two personalities are alike, any more than any two faces are alike.

There are many personalities, but only a handful of basic types, as easily identified as basic physical traits such as brown eyes, blue eyes, or green eyes. There are dominant and disciplined personalities, artistic and thoughtful personalities, demonstrative and caring personalities.

The Life Signs system is formed on nine types of personality. This broad approach hides a complex delineation of the subtle differences between us. These nine types are grouped into three categories: Feelers, Thinkers, and Doers. Each group consists of three types of Life Signs, which have similar traits.

From the heart

Each sign is often referred to by its number on the Life Signs wheel. The Reformer, for example, is type One. This does not imply that a One is better than a Two or a Six or a Nine. Each of the types is equal. Think of them as nine spokes on the wheel of a cart, with the wheel turning around. No particular spoke, or number, can be said to be at the top or the bottom of the wheel, and all of them are connected equally to the hub and to the rim.

The alliances between types can be charted on the enneagram, or Life Signs wheel (see pp.68–69), but first you should be introduced to the nine Life Signs.

The Feelers

Reformers, Magicians, and Mother Hens belong in the Feelers group. They have in common issues related to the heart; having a sense of identity and self-esteem is vital to them.

The Reformer, which is type One on the Life Signs wheel, likes to do things the right way. If the world does things the

The Reformer

For your information

The three groups

The nine Life Signs are divided into three groups: Feelers, Thinkers, and Doers. The symbols below represent the three groups.

 ● Reformers, Mother Hens, and Magicians are the Feelers. They act on inner certainties, which can be thought out, but they are equally powerful even when they remain in the subconscious.

 ● Actors, Artists, and Intellectuals are the Thinkers. They work things out, whether or not they act on their knowledge.

● Believers, Busy Bees, and Bosses are the Doers. They may have reasons for what they do, but they will do something even if there is no rationale for doing it.

wrong way, he aims to put them right. Many successful, honest politicians are dynamic Reformers—so too are some murderous revolutionaries. The Reformer has a gift for detail, a grasp of the way little things influence the great. He is opinionated, judgmental, and quick to anger if rules are broken. Critical of himself even more than of others, the Reformer strives to be at his best and sets high standards. He has an instinctive sense of order and neatness, but can be indecisive when the best ways of achieving his goals are not plain to him.

The Mother Hen, type Two on the Life Signs wheel, focuses on the small part of the world that

The Mother Hen

she can nurture and protect and takes little notice of anything else. The Mother Hen is only interested in her domain and talks endlessly of it. Her life is devoted to caring, with outstanding generosity, and her first thoughts are for those who rely on her. The Mother Hen knows she is important because others would suffer without her. She never holds back from expressing her emotions. If her unconditional love is accepted, the Mother Hen can be a wonderful, radiant person, adored for her big heart. However, if those she loves are ungrateful, then she can become possessive, overprotective, meddling, and resentful.

The Magician, type Nine, needs harmony and peace. The confrontation that energizes the types on either side of the Magician on the Life Signs wheel—the Boss and the Reformer—can be distressing to him. He brings people together and heals wounds. The Magician is a healer, using conventional medicine or the power of his personality. He is often a "middle child," accustomed to finding a compromise between warring siblings and parents. The Magician can be too fond of a quiet life, lapsing into laziness and going along with anything instead of making a scene.

The Magician

The Thinkers

Actors, Artists, and Intellectuals make up the Thinkers group. The ability—or inability—to form a sense of self is of main importance to this group. These Life Signs struggle to make decisions about their future.

The Actor, type Three, wants your attention and respect. This fuels her ambition and drive, not to mention ego. Often an only child, the Actor's self-esteem is high, and success comes easily. The Actor is sensitive to how others perceive her. Her image is polished with care, but it is not superficial. The Actor believes herself to be the way others see her, and this is self-fulfilling. If the world regards her as a star, she is a star; if her children believe she is devoted, she is the most loving parent. The Actor motivates others—everyone admires success.

The Actor

The Artist, type Four, has powerful emotions. These are heightened by an early inability to articulate strong feelings, either because he cannot find the words or nobody is listening. The Artist's struggle is to express his emotions throughout his life. If he can transform them into something that others understand—words, pictures, music—he will be fulfilled. Others will hail the Artist's talent, but the greatest satisfaction will be personal, because he has said what he has wanted to say. If an outlet or an audience cannot be found, the Artist retreats into himself, sometimes dwelling on the formless emotions or denying them.

The Artist

The Intellectual, type Five, thinks all the time. Sometimes her actions are overwhelmed by her thoughts and she forgets what she is doing. Sometimes the Intellectual stops doing something altogether—she just works out what she would do. She has scintillating or furious conversations in her head, although the

The Intellectual

world does not often get to hear them. She prefers her own company and sometimes finds it difficult to express her thoughts because there are so many things to say. This makes relationships difficult, but the Intellectual is willing to sacrifice anything, even love and friendships, if her thoughts are important enough. After all, it is the thinkers and the scientists who created the modern world.

The Doers

The Believers, Busy Bees, and Bosses are members of the Doers group. How they relate to their own instinctual energy is at the root of this group.

The Believer, type Six, has a deep need to belong within society. He is attracted to ideas, companies, and people and will be fully committed to them. He shoulders his responsibilities gladly and urges others to follow his example. Never afraid to obey, he is also capable of good leadership. If the Believer's ideal is deserving of his energy, he is devoted and reliable, an unshakable team player and a faithful partner. If he is betrayed, his world falls apart and he will defend himself by being unfriendly to outsiders. This hostility may show itself as prejudice, but it is a reaction to insecurity. The Believer is courageous, but he dislikes acting on impulse. He will stick to the rules and covet respect and status.

The Busy Bee, type Seven, is unstoppable. She buzzes with energy, enthusiasm, and excitement. The Busy Bee cannot say no—she will continue to tackle new projects, make fresh promises, and set new goals until she is out of control. This can set up a manic-depressive pattern, where the Busy Bee is trying to do too much or is incapable of doing anything at all. People are often quick to tell her where she is going wrong. If the Busy Bee can govern herself, delegating instead of trying to control every stage, and finishing one project before throwing

The Busy Bee

herself into the next, there is no limit to what she can achieve.

The Boss, type Eight, grasps a situation and takes control. He is not given to introspection or searching his soul. He does what needs to be done and recognizes that little can be achieved without the cooperation of others—and he instinctively knows how to cajole and command. The Boss's attitude is positive, certain that what must be done will be done if all is properly organized. He is indifferent to the dislike or affection of most people around him—what anyone thinks of him privately is scarcely of importance. However, he does rely heavily on the love and support of a few close relationships. If he is well loved, he can achieve more through his inspirational character than most others.

The Believer

The Boss

From the heart

When I first learned about the nine Life Signs, I was fascinated by the concept and enthusiastically tried to label everyone I knew. At first, some people seemed not to fit into any category and I became discouraged and wondered if something was missing from the system. Then I realized that I had not yet decided fully which type I was: a Three or a Seven, or perhaps a Nine?

If it took a while for me to understand and accept my own type (I am a Three), then, of course, it would be more difficult to interpret other people whom I knew less well than myself.

How the Life Signs can work for you

Each Life Sign contains many characteristics, and developing an understanding of these can help you in your everyday life.

Perhaps you recognize yourself in one of the thumbnail sketches on the preceding pages. More probably you recognize yourself in several. Keep an open mind—it is rare for people to be certain of their own type at once. That is why the most comprehensive questionnaire of its type, designed to help you determine your Life Sign, has been included as an integral part of this book (see pp.22–61).

The object to understanding the Life Signs is simply self-knowledge. At the end of this book, you won't get a diploma pronouncing you to be a Busy Bee with distinction or an accredited Reformer. What you will get is more valuable—a set of mental tools to help you through any problem that besets you.

From the heart

 The English poet John Donne once wrote "No man is an island." We all exist in relation to each other, and we all live and love and work and play within an extraordinarily complex network of human relationships.

These relationships are at the core of the Life Signs. After you learn how to apply the Life Signs to yourself, you will be able to use them to understand the people in your life—whether at home, work, or play. By understanding how and why someone will react in a certain situation, you can develop a better, more positive relationship with that person.

The many facets of a Life Sign

Each of the nine Life Signs contains a spectrum of characteristics. The best emerge when a person is happy and fulfilled. The worst surface when frustration, cynicism, and bitterness take hold. By recognizing your own Life Sign, you can assess your potential weaknesses—and identify bad habits and faults whose existence you may be denying to yourself.

The Life Signs system does not pretend that all humans are perfect, or anywhere near perfect. We may all have been born with the capacity for saintliness, but so few of us achieve it that we can be sure of only this—people, however much difficulty they face, can become better. We all possess the power to be the best we can be. This will fall short of saintliness, but it is easier to forgive our own faults when we are striving to overcome them.

This is a daunting task, and knowledge of the Life Signs will be a great aid. By recognizing the best qualities at the top of each Life Sign's spectrum, we identify our own best potentials. By meditating on the achievements of others who share our Sign, we can be inspired to achieve. If you are already fairly sure of your own type and you are impatient to skip the questionnaire (hello, Busy Bee), you can read a fuller account of each Life Sign's strengths and weaknesses on pages 70–87.

Using your knowledge

By understanding yourself you can relate better to others. Life Signs focus on self-development and achieving balance, as well as on possibly the most important issue—relationships. Life Signs are not like star signs as interpreted by astrologers; no one

Sign is exclusively suited to another type. In fact, any two individuals can build a loving, lasting partnership if they understand and trust each other.

Coping with stress is one of the greatest tests for people in this technical age. Each Life Sign reacts differently to stress, all with their own coping mechanisms. By learning about the tools that other minds use, you can add to your own mental workshop. The same is true of self-confidence, and when you understand your own instincts, you will enjoy gaining insight into those of others.

We choose our friends, but not our family—nor, very often, our colleagues. The workplace thrusts us into relationships, which, when they go wrong, can exert immense strain. An understanding of the Life Signs can help put an end to "personality clashes."

You'll find exercises throughout the book to test your open-mindedness and your spirit of mental adventure. The Life Signs system is designed to be enjoyed—so have fun learning.

For your information

Knowing yourself

The true knowledge of your own nature is the ultimate human wisdom. The words *"Gnothe seauton"* or "Know thyself!" were written above the doorway of the temple at Delphi in ancient Greece. Whoever passed through the doorway to ask the oracle for a prediction would see the words, and perhaps the wisest would turn and walk away, because there is no question so searching that can be asked of an oracle as the questions we put to ourselves. Once you understand the Life Signs and know yourself better, you can answer your own questions.

Only the remains are left of this temple in Delphi, Greece, which once displayed the words *"Gnothe seauton,"* or "Know thyself."

Dealing with other types

Jean-Paul Sartre complained, "Hell is other people." Sartre, of course, was a type Five, an introspective Intellectual who cared little for what others thought of him and cared less for them. However, life should not be difficult, and you can make hellish people seem much less irritating by seeing life from their perspective and allowing yourself to empathize.

To help you learn how to understand the different Life Sign types, try the exercise on these pages. Imagine a radio station phone-in hour. It is election time, and your local station is giving a platform to all who want to air their views. Phone-ins enable people to sound off with less inhibition than they might face-to-face, where seeing their audience's irritation would temper their hostility. On the radio, faces and body language become invisible. Listen to each of these nine people. Try not to become annoyed as you identify their Life Signs.

◆ Caller one

She knows how she will be voting. She has voted for this party all her life, and she thinks that anyone who votes for the other main party does so out of destructiveness. People who persistently vote for the opposition should be identified and barred from voting, because they are abusing the democratic process.

◆ Caller two

This person has a specific point to make. He puts it forcefully and well, but he does not appreciate that this is just one issue among many at election time. As far as he is concerned, he has argued his case, won the debate, and anyone who cannot vote "right" on this basis is too dumb to deserve the right to vote.

◆ Caller three

This caller is an amateur psephologist, someone who studies elections. She is a trend-watcher, and she has amassed an interesting file of statistics, which she would like to read out loud, if she can find the right page. The paragraph she is looking for should be right here—ah, here it is, yes…. She is cut off midway.

◆ The host

The host loses patience, about 20 seconds after everyone else, and hangs up. He is oleaginous, having an offensive, ingratiating character with a oily voice. He wants to share in-jokes with every listener. Although he is smugly polite to all the callers, he flicks barbed comments after them when their calls are over. He wants you to trust him so much, it makes you suspicious.

◆ Caller four

A campaign organizer for one of the electoral candidates, this caller is urging everyone to vote. Because she is always in a hurry, she rushes through her points. Whoever you are, whatever your politics, her candidate wants to see you at the polls. He is a fair man, ready to obey the democratic majority. Everyone must turn out. Failure to exercise your right to vote is an insult to 200 years of the pioneer spirit.

◆ Caller five

He won't be voting, because all the politicians are the same. They are out for themselves, and nobody cares how ordinary people feel or understand what they are going through. Even if there is someone new in the White House, what difference can it make to individual problems.

◆ Caller six

She loves the elections. There is so much going on. This woman can watch six news channels 24 hours a day if she wants, and there will be no boring specials from Indonesia about conditions in shoe factories. This is political life in the raw, day-long adrenaline, and she would have elections every six months if she could. She has not made a decision on whom she will vote for, but she will definitely be voting.

◆ Caller seven

With two sons in school, this caller is worried about education. In his neighborhood the high school has suffered from under-funding, with the result that both his sons are being taught in classes so large that they are missing out on vital lessons and attention. Whoever gets into power will have to address this problem, because it cannot be allowed to go on.

◆ Caller eight

The whole election is becoming very stressful to this caller, and, if she could, she would go on vacation until it was all over. She is not going to be voting, but she is probably saying that because, if some of the previous callers knew how she would be voting, they would probably want to call back and abuse her. She cannot understand why the two parties do not simply alternate, four years in power each, or perhaps eight years so that things get done; then there would not have to be elections, which would save a lot of public money.

ANSWERS

These caller profiles are, of course, stereotypes of the more negative aspects of each Life Sign type. Their personalities have been exaggerated to make them more identifiable to you. Once you identify the caller with the Life Sign type, you should be able to use your understanding of that type's personality to help you empathize with the caller. Were you able to match all of the callers and the host with the nine Life Signs? They are:

Caller one: the Believer
Caller two: the Reformer
Caller three: the Intellectual
The host: the Actor
Caller four: the Boss
Caller five: the Artist
Caller six: the Busy Bee
Caller seven: the Mother Hen
Caller eight: the Magician

The Life Signs personality questionnaire

You are about to face 144 of the most thought-provoking questions you will ever encounter. Along with a team of researchers, I have devised this questionnaire to present each reader with a mind-expanding array of situations, quandaries, and predicaments.

Choosing an answer

Each of the questions contains a paired statement. Read the question and decide which of the two statements is more applicable to your own personality. Try not to make your choice based only on how you feel today—think about how your character has been throughout your adult life, and use that as a guide. You are establishing the general trends that provide the motivating forces within your personality. Recent fads and current whims are less relevant than the well-established factors that make you the person you are.

As you read a question, it will help to visualize each of the options as vividly as possible. Imagine each scene projected onto a movie screen in your mind. Concentrate on the colors and the sounds; then allow your imagination to taste the flavors, touch the textures, and smell the scents.

The questionnaire is designed to reveal your hidden facets, as well as the obvious ones in your nature. As you study the choices, it will seem in some cases that neither statement is relevant. That is to be expected. Each question balances one of the nine Life Signs types against another, and, if your character contains little of either of those particular types, the question may be difficult to answer.

Try to answer as many questions as you can. Pick the statement that you feel is more applicable to you; however, if both are equally inapplicable, then skip the question. A low score in some types will help to emphasize the type that predominates in your character. Do not choose an answer at random, because inaccurate responses will skew your result. It is better to leave out a question altogether than to give a careless answer, because a skipped question will simply add nothing to your total for each of the types, while wrong answers will artificially raise a score.

Remember that you are the beneficiary of your own truthfulness. An honest answer will contribute to an honest profile. Conversely, guesses are as bad as lies. Imagine, if it helps, that you are answering these questions not only to yourself but to a stern judge, who does not mind which option you pick but who will be upset if you treat the questionnaire flippantly.

The four sections

The questionnaire is divided into four sections. By going through all four of them, you will be able to most accurately identify your Life Sign. If you are impatient, you can get a somewhat reliable result by completing fewer sections; however, you should remember that the more sections you complete, the more accurate your results will be.

Each section consists of 36 questions. If you choose not to complete the full questionnaire, it is important that you complete the section that you are in; for example, 36 questions for section one, 72 questions for sections one and two, 108 questions for sections one, two, and three, and 144 questions for all four sections.

If you try to calculate your Life Sign based on, for example, 50 or 90 answers, you will get a completely inaccurate result. This is because each section of 36 questions pairs off every Life Sign type against every other type. There are nine Life Signs, so the pairings are types 1–2, 1–3, 1–4, 1–5, 1–6, 1–7, 1–8, 1–9, 2–1, 2–3, 2–4, until 8–9. If you answer only part of a section, you may miss some of the questions that will indicate your true Life Sign.

Hidden results

The questions are presented in a random order, because knowing the type may influence how you answer the question. For the same reason, the type numbers and names have been replaced by symbols (see the key below). The symbols have been randomly matched to the nine Life Sign types. A key to reveal the types is provided after the first section and at the end of the questionnaire.

After answering the questionnaire—or a section—count how many of each symbol you have checked off. For example, you might have 21 ◗s, 16 ❖s, 12 ◆s, 25 □s, 15 !s, 20 ▲s, 12 ⊙s, 8 ✳s, and 15 ✪s, for a total of 144 answers. There are more squares than any other symbol, so the square identifies your type. Using the key at the end of the questionnaire, it will reveal which Life Sign corresponds to the square.

Do not throw away your record of check marks. You will be returning to it to discover other Life Signs that have a say in your character, such as your wing (see pp. 68–69).

Key to symbols

Each time you make a choice, keep a note of your answer. You can put a check mark in the space provided next to the symbols below, circle the symbol next to your choice in the questionnaire, or, if you prefer not to mark the book, copy the symbols below onto a notepad.

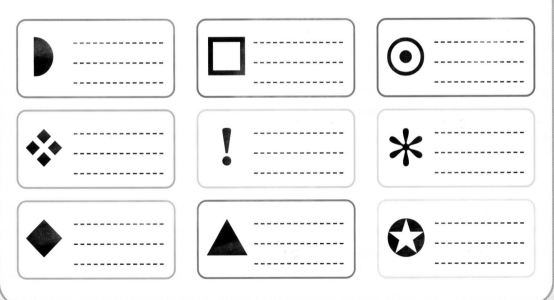

SECTION ONE

1 On a subway in a large city, you overhear a group of tourists planning their itinerary. They are going to run into problems. The sights they want to see are closed for renovations, their guidebook is out of date, and they are heading in the wrong direction, toward the less desirable end of town. Do you:

A. Correct their mistakes, taking it upon yourself to offer some guidance. You don't believe free advice is necessarily worthless, especially when you are the one giving it.

B. Let them discover their mistakes. They might enjoy the adventure of the day in spite of their guidebook. In any event they haven't asked for help, and they probably won't welcome it.

2 A landmark birthday looms before you, and your generous family is promising the treat of a lifetime. You thumb the brochures and think about the attractions of two outrageously expensive treats. Which one would you choose:

A. The 200-mph (320-km) hurtle around a twisting Grand Prix track in the cockpit of a Formula 1 racing car, suspended less than two inches (50 mm) above the blazing tarmac.

B. A gentle drift into the clouds, accompanied by your family, in the wicker basket of a hot air balloon silently floating over the countryside, where you can see the world from an exhilaratingly new, yet comfortingly peaceful, perspective.

3 Your assignment is to climb a high, dangerous mountain. Do you do it:

A. With friends, roped together for safety and strength, so that your life is constantly protected and supported by them, just as you help to protect and support their lives—although if one falls, you could all go crashing down together.

B. Solo, putting your trust solely into your own skills and courage, and enjoying the exhilaration of independence.

4 If you could rule the world, would it be in the style of:

A. The fearless, dogmatic, never-say-die style of the British Prime Minister Winston Churchill.

B. The high stakes, charismatic style of President John Kennedy.

5 Your office is being redesigned, and your opinion will be an important factor in the new look. Would you prefer to see:

A. A network of cubicles, where each worker can enjoy a little personal space, free from visual distractions, where unnecessary small talk will be minimized and each person is free to focus on the current project to be worked on.

B. An open-plan environment, where people can exchange views and converse freely, offering help and support, although this interaction could dilute each person's individual focus.

6 Imagine yourself as a rock star. Going into the studio to lay down your crucial third album, you know you've got some great songs—the best you've ever written. The band and the producer are thrilled when you sit down with an acoustic guitar to debut the material. Do you:

A. Perform with every ounce of passion in you, then leave the rest to the experts—returning to the studio when the sound engineers have done their work, so that you can review the music and point out where changes and improvements have to be made.

B. Remain involved at every stage, working long hours over the mixing desk, creating the electronic samples yourself and overseeing every detail, including the cover design.

7 You are visited in your dreams by an unusual angel with large, red forearms and a tight-fitting wig, looking like a cleaner in a rundown roadside restaurant. She announces herself as your angel of judgment, and you are apprehensive about what her judgment might be. Which do you fear more, that she will tell you:

A. Your trouble is you waste too much time thinking of yourself.

B. Your trouble is you waste too much time on the comfort of others.

8 Which great genius do you find more inspirational:

A. The world's greatest scientist, Albert Einstein.

B. The world's greatest conqueror, Napoleon.

9

You have finished the first draft of your novel, but you feel compelled to slip it back into the desk drawer. For the time being, you are not planning to show it to anyone. Is this because:

A. You are plagued by doubts—the book may not be as good as you thought it was while you were writing it.

B. You are a perfectionist, and you don't want anyone to judge your work until you have taken every pain to make it as good as it possibly can be.

10

A close relative has bought a run-down house, and she is dedicating herself to its renovation. She appeals for your help, and, of course, you are glad to give it. But are you:

A. Content to follow her instructions, making yourself helpful with the painting and other decorating jobs and offering your opinion on how the work should be done, but also recognizing that she must have the final say because the house is hers.

B. Frustrated that you can't take control, but inspired to create something out of nothing and turn a wreck into a valuable home. In fact, you consider undertaking a similar project.

11

You are chosen to negotiate a pay raise. Are you seen as:

A. Someone who is a poor performer in heated arguments and not such a great candidate for the negotiating team; however, you are a clear-headed thinker who will see through the sweet-talking jargon to get to the real deal.

B. A bold, forthright debater who loves a verbal battle and will be a natural choice to mediate on behalf of the whole team.

12

Who do you consider the true Southern Belle:

A. Vivien Leigh, the beauty who played Scarlett O'Hara in *Gone with the Wind*.

B. Bette Davis, the overlooked actress who echoed the part of Scarlett in her masterpiece *Jezebel*.

13

You set aside the morning to choose a new wardrobe for the fall. It is a major piece of shopping, and you'll be investing a substantial sum in clothes that will have to see you through not only this season, but the following spring and fall, too. You'll be wearing these clothes a lot, but when you go shopping will it be:

A. A quick decision—you'll be in and out of the stores in no time.

B. A horrible agony of indecision, with visits to a number of stores.

14

You have completed a product development review, outlining how your company should change its main product. You have compiled all the statistics on your competitors' wares. However, you wake up with a strong intuition, almost a superstitious urge, to change the recommendations in your report. It is an irrational, but powerful sensation. Do you:

A. Go with your instincts, even when colleagues advise that you may invalidate your whole report and do your reputation serious harm—not to mention the risk of leading the company into uncharted waters.

B. Ignore your forebodings because you feel that, while your report may not be reaching the right conclusions, you would be in danger of making things even worse by following mere intuition.

15

You have been asked to take control of a reorganization at your office, which has been disrupted by personality clashes, and your plan has been a success. You got the job done, but no one knows how—except you. Did you succeed because:

A. You set aside the emotional turmoil and, with a calm, determined smile, simply went ahead with an impossible task and made it possible.

B. You held a meeting, explained how you felt, and invited the emotional responses of everyone else. When you had worked through your feelings, you felt a liberation, which allowed you to pursue the objectives with fresh energy.

16

Which cartoon character do you more closely associate yourself with:

A. Superman, who fought to help defend mankind against evil people.

B. The world's most mischievous schoolboy, Dennis the Menace.

17 Your children are learning a foreign language at school, one that you don't speak yourself. Do you decide to:

A. Learn it with them, offering your support and enthusiasm, renting videos in the language and discovering the national culture and mythology, perhaps booking vacations to parts of the world where that language is spoken.

B. Let the children study on their own, because teaching languages is the school's business, and learning this language was never on your agenda. Getting involved will just distract you from the tasks that are your role in the family.

18 Think for a moment of the young princes of the British royal family, who suffered the untimely death of their mother, Diana. What do you think are the most important qualities that their father, Prince Charles, should instill in these young men:

A. A traditional sense of duty to their birth, their heritage, their family, and their nation.

B. The flexibility to adapt to a new age of media manipulation, where the role of royalty becomes less to do with social responsibilities than with show business.

19 People can't always get through to you, and you know it is true. But is this because:

A. You are a daydreamer, who often tunes out and gets lost in the movies that are running in your own head—so when someone addresses a question to you, all too often you simply don't hear it.

B. You are an intensely emotional person who is sometimes hard to reach because no one else can feel exactly as you feel. Sometimes, when you are feeling down, you just don't want to reach out and join the rest of the world.

20 Which of these powerful women do you think did more for the world:

A. Mother Teresa, who cared for the poor of Calcutta in India and saved countless lives.

B. Margaret Thatcher, the Iron Lady of British politics, who helped to end the Cold War.

21

At a party you are offered an illegal drug. Everyone else seems to be taking it—there is no pretence about it. What is your response:

A. To take the drug and break the law, because you've always said you'll try anything once and there is no point in living if you don't live to the maximum.

B. To refuse the drug, because you prefer to stay in control and live by your own rules and principles.

22

Your assignment is to sail around the world. Your sponsors have released unlimited funds and your employer is offering an unlimited sabbatical—effectively, you can take as long as you want. But you are entered in a race, and the expectations are for you to tackle this in the most competitive style—everyone wants you to complete the circumnavigation in the fastest time possible and win the cup. Do you:

A. Accept the challenge and exert yourself to the maximum to be the first to finish.

B. Seize the chance to indulge yourself, meandering around the world via its most alluring ports, happy to see someone else take the prize.

23

You have a nice apartment and a steady income—and the chance to fulfill the adventure fantasy of your lifetime. Maybe it is sailing round the globe or acting in a repertory theatrical company or racing in the Indianapolis 500. Whatever it is, the chance won't come again. But to take that chance means jeopardizing your job and home. Does the secret voice that whispers advice in your head say:

A. Seize the day and fulfill your fantasy.

B. Don't risk throwing away your security.

24

Which of these two leaders do you relate to more:

A. Lawrence of Arabia, the tortured British commander who endured many hardships during World War I.

B. Julius Caesar, who inspired his troops to greatness and went on to seize absolute power.

25 You set high standards for yourself, and you find nothing more irritating than other people badgering you with their ideas of how to do things. You are approached by the school concert committee to take charge of car parking arrangements, and you work out the most efficient use of space and time; however, a number of teachers and school officials will want to park in their accustomed spaces. Are you:

A. Firm and insistent that everyone must do it your way to avoid creating chaos.

B. Relaxed about allowing people to park where they feel they should, leaving them to clear up their own mess later on.

26 You have always felt you had many of the qualities required of a great teacher. Now, in a major career change (assuming you are not a teacher already), you are going to prove it. Do you feel your latent skills are better suited to teaching:

A. Gifted children whose thirst for learning is never satisfied, and whose minds will constantly be racing ahead of your own as you help them fulfill their potential on the fast track to college and high-flying careers.

B. Children with special needs and learning difficulties, who will often find it hard or even impossible to grasp the concepts you are teaching. They may make difficult physical demands upon you as well, yet they possess their own potential, which richly deserves to be fulfilled.

27 A television interviewer sits in an easy chair facing yours, proffering the microphone respectfully. She asks, "You have enjoyed exceptional success during your long life. To what do you attribute this?" Do you answer:

A. I have always possessed an instinctive gift for understanding how people will react to me and what I do or say, so I have always been able to adjust my behavior to leave the best possible impression.

B. The key has been that I don't care what anyone thinks of me. I just go right ahead and do what I believe to be best—and more often than not, it works.

28 Which of these childhood fantasy worlds would you prefer to visit:

A. Willy Wonka's fantastic chocolate factory, with its chocolate pool and waterfall, created by Roald Dahl.

B. Harry Potter's Hogwarts, the magical school of wizardry and witchcraft, created by J. K. Rowling.

29

On a cross-country journey, your train breaks down for the second time. It is getting late, everyone is grumbling about missed connections, and several families have tired, fractious children. The train staff is unhelpful, and it is clear that the fastest solution (although not, of course, the safest) would be to leave the train, walk half a mile or so to the nearest town, and organize bus transportation for those who need it. Are you:

A. Willing to take responsibility and encourage people to join you in arranging bus transportation.

B. More comfortable waiting for the train to move or for someone else to arrange the bus—you know that you would find it hard to organize fellow passengers who are not your friends.

30

You are the new member of the cast of an established television soap opera, joining an established team. Do you:

A. Make an effort to fit in and find friends among both the actors and the crew, with a special determination to be accepted and liked by the crew.

B. Focus on your performance, knowing that others in the team will come and go, and that your first loyalty must be to yourself and your fans.

31

You are working at home over the weekend, determined to make progress on a project with no deadline. A friend from the office phones and invites you to the movies—six of your colleagues are going to see an Oscar-nominated spectacular. Do you:

A. Put aside your work and join in a spontaneous evening of fun—after all, it is good to be flexible.

B. Stick to your plan to get some work done, because it is important to stay focused on your project.

!

32

Which one of this former royal couple inspires you more:

A. Princess Diana, who spoke up for AIDS awareness and land-mine victims.

B. Prince Charles, who is a believer in organic farming and helps young adults find job opportunities.

33 You are the manager and head stylist of a hairdressing salon—you prefer the title Director of Coiffure at the Cut Above Group. You have worked your way up from the days when you swept up the cuttings and made the coffee. What is more important to you:

A. That the rest of the team recognize you as the one in charge and defer to your judgment, doing as they are told and never answering back to your demands.

B. That the customers know you are No. 1, with your picture and your awards on the wall and your appointments booked for 12 weeks in advance.

34 During a long drive, you and two friends start to debate the merits of vegetarianism. The argument gets lively. One of your companions calls the mass slaughter of animals for food "a Holocaust" and the other hits back that it is unnatural for human beings to deny themselves meat. Is your instinct to:

A. Join in with gusto, clearly voicing your own opinions and attacking any weak arguments without compromise.

B. Hold back, refraining from saying everything that comes into your head. There is no sense in hurting your friends' feelings when nothing serious hinges on this argument.

35 You are staying in a Scottish castle, haunted by the ghost of Lady Audrey, who killed herself when her father refused to let her wed a dashing outlaw. Is your reaction one of:

A. Utter skepticism, both to the notion of ghosts and to the idea that any highborn woman, however passionately romantic, would commit suicide rather than be parted from a villain.

B. Delightful sadness, your heart wrung by a story that is so melancholy that you want it to be true—even if that means a ghost might walk through your bedroom during the night.

36 These basketball heroes play with distinctly different styles. Which one do you prefer:

A. Michael Jordan, the wizard whose natural talent makes him one of basketball's greats.

B. Shaquille O'Neal, one of the toughest players, whose own teammates fear him.

End of section one

Preliminary scores

Congratulations on completing the first group of questions. If you would like to use the first part of the questionnaire as the basis for determining your Life Sign, stop here and count how many of each symbol you have accumulated. Now look below to find the symbol with the highest total—it will correspond with your Life Sign.

Before counting your results, remember that a section of 36 questions pits each Life Sign against the other signs only once. The overall result will be a clear indication of your own type, but you'll get a more accurate picture of your personality if you complete two sections (72 questions), three sections (108 questions), or—best of all—four sections (144 questions).

If you would like to continue the questionnaire, don't look now to see which Life Sign rules your personality. It is also better if you don't decipher the symbols used to disguise the nine Life Signs. Preconceived notions can be powerful beasts, and if you have a fixed idea in your head that you are one type or another, you will find it difficult to approach new questions with an open mind. Simply turn the page and continue with question 37. If you answer all 144 questions, turn to page 61; for 72 or 108 questions, return to this page to use the key below.

Key to symbols

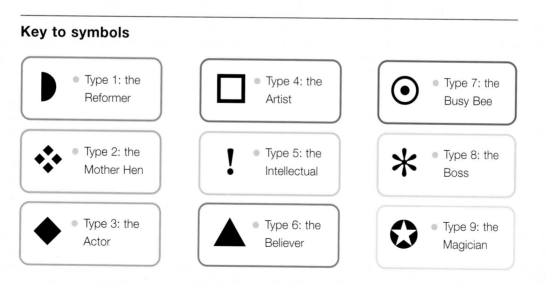

Type 1: the Reformer

Type 4: the Artist

Type 7: the Busy Bee

Type 2: the Mother Hen

Type 5: the Intellectual

Type 8: the Boss

Type 3: the Actor

Type 6: the Believer

Type 9: the Magician

SECTION TWO

37 Your hypnotherapist regresses you to a past life during the early years of the American West. Do you recall being:

A. A pioneer leading a wagon train, blazing a trail across the prairie, building a new nation for your family from the raw materials of a virgin country.

B. A bar-room pianist, indulging an easy-going musical gift as you drift from town to town along the new frontier and parlaying your talent into liquor, gambling, rough-house brawls, and romance.

38 It is Friday evening, and, before you leave your desk, you calculate your monthly finances. To your horror, you realize that your withdrawals are about to plunge your account into overdraft. If only you thought of this earlier—but you have been absorbed in work and your bank is shut until Monday. Do you:

A. Drown your anxiety in some fun activity, such as buying clothes— since you are already overdrawn you might as well enjoy it.

B. Put the problem out of your mind. There is no use worrying about something that is currently beyond your control.

39 Would you prefer an entertainer to end his career in the style of:

A. Frank Sinatra, who made endless comebacks.

B. Bing Crosby, who left and never came back.

40 You have decided to run for mayor. You believe you can do a great job because:

A. You are confident, eloquent, a good advocate, and nobody's fool. You have a sharp mind and a clear understanding of the ways of the world.

B. You will do what is right, fair, decent, and honest, always upholding your moral code without fear or stooping to favoritism.

41

You are leaving your employer to start your own business, and your colleagues have organized a big send-off. It is a touching occasion, with warm-hearted speeches, a presentation, and even a framed cartoon of yourself. You can't go without making a speech. Do you:

A. Tell everyone how great they've been, how dearly you value their friendship, and how you hope they will keep in contact, before going around the room, making your farewells to each person.

B. Confine yourself to a few well-chosen words before making a dignified exit, secure in the knowledge that they already know how much you have valued their comradeship.

!

42

It is team-building time at the office, and you and your colleagues have been given an assignment to bring you closer together—each one of you has to parachute from an old plane, 10,000 feet (3,000 m.) high in the sky. There is no avoiding this—but do you do it:

A. For the thrill, the once-in-a-lifetime experience and the almost physical joy of knowing that, however afraid your companions may be, you are loving it.

B. To demonstrate your solidarity with your comrades, and because a bold leap could be good for your career, whereas a feeble jump will probably count against you during the next round of promotions.

◆

43

Which of these first-time space-age achievements do you see as being greater:

A. Putting Yuri Gagarin into space.

□

B. Enabling Neil Armstrong to walk on the moon.

44

Your company is developing a terrific invention, which could solve the world's water-pollution problems. It is safe, cheap, effective—but not quite ready. You know that a few rival firms are working on similar devices, although your spies are not sure how well they are doing. Meanwhile, millions of children in underdeveloped countries are dying every year from dysentery. Should you:

A. Keep the plans secret until they are perfected, running the risk that others will beat you to the finish line.

!

B. Start broadcasting the news right away, relying on your team's ability—under your guidance—to perfect the device in the field.

*

45 The Bible says, "Greater love hath no man than this, that a man lay down his life for his friends" (John 15:13). But when the British Prime Minister Harold Macmillan held a brutal reorganization of his Cabinet, a rival twisted the quotation: "Greater love hath no man than this, that a man lay down his friends for his life." Would you ever:

A. Sacrifice your friends if you knew it could be essential for the public good.

B. Sacrifice yourself, and perhaps put the public good at risk, instead of betraying your friends, although you knew they probably didn't deserve being protected.

46 A 33-year-old close friend seeks your advice. His partner, who is 30 years old, wants children. He wants to wait for a few years, giving his career and his earning ability more time to develop. But he has been putting off parenthood for a long time, and there is a danger that the relationship might not take much more of his delaying tactics. Do you tell him:

A. Go for it—being a father will bring out the best in you, and you can't go through life being afraid of the big decisions. Being a family means much more than finances.

B. Don't be rushed. If you don't think you are ready for fatherhood, then you are not ready. You shouldn't jeopardize your entire career to patch up a relationship.

47 Which of these actresses has the social life you prefer:

A. Greta Garbo, who wanted to be left alone.

B. Bette Midler, who likes to be the party queen.

48 You are planning to travel across the United States by Greyhound bus. Is this:

A. The culmination of a long-held ambition, backed up by painstaking planning with route maps and bus schedules, with suitcases of clothes and food that will see you through every foreseeable problem—you trust to preparation.

B. A spur-of-the-moment adventure, doubly fun for being spontaneous. Although you know you might run into trouble ahead with a scantily packed bag and little idea of the network of bus connections, you put your trust in luck.

49 You are having a "down" day. Tired and worried, you can't seem to lift yourself to your usual positive level. This is taking its toll on people around you, but you can't help your nature. Are others more likely to be upset and irritated by you because:

A. You are letting your pessimism show in complaints and you are badgering others over unresolved questions.

B. You are demanding impossible fixes for problems that didn't bother you yesterday—you are restless and full of unhelpful suggestions.

50 Your help is needed by the local amateur theatrical group. You have the ability they need: You can organize the stagehands, play the starring role, write the music, or direct the show—or maybe you can do all of the above. But the show spirals into a tear-laden crisis. Is this because you:

A. Promise too much and stretch yourself impossibly in every direction, encouraging everyone to rely on you.

B. Offer too little time and energy, preferring to remain semi-detached from a project that wasn't yours from the conception.

51 Which of these artist's work do you prefer:

A. The constantly changing canvas of Pablo Picasso.

B. The stone or metal sculpture of Auguste Rodin.

52 Your partner wants to move, staying in the area but transferring to a property that is better suited to the current size of your family. This is not something you have discussed before, so it comes as a surprise. You have always imagined staying in your present home unless you moved to another town, city, or country. Your reaction is one of emotional turmoil. You want to respect your partner's needs, of course, and part of you finds the idea attractive—but another part of you is less sure. Do you resolve your uncertainty by:

A. Taking a lot of advice from family and friends, listening carefully to the responses of people who have your family's best interests at heart.

B. Ignoring your doubts and dedicating yourself to the move, relying on your own counsel that wherever you choose to make a home, there your home will be.

53

The marriage of friends you have known since college days is in deep trouble. Both partners confide in you, and you spend many hours on the phone, listening to a painful catalog of grievances. You believe the partnership can be strong enough to weather this storm, and you urge both of them to make it work. However, they split amid bitter acrimony, and both of them blame you for interfering. They came to you pleading for help, so you are angry—but is it because:

A. Your advice has been ignored, your guidance has been thrown away, and all your hopes and efforts have been wasted.

B. You have had no thanks for your efforts—worse, you are being blamed for a break-up you did everything to avert.

54

You are standing on a crowded commuter train when a man on the seat beside you starts complaining to a companion about how terrible the video was that he watched last night. He hated everything about it: the acting, the dialogue, the plot. After a few seconds you realize that he is disparaging one of your favorite recent films. However, you may be a little biased, because you are privately proud that an old schoolfriend you haven't seen for years wrote the script. Do you feel:

A. Angry, and seethe silently, or even speak up to defend the movie because you feel great loyalty to it.

B. Calm, because you don't know this man and you respect neither his opinions nor his manner of broadcasting them around the train—and, anyhow, his opinion can't change yours.

55

Which of these fictional styles of writing do you prefer to lose yourself in:

A. J. R. R. Tolkien's magical world of invention.

B. Charles Dickens' marvelous world of exaggeration.

56

You watch a documentary about a crisis in a Central American country that has been devastated by natural disasters. You feel compelled to help, but there are several charities appealing to you to volunteer your personal help, as well as your money. What is more important to you:

A To assist with fund-raising by working in a thrift shop or going from door to door asking for donations, thereby raising money for immediate relief.

B. To offer expertise and advice to enable the people to put themselves back on their feet and arrange safeguards against future catastrophes.

57

Bells are ringing in the New Year, and through the distractions of a lively party a realization comes upon you that in the next few months you want to make a serious attempt at improving your attitude toward life. Must you:

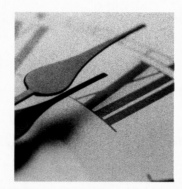

A. Be easier upon yourself, more flexible and less obsessive about rules and procedures, in order to get more done.

B. Be stricter with yourself and more disciplined, staying inside the boundaries of your rules in order to get more done.

58

You are going on a date—and this person is someone you instinctively like and admire. There is a strong attraction and a feeling that this is someone who could be a possible partner for life, so it is a daunting date. What do you do to impress:

A. Remain reticent about your achievements, dreams, and talents. You don't want to come across as arrogant or self-obsessed.

B. Give yourself the best possible reviews—how will your date know about your best characteristics (which are many) if you keep them all secret.

59

Brains or teamwork—which Hollywood train robber had the right approach:

A. Butch Cassidy (played by Paul Newman), trying to think things through.

B. The Sundance Kid (played by Robert Redford), relying on the bond between the two robbers.

60

Your light aircraft crashes in high, snow-clad mountains. Everyone is alive, although two are injured, and you know everyone must act as a team or you are all doomed. What do you do:

A. Take command, forcing people to survive and taking stock of your resources so you can organize a rescue.

B. Watch, record, and understand, so that the story can later be told, both of the external disaster and of the inner struggles.

61 It is casual Friday. While your colleagues will not be wearing their business suits and ties, they will not be coming to the office in gardening dungarees and flip-flops either. You can adapt to the once-a-week uniform easily, flashing the logos on your designer sneakers and loose-fitting sportswear. But do you:

A. Feel more comfortable with clients in your casuals.

B. Project your professionalism more easily in the serious business suit.

62 You are about to have a large house-warming party, and you know that your home will be packed. Do your friends never pass up your parties because:

A. You are a generous host who makes sure that everyone has plenty to eat and drink and is lightheartedly entertained.

B. You are an inveterate jokester, a fun-loving party animal whose stock of crude stories and back-slapping humor will keep everyone hilariously entertained until dawn.

63 Which of these two men of the 20th century do you find more interesting:

A. Muhammad Ali, "The Greatest" boxer, known as much for his quotes as for his boxing skills.

B. Stephen Hawking, the scientist who wrote the best-selling *A Brief History of Time*.

64 Your aunt is celebrating a milestone birthday, and your family expects you to attend a large get-together. However, you will have to travel a long distance, and you have never been particularly fond of this aunt. The party also clashes with a talk at your local theater, which you've been looking forward to—and you already have tickets. Do you:

A. Find a way out of it—if you make a good enough excuse, no one will really miss you.

B. View the trip as your duty. You don't like it, but you can't miss it.

65 The Chinese philosopher Lao Tsu said there are four types of leader: the hated, the feared, the loved, and the invisible. He valued the invisible one most, who makes the people believe they achieve everything themselves. But Lao Tsu never worked in a capitalist economy, where invisible leaders were liable to be downsized. You know that the best leaders today make themselves loved by their workforce. Is this best achieved by:

A. A firm hand, which offers rule and guidance and imposes discipline and strict boundaries.

B. An open hand, encouraging the workforce to have fun and be creative in an atmosphere of acceptance.

66 You are dining with your partner's new client in a busy, noisy restaurant. The client is a backslapping, storytelling type of person, and over the hubbub you catch what sounds like the racist punchline of a joke. You aren't sure if you can believe your ears. Do you:

A. Ask the client to repeat the punchline and, if it is as bad as you fear, point out that racism is not funny.

B. Hope you misheard the joke and maintain a diplomatic deafness—your partner won't thank you for picking fights with a client.

67 Which of these 1970s television cops would you regard as the coolest:

A. The go-for-it, streetwise Starsky, played by Paul Michael Glaser.

B. The think-it-through, better-educated, soft-spoken Hutch, played by David Soul.

68 Every year you have kept a date with a few old friends. It has become a tradition—but, unfortunately, it is not much fun any more. This time you say so. Although you are glad that you did, your friends all blame you for ending an era. Do you:

A. Fear you have betrayed yourself by revealing your emotions. You could have kept quiet and let the tradition die on its own.

B. Wish your friends could appreciate that you decided to say what you did because you love them, and you canceled the date so the friendship could continue in a different form.

69 When you were growing up, what did you long for more:

A. Independence from your parents and the chance to follow your own path through life.

B. Your parents' applause and praise, the knowledge that you were fulfilling their hopes and aspirations for you.

70 Congratulations! You have won a career makeover in the lottery run by an employment website. Do you opt to be:

A. An investigative journalist, asking searching questions of politicians and businessmen after a major disaster at a chemicals plant.

B. A trauma counselor, helping victims and bereaved families deal with the aftermath of the catastrophe.

71 Which 19th-century heroine do you admire more:

A. The pioneer nurse Florence Nightingale, who braved the war zone to help wounded soldiers.

B. Queen Victoria, who inspired people all around the globe to give homage to a common empire.

72 You are a member of the clergy, preparing a sermon for one of the most important festivals of your religion—be it Easter, Yom Kippur, Ramadan, or some other sacred occasion. Is your address:

A. Full of fun and fire, a performance of rapid allusions and electric energy, part stand-up comedy and part prophetic splendor.

B. Solemn, reassured and reassuring, full of power and inspiration, but with no surprises.

End of section two

42

SECTION THREE

73 You have just enrolled your child in a new school, where the parent–teacher association is in chaos. The principal suggests your skills would be invaluable on the committee—but your response upsets her because:

A. You spell out all the problems, outline your preferred solutions, cast doubt on the ability of some of the others involved to carry through your plan, and immediately assume command.

B. Once you know that a group of people with egos are involved, you want to keep your distance.

74 Who do you feel did more for the world:

A. Henry Ford, the American automobile engineer who pioneered "assembly-line" mass production techniques.

B. Alexander Graham Bell, inventor of the telephone.

75 You overhear a colleague making snide criticisms about your hairstyle. You are not friends, but you work together—however, without a friendly atmosphere your work will suffer. Do you:

A. Have a fight and clear the air, because you can't keep your feelings hidden or let the remarks pass.

B. Act as though nothing has been said and keep up an appearance of friendliness, while privately noting your colleague's untrustworthiness.

76 The international company for which you are a senior vice president is appointing you as spokesman of a delegation to meet a potential production team in the Far East. You will be talking to the workers' representatives, because your company believes in cooperation—not exploitation. You know the workers have legitimate concerns. You have two strong arguments for the workers, both of which you'll use fully—but will your main efforts be directed to:

A. Straight talking, letting them know that your company can go elsewhere, which would have serious economic consequences for their region.

B. Tantalizing visions and promises, reminding them how good their new lives will be if they allow you to bring economic stability.

77. At a party to mark the departure of a popular colleague who is moving to a rival firm, you realize that other people are saying their good-byes with hugs, not handshakes. Do you:

A. Make your hug good and firm, with a pat on the back and a squeeze on the arm.

B. Make your hug no more than a brief touch on the shoulders.

78 Which celebrity best represents the archetypal rock star:

A. Mick Jagger, one of the Rolling Stones, first presented as a 1960s bad boy as a counterpart to the "good" Beatles.

B. Madonna, the "material girl" known for her outrageous stage costumes.

79 You have a pair of free movie tickets, and your companion is happy to let you choose the film. Two movies are showing. Which do you pick:

A. *Anna Karenina,* a great, mournful Russian classic, where you will need a box of tissues.

B. *Forrest Gump,* an uplifting piece of trivial fun, which is guaranteed to require a carton of popcorn.

80 You witness a domestic argument in a shopping mall. It is heated and there is some pushing and shoving, but it doesn't look as though either partner is about to explode into serious physical violence. Is your instinct to:

A. Stay out of it, because it is none of your business. You might make things worse by offering assistance, and you might even get embroiled and hurt yourself. **!**

B. Step in, telling the couple to calm down because they are in a public place—a civilized society requires civilized behavior from bystanders as well as from the main actors.

81

Your six-year-old's teacher would like to meet with you because some of the children have been using bad language in class. Another parent claims that your child has been teaching rude words to the others. You have spoken to your child, and you are ready to defend her—however, the truth is you are not certain of the facts. The culprit could be another pupil, or it could be all of them. As you drive to school, you assess the possible problems with the way you present yourself. Is the main risk:

A. Your uncertainty with the facts will reveal itself in contradictory statements. You will not have enough confidence and will lapse into tongue-tied embarrassment.

B. You will be so talkative, assertive, and confident that the teacher will regard you as pushy and instinctively oppose your viewpoint.

82

Which celebrity style do you prefer when watching a talk show:

A. The sympathetic, emotional Oprah Winfrey.

B. The caustic, witty Joan Rivers.

83

Imagine yourself as a teenager at college, on the point of falling in love for the first time. There are three romances in the air, three possibilities. The situation ends in disaster. Is your downfall due to your being:

A. Too uncertain of yourself, unsure of what signals you are giving and frightened of rejection, delaying your response so long that all the possibilities fizzle out.

B. Too greedy, trying to date them all and keep each a secret from the others. You are caught in your deception, and you end up with no romance at all.

84

You enroll for a philosophy course at your local college's night classes, where the history of human thought fascinates you. Are you more likely to:

A. See the world as it plainly is, maintaining a strong sense of reality, simply brushing aside insoluble riddles of existence.

B. Begin to doubt everything—your past beliefs, your current values, the purpose of your life, the meaning of human culture, and the reality of the very fabric of the world.

85

You stumble across the transcript of a meeting. There are no names, dates, or times, but you recognize the subject under discussion and you are sure yours is one of the voices recorded here. Are you more likely to have said:

A. "Option One looks good, but I'm not convinced yet. In fact, the more I think about it, the more attractive the second option seems."

B. "For goodness sakes, stop clucking like a lot of hens and pick Option One, because if you can't make up your mind I'll make it up for you!"

86

Which member of the Beatles do you prefer:

A. The sentimental Paul McCartney, who wrote *Yesterday*.

B. The sharp-tongued John Lennon, who wrote *Imagine*.

87

You must attend a product launch. There will be hosts of people from the media, client companies, and supplier agencies, all with their name tags. There may be useful people who could help in your future career. Do you view the event as:

A. A chance to network, to make the acquaintance of a wide range of potentially useful contacts. You will take a box of business cards with you.

B. A tiresome succession of hands to be shaken and backs to be slapped, with people who will forget your face before they have even finished reading the name on your lapel.

88

You are planning a long tour of Europe. It is a major vacation for you, made possible by a lottery win, and most of the places you will see (if not all of them) will be entirely new to you. Do you:

A. Prepare thoroughly before you travel, phoning ahead to check the availability of accommodation, planning an itinerary, purchasing an ample supply of traveler's checks, and investing in a suitcase full of guidebooks.

B. Treat the experience as a wild adventure, a chance to go on the run from reality, traveling light with a pack of credit cards and no itinerary.

89 After a dinner party your companions begin to discuss a news story about a controversial medical treatment. One guest reveals her own experience of several years ago. Are you more likely to:

A. Listen and offer nonjudgmental supportive comment, pleased that she is confiding in you.

B. Set out your own viewpoint on the subject in a forthright style, debating vigorously with those who disagree with you.

90 Which inspirational leader do you admire more:

A. Nelson Mandela, who emerged from prison to bring together the whole of South Africa, black and white.

B. Mahatma Gandhi, who led Indians to independence from British rule through peaceful means.

91 You put down the phone— that is another friendship blown to smithereens. Was the fight with your former friend because:

A. You felt slighted, under personal attack, and the object of insults, which your self-regard would not permit you to ignore.

B. You have forgotten the social niceties once again such as remembering birthdays and phoning when you said you would.

92 You dream that you have died and your soul is instructed to present itself before the recording angels in a bureaucratic celestial office building. A weary junior reincarnation official informs you that, owing to population cut-backs, your spirit is being downsized into the inanimate objects department—however, there is at least an element of choice. Would you prefer to come back as:

A. A neon sign above a metropolitan apartment building, blazing out dynamic directions to the milling populace below.

B. A first-aid pack at giant public gatherings, such as concerts and sports events, dispensing comfort and care.

93

You buy a radio station and install yourself as the boss. Do you:

A. Give yourself your own show, surrounding yourself with a posse of friends and making it your mission to win the ratings war as you steer the ship.

B. Get down to reinventing the station's format and public face, homing in on the listener's needs and wishes through focus groups, statistics, and your own inner vision.

94

If you could live one day as a musical giant, would you be:

A. Elvis Presley, the king of rock and roll.

B. Louis Armstrong, the king of jazz.

95

You are sitting at the breakfast table, staring out of the window but not really seeing what is outside. Is your mind occupied by:

A. Practical matters such as money and school clothes, what you will eat for an evening meal, and which chores have to be done before Sunday.

B. Daydreams, your thoughts spinning through stories and situations. If you were asked to stop and trace the skein of your musings back to their starting point, it might be impossible.

96

You are lying on a comfortable couch in a dim study, much like a psychologist's office. The door opens and you see, startlingly, the genius of psychoanalysis, Carl Gustav Jung. He is impossibly old and white-haired, but his watery eyes are still bright behind pince-nez. He reminds you that he was the first to categorize people into two essential types. Which group do you belong to:

A. Extroverts, who are typically gregarious and unreserved.

B. Introverts, who are typically shy or reserved.

97 It is rush hour and you are driving through a part of town you don't often visit. You need to turn across the oncoming traffic, but there is no gap, and no likelihood of a gap. You could:

A. Because you can't wait all night, nose into the opposite lane, forcing someone to brake and let you through—although this might cause an accident that would be completely your fault.

B. Wait for someone to have the courtesy to let you through, because that is certainly what you would do for another driver in your situation—and surely there is another well-mannered driver out there somewhere.

98 Which style of actress do you prefer:

A. Audrey Hepburn, who personifies feminine grace.

B. Katharine Hepburn, known for her feminine wiles.

99 You make new friends during a brief vacation. You are relaxed and very much yourself, at your best. It is a fun friendship, without any implications for your work or your family—just pleasant conversation and companionship. How do these friends see you:

A. Assured, confident, fun-loving, and well-dressed.

B. Eccentric, unique, amusing, and interesting.

100 You see a framed sign on the wall of a colleague's office, with the saying: "Genius is 1 percent inspiration and 99 percent perspiration." Do you feel:

A. That's okay, but not many people can supply that vital catalyst, the single hundredth that breathes life into the mundane. I'm one of those who possesses the talent for inspiration.

B. That's okay, but not many people possess the dogged determination to produce every ounce of perspiration and see a project through from start to finish. I'm one of those who has the grit it takes, and the final percentage point of inspiration is all luck or illusion anyway.

101

The builder who repaired your roof has just handed you his bill—and it is 10 percent over the estimate, which he claimed was a competitive price. He has been an intrusive presence in your home, and you will be glad to see the back of him—and that estimate was only a verbal quote. Do you:

A. Pay the extra money to avoid a confrontation. You are unlikely to win an argument and just want to get rid of him.

B. Flatly refuse to pay any more than the price he quoted.

102

Which president of the United States do you think was the better mirror of the nation's character:

A. The unswervingly honest George Washington, who could not tell a lie.

B. Ronald Reagan, who delivered lines written by others in a heartfelt performance that inspired a nation.

103

You are full of great ideas, which are not always realized. Is this because:

A. You always lack sufficient time. Other responsibilities usually intervene, and the right moment often fails to present itself.

B. You never meet people who will help you make the right contacts and give you the support you need.

104

As you drive home from an enjoyable dinner party, you reflect that several of the guests seemed honestly entertained by your presence and attracted to your personality. You feel flattered and self-confident. Do you think your success tonight stemmed from:

A. Your lively conversation and the genuine interest you exhibited in your companions' lives and in their conversations.

B. Your reserved demeanor, your air of mystery, and your intriguingly secretive smile.

105

You are a director of a manufacturing firm with about 60 employees. It is going through a difficult time, hit by recession, aggressive rivals, and late payments. Morale is low among workers, who are worried about losing their jobs. Are you:

A. A rock whose solid presence is a constant source of comfort and confidence to employees and clients.

B. A clever tactician, who hides increasing anxiety behind a mask of optimism, maintaining a facade of calm control, knowing that others will judge you on how well you handle this crisis.

106

Which of these celebrities do you prefer:

A. Cary Grant, the witty and suave matinee idol.

B. Jimmy Stewart, the stuttering, straight-from-the-heart hero.

107

You are one of many employees working in a large, pre–World War II wealthy household. You are part of the housekeeping staff that performs domestic duties. How do you see your role:

A. To fit in with the team, obey orders, and find your place in the complex hierarchy among employees, filling that place to the best of your ability.

B. To serve the family faithfully and selflessly, straining to ensure that none of them ever wants for any comfort.

108

Job-hunting through the want ads in your newspaper, you see two intriguing posts advertised. Which one would you apply for:

A. "We need an organizer! If you can keep track of supplies and catalog stocks and regulate output, if your middle name is 'logistics,' if you can keep a firm grip on the cash flow and a close eye on the spreadsheets, we need you!"

B. "We need a generator! If ideas flow from you like sparks, if you can see solutions in problems and fresh concepts in stale strategies, if your mind and your eyes and mouth are always open, we need you!"

End of section three

SECTION FOUR

109 Which of these two renowned painters do you prefer:

A. Vincent Van Gogh, the starving artist who pioneered expressionism.

B. Salvador Dali, the dazzling showman who was a master of surrealism.

110 Your ship goes down and two years later you are rescued from a desert island. On returning home, you find your obituary in a newspaper. What did your friends say:

A. You were passionate, sometimes difficult, subject to mood swings, but never half-hearted.

B. You had wisdom balanced by an even temper, a cool and unruffled personality whose depth of emotion was masked by an equable nature.

111 Following the sad death of your elderly and beloved dog, your friends urge you to acquire a new pet. You are reluctant. Is this because:

A. Your heart is still full of your old friend and it would be a betrayal to transfer your affections to another animal.

B. You don't feel it is wise or desirable to make a 15-year-long commitment to a pet when you have no idea what the future might bring.

112 You are on vacation in a European seaport, dressed casually in a pullover and jeans. You look like a native—or so you think. When you walk into a bar to get a bite to eat, every head turns and you realize that you are not in the type of bar where they serve hamburgers with beer—instead, they serve whisky with beer. Do you:

A. Ignore the stares, look tough (maybe you don't have to try too hard), and order a drink before you leave—after long enough to make it clear that you are not intimidated.

B. Exercise your right to be in this place, and explain to the bartender that you are a visitor looking for somewhere to eat—perhaps he knows a good restaurant.

113 Which of these authors do you prefer:

A. Jane Austen, the author of comedies of manners.

B. Agatha Christie, the author of detective mysteries.

114 At a party you are introduced to a fellow guest by your enthusiastic hostess, who exclaims, "I just know that you two are going to get along wonderfully!" What is your instinct:

A. To let the other person show you what you might have in common, to sum up this new personality quietly before you start to make an impression of your own, emphasizing the characteristics that you calculate will show you to your best advantage.

B. To launch into animated conversation immediately, eager to show just why your hostess is so sure you will be a convivial and entertaining guest.

115 Human DNA is identical to within a couple of percentage points to gorilla DNA. Between human individuals, our DNA differs by only fractions of a percentage point. Yet forensic science can identify each person by their unique gene structures. Does this convince you that:

A. We are all essentially the same, part of the oneness of humanity, and that our differences are ultimately inconsequential.

B. All differences, however small they appear to be on paper, can be crucial, and that the essential glory of being human lies in our individuality.

116 You are in a lifeboat with six other passengers who have escaped from a sinking cruise liner. There is no radio, no map, and no sign of land, but there is plenty of food and water stored in the lifeboat. You sense your companions are glad to have you aboard and you know, because of the store of provisions, that it is not because they want to eat you. Is it because of:

A. Your quick, inventive mind, which will instantly see and summarize the possibilities facing all of you and the likely solution.

B. Your dauntless style, untouched by the vastness of the ocean, which will inspire and give support to your companions as you cheer them up, organize them, and, in moments of crisis, take command.

117

Which comedian do you relate to the most:

A. Stan Laurel, the thin, nervous funny man.

B. Oliver Hardy, the tubby, commanding straight man.

118

On a short flight you meet a couple from the other side of the Atlantic. They are friendly, in a vacation mood, and full of questions about you and your family's lifestyle. Do you find yourself:

A. Handing out your address, showing them family photos, telling your life story, and inviting the couple to stay with you whenever they are in the area.

B. Answering their questions with polite reserve and careful vagueness, happy to enjoy a conversation but unwilling to give away too much of yourself.

119

In the small hours of the night, you wake up with troubles on your mind. You can't get out of bed to deal with them right away, but there might be a solution for the problem if you can analyze the situation properly. Do you:

A. Lie awake, turning over the difficulties in your mind, unable to rest until you find the answer.

B. Put the problem away for consideration in the daylight, when you will feel more positive and less threatened, and turn instead to thoughts of something more pleasant, such as happy memories or the novel you have been reading, until you drift back to sleep.

120

Your neighborhood committee has voted to refurbish a local playground. Everybody has an idea about how this should be done, and what should have been a one-meeting decision has already spread itself over three evenings. Is your instinct:

A. To pick one idea, any idea, and move on with the plan, because the children don't have enough safe places to play.

B. To listen to everything, because other people will be reluctant to change their minds once a decision is made, even in the face of compelling new ideas—and because the children's safety can be guaranteed at this stage by careful planning.

121 Which of these fictional characters do you prefer:

A. Robin Hood, the bold outlaw.

B. Little John, the outlaw's faithful friend.

122 You are about to ask for a pay raise. You need it and you deserve it, but you know that if you don't get it, you will stay in this job for a while. Your boss is a short-tempered, stressed-out person. You know her well and can gauge the good and bad moods. When you press your claim, it fails. Is this because you are:

A. Too assertive and too ready to risk a flare-up, because you know your best tactics in any argument are to state your case and meet every challenge.

B. Too meek and too ready to back down and seek conciliation—you know that if it comes to a fight, your boss is always going to come out winning.

123 You are proud of your family photos. You have an eye for a picture, and when you offer a few prints for a local exhibition, it seems almost natural that a hotshot collector invites you to put a bigger show together. What follows is a total surprise: National newspaper reviews, a $10,000 arts prize, clamor from art lovers for limited edition prints. Is this acclaim:

A. Long overdue, the recognition you were born to enjoy and your chance to bask in the spotlight of newspaper interviews and talk-show appearances.

B. Something that doesn't seem right and a disturbing change to your life. You feel as if you have wandered into the wrong room and, although you are happy that your photos are admired, you feel detached from the praise.

124 Your neighbor has a tip for the Kentucky Derby, the greatest horse race in the United States and one of the greatest in the world. This tip is a long shot, but your neighbor seems confident. His son has just come back from a vacation at the stables where the horse is training. Do you:

A. Make a bet and feel good about following an impulse, accepting any nervousness as part of the day's fun and excitement.

B. Check the horse's past performance, perhaps even read up on the course's track record for this type of runner, and only place your bet after long, careful consideration.

125 Which of these actors do you prefer:

A. Humphrey Bogart, the classical tough guy.

B. Tom Hanks, the actor who brings tears to the eyes.

126 How do you envision the future? Do you foresee:

A. Global warming, limited nuclear wars, overpopulation, market crashes, and the increased spread of AIDS.

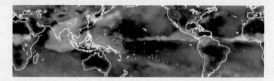

B. Cures for cancer, ecological lifestyles, better nutrition in undeveloped countries, and an end to Third World debt.

127 During a transatlantic flight, your airplane suddenly lurches and abruptly falls. As the passengers around you are thrown screaming from their seats, you are filled with the sickening certainty that you are about to die. The plunge ends as unexpectedly as it began, and the plane flies on to safety. Afterward, do you:

A. Scrutinize your emotional reaction, reviewing every detail of the event and coming to terms with a number of feelings you never before imagined—perhaps even undergoing therapy to deal with post-traumatic stress. □

B. Shrug off the incident as something unpleasant that has happened and is now in the past. !

128 There is a war on, and you receive an urgent call—you are appointed to lead a well-established unit. Your skills are unique and invaluable. The unit's previous commanding officer, a much respected leader, was killed in action. Do you:

A. Try to step into your predecessor's boots, offering sympathetic leadership to troops who have already bonded into a single, highly efficient machine.

B. Confront the troops, making them face the new chapter in their unit's history, forcing them to understand they must adapt or die.

129

Who had the right technique to make changes in the world:

A. Martin Luther King, Jr., the civil rights leader who had a dream for all Americans.

B. Bob Geldof, the visionary musician behind the international rock concert known as Live Aid, who knew that something had to be done to save a nation from starvation.

130

You are a castaway on an island as a contestant in a reality TV show. After one week you are on the point of collapse from exhaustion. Is this because you have been:

A. Playing to the camera every hour of the day, making sure the viewers know you and recognize your unique talents.

B. Trying to do everything for everyone, keeping the peace and building the fires, listening to complaints and cooking the fish—not to appear saintly to the viewers but because it is not in your nature to leave others floundering.

131

At an interview for a job you desperately want, the interviewer is proving tough. After a succession of difficult questions, he demands, "What is it that makes you a special candidate? What do you bring that's better than the rest?" Do you answer:

A. I am 1,000 percent dedicated, never late and never sick, and always committed to working hard in the most trying of situations.

B. I am clear-sighted and gifted with excellent judgment, with an analytical mind that can see all sides of any problem.

132

You are using your cell phone on the train, when you become aware of the mocking voice of another passenger. "I'm on the train!" he is shouting into an imaginary phone, "You're breaking up. I'm on the train!" Without turning around, you cannot be certain that this is aimed at you. Do you:

A. Look around and, if you are sure that the mockery is intended for you, stand up to confront the man.

B. Ignore the provocation and carry on with your conversation.

133 Which of these music legends do you prefer:

A. Jimi Hendrix, the uncompromising rock guitarist.

B. Bob Marley, the all-embracing reggae artist.

134 You have the chance to spend New Year's Day in the Far East. It is a terrific opportunity to enjoy a busy trip to fascinating new places. But it does mean you will be away from your family for most of the holiday season. Which is more important to you:

A. Being a valued constant in the family equation, always on hand to help out and entertain.

B. Taking chances while they are there. You don't want an old age spent regretting missed opportunities.

135 A gypsy's cruel curse upon you means you are fated to be reincarnated as a politician. What kind of politico will you be:

A. A showboater, not above deal-making and back-scratching, destined for high office, high risks, high income, and high profile.

B. A loyal public servant, forgoing the lure of power to serve the voters who elect you, deeply immersing yourself into the fascinating detail of other people's lives, turning the accursed career into a voyage of discovery.

136 You are sorting through a drawer and find a creased photograph from a wonderful vacation. Which scene would you prefer to see:

A. A restaurant in a faraway city, a lost lover sitting across the table with a sad smile, a sunset reflecting in the polished wood of the table.

B. A picnic rug spread in a field, the remains of lunch scattered on the grass, with close relatives watching as children run happily under a sunny sky.

137

Who portrayed the ideal cowboy:

A. John Wayne, the defiant, all-or-nothing tough man.

B. Gary Cooper, the peace-loving hero who fights only when he must.

138

The past is a foreign country, claimed the British novelist and short story writer L. P. Hartley. When you look back at your own past, do you see someone:

A. With different political beliefs, different sexual morals, and different attitudes to drugs and religion.

B. With the same outlook and character that you possess now.

139

You are a newspaper reporter, filing the front page story close to deadline. The atmosphere has reached fever pitch, and from across the room you hear the editor fulminating—she wants your copy and she wants it five minutes ago. Do you:

A. Take refuge in a calm inner shell, maintaining a steady focus on the words that must be written and the facts that must be assembled, knowing that distraction could drive you to inaccuracies.

B. Stand up for yourself, shouting back and making it plain that the story is what matters, and that it is your story and you won't be harassed into filing substandard copy.

140

You are on your own in your home, looking out of the window at a torrential downpour, when there is a buzz at the door. You look through the peephole and see a woman you don't know, dripping wet. When you open the door, she explains that her car has broken down. You can see it at the curb—a vintage Porsche, probably old enough to break down with expensive regularity.

The woman is well spoken and tells you she has called the repair services on her cell phone. A mechanic will be along in 90 minutes but she wants to know if she can possibly wait in your home. Do you:

A. Tell her politely but firmly that you don't know her and suggest that she wait in her car.

B. Invite her into the kitchen, give her a towel, hang up her coat, and make a pot of coffee.

141

Which of these Hollywood actors do you prefer:

A. Jim Carrey, the comedic star of *The Grinch*.

B. Russell Crowe, the heartthrob who starred in *Gladiator*.

142

At the end of a long day you fall into bed. Your partner is already asleep. What comes more naturally:

A. To lie awake, replaying in your mind everything that has happened to you since the morning, before you at last drop off—and replay everything once more in your dreams.

B. To slip easily into slumber, blanking out the day's events and enjoying a rest barely broken by dreams, which you will not remember when you awake.

143

You watch the relationship between your sister, a single parent, and her 13-year-old son. She is possessive and clinging, and she won't allow him the space he needs to grow up. He is melodramatic and hurtful, always seeking to enrage her so much that she will turn her back on him. You know that he secretly blames himself for his parents' breakup and accuses himself of driving his father away. When you look at yourself, which one of them do you more closely resemble:

A. The possessive parent.

B. The insecure child.

144

Your boss calls you in with a proposition, which she doesn't reveal at once. She suggests you tell her what changes you would introduce to make your job more enjoyable, and she asks you to say what—and whom—you most dislike about the company. Do you:

A. Feel sorely tempted to answer fully, because you are so intrigued by the unspoken proposition, which you suspect might include major new responsibilities and a substantial increase in salary.

B. Feel too wary to answer with more than bland generalizations, because the proposition might amount to nothing and the whole setup could possibly be a trap.

End of questionnaire

Complete scores

Well done! You have successfully completed a voyage through your personality, which is unique in the history of self-analysis. Not only have you explored the length and breadth of your character and reached into some of its more mysterious depths but you have also given your brain a total mental workout.

Your imagination is healthier, your powers of visualization are more vivid, and your daydreaming nodes are at their peak of fitness. You will be using all these mind powers and more as you work with the advice and exercises in this book.

You have worked hard for this moment—so enjoy yourself, as you are about to discover your Life Sign. Start by counting the symbols you have marked. The symbol with the highest total represents your Life Sign. Look in the key below to find the appropriate symbol—it is shown with its corresponding Life Sign. Once you have determined your Life Sign, you can discover more about yourself in Chapter 2.

Key to symbols

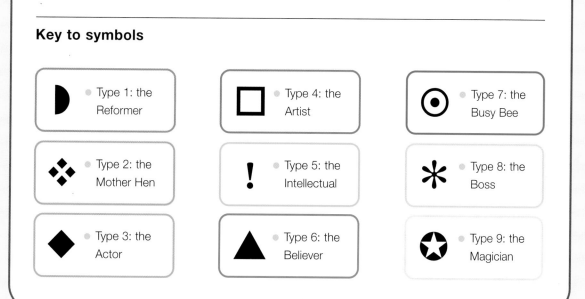

- Type 1: the Reformer
- Type 2: the Mother Hen
- Type 3: the Actor
- Type 4: the Artist
- Type 5: the Intellectual
- Type 6: the Believer
- Type 7: the Busy Bee
- Type 8: the Boss
- Type 9: the Magician

Reading the results

Now that you have determined your Life Sign, you will want to learn more about your Sign's characteristics. Each Life Sign contains a spectrum of traits. Some of these will seem to mirror your own personality's aspects, others will remind you uncomfortably of yourself at your weakest, and yet others will inspire you with the knowledge of what is possible for you. What you will discover is a set of tools to help you get the best out of life, relationships, and your own willpower.

Analyzing the answers

You can tell a lot about your own—or someone else's—personality by studying a chart of answers to the questionnaire in the previous chapter. The results will not only identify the type, or Life Sign, that best fits a person, it also brings to life the other less domineering traits of a person's personality, including her wing (see pp. 68–69).

You will find below studies of how four people have responded to the questionnaire. Their responses and the following analyzes will help you to interpret your own answers. Because you know yourself better than anyone else, it is best to start with your own questionnaire. With practice, you can soon interpret the answers of others who have filled in the questionnaire.

Key to the Life Signs

 Type 1: the Reformer

 Type 4: the Artist

 Type 7: the Busy Bee

 Type 2: the Mother Hen

 Type 5: the Intellectual

 Type 8: the Boss

 Type 3: the Actor

 Type 6: the Believer

Type 9: the Magician

Example questionnaire 1
The developing personality

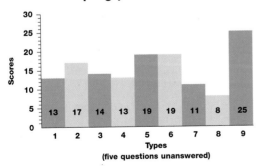

Scores

| 13 | 17 | 14 | 13 | 19 | 19 | 11 | 8 | 25 |

1 2 3 4 5 6 7 8 9
Types
(five questions unanswered)

◆ **Jenny**

A young 22-year-old woman, Jenny's life is careering through huge changes in only a few short years. Not long after she finished college with a degree in English and business studies, Jenny was given a job as a junior executive with an advertising agency in Toronto, where her parents live. Within weeks of starting her new job, Jenny discovered that she was pregnant, However, Jenny and the father, also a new graduate, had agreed to end their relationship, and the father has taken off to spend two years traveling around the world.

Jenny's parents urged her against an abortion, and they promised to help bring up their grandchild. Her new employer also guaranteed to keep her job open if she took maternity leave. The baby is now four months old, and Jenny is preparing to return to work while her mother handles the childcare. Jenny says she has been guided to all the right decisions and regrets nothing, but she does not feel that she made those choices herself. In fact, she feels that she is the last person to have any control over her life.

Jenny's chart reading

The turmoil in Jenny's life is reflected in her chart reading. She has scored artificially high in the Magician sign. I say "artificially," because mature Magicians are almost nonchalantly in control of their destiny, deftly juggling everything life can throw at them—and while Jenny is coping well, she is not nonchalant. The high type 9 reading reflects her desperation to keep everyone on her side and helping her—without the support of her parents and employer, she knows she could be in trouble. Jenny has relinquished all command, and this is revealed in the rock-bottom Boss score, and the low Busy Bee and Reformer tallies.

Jenny's true character is revealed by a pair of strong scores on types 5 and 6. She is an Intellectual with a powerful Believer spirit. It is this combination of analytical brains and team energy that has brought Jenny to the attention of her new boss. He recognizes in her the early stages of a strong executive character, and he clearly believes her experiences will bring out the latent best once she settles back into her job.

Example questionnaire 2
The over-developed personality

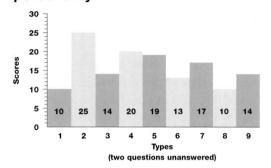

Types
(two questions unanswered)

◆ **Virginia**

At the age of 77, Virginia, a retired teacher, has just become a great-grandmother. She has, as she will certainly tell you if you meet her, 4 children and 11 grandchildren. Her husband died four years ago, and she has shown no interest in rekindling her social life, but she is not bored because every night brings a baby-sitting assignment or a plea for help with cooking, housework, and homework. Virginia is every family's dream grandmother. If you could buy relatives like this, she would be beyond price. Her children have noticed that Virginia is taking less interest in theaters and current affairs than formerly, but they conveniently feel this reflects her recent loss.

Virginia's chart reading

At first sight Virginia appears to be a clear-cut Mother Hen. However, I am always suspicious when I see a result like this, and I look to the secondary scores. Why is she scoring so high in the "helpful grandmother" mode? Most likely because it suits everyone around her. What this chart shows is a personality that developed fully, and then it began to channel a great deal of energy into an emerging area for the benefit of her children and grandchildren. In other words, Virginia is now over-developed in one area of her personality, and she would enjoy a return to her core traits.

Virginia has high, balanced scores at types 4 and 5. She is naturally an Artist with a powerful mind, capable of reflection at great depth. It is no surprise that she used to love the theater—her profile, which also contains a healthy Busy Bee influence, is perfect for a woman who might turn to painting or writing in her retirement. As a teacher she would have been an inspiration, and no doubt many of her pupils remember her with affection mixed with a little awe. Virginia's family should stop exploiting her natural family instincts and encourage her to spend more time enjoying herself as she once used to. After all, Virginia does have her own life to consider.

Example questionnaire 3
The balanced personality

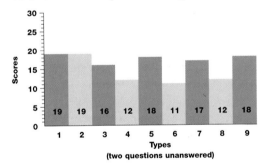

Types
(two questions unanswered)

Type	1	2	3	4	5	6	7	8	9
Score	19	19	16	12	18	11	17	12	18

◆ John

An architect, John is the father of three children. He is firm but almost endlessly patient with his children, giving his two sons and a daughter plenty of freedom within clear limits. When confronted with a problem, he likes to respond rationally, thinking his way through rather than laying down the law.

John's colleagues look up to him and accept his wisdom, respecting his experience, although they do not regard him as their leader. His flair for democracy enables his team to find their own solutions and to feel that they have taken charge of some projects. John's leadership talents are of the rarest type—almost invisible. Yet, when his input is closely examined, it becomes obvious that without his talents the job could not have been done.

John's chart reading

This person has an exceptionally well-balanced personality with a strong showing in the emotional Life Signs. His scores in the Feelers group—types 9, 1, and 2, are almost evenly balanced, with a pronounced Intellectual wing. His dominant sign is probably the Reformer. He knows what he thinks, and he trusts his judgment. But he also has great respect for other people's opinions, and he knows how to assimilate their views without conflict.

Although John is not introspective—hence the low type 4 score—he is unafraid of showing his emotions, and he has a flair for acting on instinct. He does like to get things done, and occasionally he takes on more work than he can comfortably handle. In fact, John would say that his greatest fault is to get involved in projects that should be a lower priority to him—but he is protected by an acute awareness of his core energy levels.

Curiously, John does not regard himself as a team player, and he prefers to work on his own instead of sitting on committees and attending meetings. He is not a "clubbable" type—he will never join a political party or declare allegiance to a particular sports team (although he works out at the gym and sometimes goes running).

Example questionnaire 4
The unbalanced personality

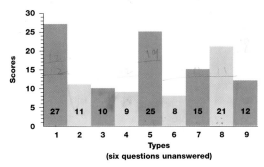

Types
(six questions unanswered)

1	2	3	4	5	6	7	8	9
27	11	10	9	25	8	15	21	12

◆ Tony

Divorced, with one child, Tony seldom sees his son, whom he regards as academically slow. Already on his third career, Tony is currently enjoying a rare period of financial stability. He has previously risen to two senior executive positions and has been fired from both of them. Now he is working as a college lecturer. His intelligence and experience is doubted by no one; however, he is hardly the most popular member of the staff.

Since he was a boy, the most commonly used adjective to describe Tony has been "arrogant." He does not see it that way himself—he simply feels that he is highly intelligent, with a logical mind and a healthy sense of right and wrong. Bullied as a child, and cruelly treated by his father, Tony reacts sharply to any criticism—real or imagined.

Tony cares little for what people think of him (hence, the low type 3 score), despises self-analysis (getting him to take this questionnaire required much begging and flattery), and makes no attempt to hide his poor opinion of his colleagues. He believes he is too good to be teaching, and the first people to know about it are his pupils. Tony is good at issuing instructions, delegating duties to the students

and making it plain what their fate will be if they fail to meet his assignments. They always do fail, of course—it would be an insult to Tony's superior intellect if others could match his high standards. But his refusal to pass students whom he feels simply do not make the grade is threatening to bring serious problems in his career—after all, the college's aim is to educate rather than humiliate. Unable to compromise, Tony will probably walk out of his job before he is asked to leave.

His inability to negotiate often leaves him feeling frustrated, even powerless. This can lead to eruptions of violence, such as the ones that ended his marriage.

Tony's chart reading

The Life Signs questionnaire has pinpointed serious areas of difficulty in Tony's personality. He has high scores in the strong personality types—the Reformer, the Intellectual, and the Boss—but he lacks the compassion of the Mother Hen, the Artist, and the Magician. He has also scored low when it comes to the Believer and the Actor. It is not unusual to have a low score in one or two of the Life Sign types, but low scores in several types shows an extremely unbalanced personality that will have trouble when it comes to communicating with others. Depending on the types involved, the person can be too aggressive or too withdrawn.

Unfortunately, without the willingness to accept that he has faults, Tony cannot develop. As long as he is unable to accept responsibility for his own character, and while he continues to blame short-sighted employers, stupid students, and idle colleagues for his problems, there will be little hope of a breakthrough. Tony is in danger of retreating altogether from reality, perhaps suffering a mental collapse.

The Life Signs wings and other connections

One of the principles of the ancient system of the enneagram is that each personality type is closely allied to a second type.

A complementary second type, often referred to as a "wing," is usually located beside the main Life Sign type on the enneagram wheel. For example, a Three's wing, or second type, would be a Two or a Four; a Seven's would be a Six or an Eight.

This concept was only partly correct, because it failed to take full account of the complex lattice of connections that combine to form the star at the center of the wheel. Each type is only one step away, not only from the types, or wings, on either side, but

also from the types directly connected to it by a line. Two lines meet at every point on the wheel, so there are four one-step links to other Signs. For example, a Nine links directly to Eight and One, as well as to Six and Three.

The two-step links

Not only are there four one-step links for every Sign, but there are also four two-step links. The Nine, for example, can reach Two and Four, Five and Seven, in

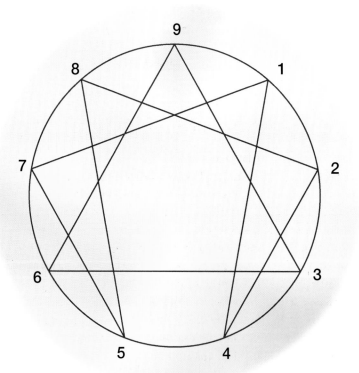

The enneagram
An ancient symbol, the enneagram (left) consists of a total of nine points, which are connected by lines forming a star pattern. This pattern is encompassed in a circle. In the example below, the two possible wings for type Five are types Six and Four. Type Five is also linked to types Seven and Eight by the lines within the circle.

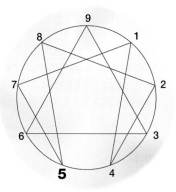

just two steps—by using one of the lines in the triangle to reach Three or Six, then moving another step to either side to the wings for Three or Six. You can try this for all the Life Signs. It is an elegant mathematical constant woven into a pattern that predates mathematics.

But what does this all mean in practical terms? Simply that whatever your main Life Sign, your personality will be powerfully influenced by a second Sign. However, you can also be influenced to a lesser degree by other Life Signs that are two steps away from your Sign. No matter where your Life Sign is on the enneagram wheel, you may be influenced by any of the other Signs.

Your second Sign

Although it is not always the case, your second Sign is likely to be the second highest scoring type from your questionnaire results. Take another look at your score—you are certain to find that the second-highest scoring type is one to which you feel a strong affinity. You may even feel that this is your main type, but don't leap to that conclusion. The questionnaire is carefully balanced to assess all aspects of your personality, including the dormant and subconscious elements, and it takes full account of potential characteristics that may not have fully developed within your personality. The second Life Sign, or wing, is frequently associated with the face that you present to the world, and it may be the type that your acquaintances would more probably associate with you. Only your closest friends may recognize that the wing is a more minor element in your whole character.

In most people, the wing is one step on the wheel from the dominant Sign. An Artist's wing will usually be Three or Five, One or Two. It is uncommon to find an Artist who is a restless ball of energy or a natural leader or who has a guiding urge to be accepted as part of a group; it is also rare to find an Artist who naturally smooths over difficulties and patches up arguments. To match one of those templates—for example, to be a Four with a wing of Six, Seven, Eight, or Nine—is unusual but by no means unheard of. It simply involves a two-step connection. People with two-step wings are rare, because their complementary traits often seem to be contradictory. This gives them an added individual flair in their dealings with life, and they can often have extraordinary flights of creativity.

Something to think about

At the center of the Life Signs wheel is an equilateral triangle (with sides of equal length), joining Three, Six, and Nine. If there were three equilateral triangles, Two would be linked to Five instead of Four and Seven would be linked to Four. The four one-step wings to four two-step wings relationship would be maintained, but it would imply that Artists and Busy Bees were complementary types and that Mother Hens were akin to Intellectuals. These pairs can be found, but they are unusual. Try counting the other triangles in the design. How many did you find?

Answer

There are 22 smaller triangles in the pattern, two mirror images of 11 triangles.

This 11–11 arrangement is significant. Many mystics regard 11–11 as an indicator of deeper mysteries, a naturally occurring design, which develops, like crystals and snowflakes, from the natural order of things. It is particularly intriguing that this mathematical rhythm can be discerned in patterns that have been drawn by men long before numbers were known or words were written.

Type One, the Reformer

Of all the Life Signs, the spectrum of possibilities for the Reformer is the widest.

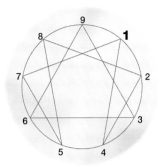

When everything goes well for the Reformer, he is powerful, successful, and content; however, when it goes wrong for him, he can spiral into catastrophe. Other Life Signs—such as the flexible Actor and the flitting Busy Bee—can bounce out of trouble, but the Reformer is always in danger of becoming locked into that spiral, unable to escape except by reversing the flow.

For the Reformer, self-knowledge is essential. At his best, he will use all his strengths and still be able to step out of his persona when difficulties loom. This is possible when a Reformer accepts his character by recognizing that if he allows himself to become fixated on problems, the problems will take over his life. It must have been a Reformer who coined the adage, "Don't sweat the small stuff (and it's all small stuff)!" That advice gives the Reformer what he needs most of all—a sense of perspective.

Ready for the challenge

It is easy to celebrate the natural accomplishments of the Reformer. His fastidious, opinionated, rational approach makes him an ideal teacher. Any child who is taught by someone with an innate sense of right and wrong, a perfectionist with a sense of good order and a tireless desire to see others reach high standards, will grow up to thank that teacher. As a politician, lawyer, police officer, journalist, or charity worker, the Reformer will exhibit the best in human nature to cope with a difficult, essential role. For example, the crusading zeal a Reformer brings to raising media awareness of child poverty will save countless lives. However, the Reformer is not seeking stardom—he will never care for the good opinion of the world if he feels that the world happens to be in the wrong.

Reformers are often attracted to the field of psychic phenomena, because they enjoy championing ideas that are unfashionable. When I read a balanced, enthusiastic report of a seance or a telepathy experiment, I know the reporter is a Reformer. He is unafraid of the ridicule of colleagues and is committed to printing the truth.

The best war reporters and investigative journalists are also Reformers. Their sure knowledge that they are pursuing the path of justice will armor them with skin as thick as a rhino's hide. One close friend, a political correspondent in Israel, once boasted to me "Both sides hate me, the hawks and the doves!

From the heart

The Reformer can feel frustrated when problems that cry out to be solved are beyond reach. You can try this exercise to help get rid of that frustration: Picture a plain wooden box in your hands. It is solid but light and has a yellow plastic lining. Imagine the infuriating problem floating over the box and dropping in, and you slam the lid and lock it in.

Now imagine taking the box above your head and hurling it away with all your force.
The box tumbles away over the horizon until it is gone and is nothing to do with you any more.

I'd be worried if either of them started liking me—that would mean I was being seen as biased."

Reformers don't do well as diplomats. If someone at a party opposes everything you say and refuses to make any conciliatory statement, then you know that you have met a Reformer—and one who enjoys exercising his combative talents too much. If you recognize yourself here, remember that you don't have to fight every battle. Sometimes it is enough to make your point by refusing to agree. Other people are entitled to opinions, too.

The perfectionist

The Reformer is inclined to perfectionism. It is good to be perfect at the end of a project, but it can be bad at the start; anything that must be exactly right before it begins will never get off the launchpad. The Reformer can be indecisive, failing to finish a project instead of completing something that is less than 100 percent. The best lesson for the Reformer is to learn to let go. He should not judge himself by endeavors that are not completely successful, but, instead, hold onto the hope of doing better next time. He must be aware that it is a short step from endlessly changing a work project to becoming addicted to work.

A Reformer does not find it easy to adapt to change as he grows older. He often wants to turn the clock back and will complain that the current popular music is simply noise, and they don't make television shows like they used to. Although this inflexibility threatens all the Life Signs, it is especially dangerous to the Reformer; but he can guard against his inflexibility by recognizing the symptoms.

The judgmental force of the Reformer

For your information

The stubborn Reformer

For an example of an inflexible Reformer subject to prejudice, read Anthony Trollope's *He Knew He Was Right*. Louis Trevelyan falsely accuses his wife of a liaison with an old friend. Everyone who knows Louis begs him to see the truth. But he is so threatened by the emergence of women's rights in London that he kidnaps his son and flees to Italy. Friends try to help Louis, but he refuses their help, demanding that his wife acknowledge his dominance as head of the family. Trevelyan is intelligent and loves his wife and son, but he cannot act against his own misplaced convictions. In real life, the Reformer must learn to respect his partner's opinions.

In partnership

An embittered Reformer is dangerous. A woman whose partner is a failed Reformer will recognize the intolerance that can turn into racism, the self-righteousness that is always ready for an argument, the hypocrisy that leads to hatred, and the inarticulateness that finds an outlet in violence. This Reformer cannot be changed from the outside—the change must be born of an inner desire to succeed. At the opposite end of the spectrum, a woman whose Reformer partner is principled, conscientious, and ethical need never fear any violence, for she will always be protected.

Type Two, the Mother Hen

Love is the driving energy of the Mother Hen, and love is the most complex emotion in the universe.

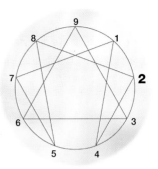

We all have an imaginary concept of the ideal mother love, but we rarely stop to think of the tumultuous feelings in a mother's heart. This all-powerful love also embraces fear, desire, ambition, and anger. For those whose entire being is centered on this energy, the whole of life is a turmoil of feelings.

The nurturing type

The key to the Mother Hen's personality is her urge to nurture. She does not feel complete unless she is caring for others. This tendency often emerges early in life—perhaps, she couldn't sleep until her dolls were all safely tucked up, or she looked after younger siblings or an infirm parent. Before she leaves her teenage years, the Mother Hen will learn to define herself in terms of the care and nurturing that she has bestowed on others.

The embracing hands of the Mother Hen

Male vs. female

Although I am referring to the Mother Hen as female, it is important to note that there are male Mother Hens. I personally know at least three fathers whose devotion to their children is a clear expression of their Mother Hen personality, either as a wing (see pp. 68–69) to the main type or as the core itself. Unfortunately, male Mother Hens are not encouraged in many Western cultures to demonstrate their real nature—nurturing is still considered effeminate by an overwhelmingly macho society. When children come into the picture, however, a real Mother Hen—male or female—will find it impossible to deny the urge to care.

Some cultures, such as southern Mediterranean societies, still vigorously promote the notion that all women should be Mother Hens. This belief is common among many Jewish families, too. My own wife, Hanna, is a wonderful example of a fully developed Mother Hen, and all my family (especially, I confess, myself) have benefited beyond measure from her years of caring.

From the heart

You cannot change the past. Imagine you are captain of a boat, looking over the stern at the wake. Nothing you do can recall the water you leave behind. Your duty is to steer the boat ahead. Let the past go, and aim for the future.

The Mother Hen's nature

The Mother Hen is naturally in touch with her psychic nature. She empathizes easily with people she scarcely knows, sharing their emotions. She is warm-hearted, generous, concerned, and thoughtful. However, the Mother Hen's loved ones know she is often overly expressive of her emotions. She will talk tirelessly about how she feels and what she wants to do, sometimes substituting talk for action. Although her intentions in this overwhelming display of emotion may be good, the effect is often to browbeat others, coercing them into doing things her way. She knows how to use flattery to cultivate people, but she can also be snide behind their backs, with a sharp tongue when she imagines she has been slighted. Because some societies are condescending toward Mother Hens, showing them a different kind of respect to that afforded to Bosses or Busy Bees, this type seeks to protect herself with words—which can lead to spreading gossip and undermining reputations.

A Mother Hen needs to be needed. She places a high value on her friends, a higher value still on her family, and at her best can be utterly unselfish. This side of her character, when carried to an extreme, becomes saintly. Think of Mother Teresa of India, whose kindness to the poor seemed to invest her with an immense and radiant aura. Mother Hens who are truly humble and altruistic are often natural healers, able to cure sickness simply by being with a patient, and this leads many Mother Hens—again, male and female—into nursing and childcare.

Too much love

All Mother Hens must beware of being too possessive. They find it hard to release a loved one from their care. Sometimes this undying loyalty brings lifelong pleasure and comfort, as in the case of a nanny who stays in contact with the children she helped to bring up well into their adult lives, perhaps even nurturing their children. But this love can become cloying, a burden, when it is unwanted. Some adults feel they cannot progress emotionally as long as their mother's intense, protective love is swaddling them. Sometimes, to be kind to another, the Mother Hen must be cruel to her own heart.

The Mother Hen wants to sacrifice herself for those she loves, but she can become self-deceiving if others reject her love. She does not understand that love this intense and all-enveloping can be too much for some other types. Artists are stifled by this emotional blanket, and Intellectuals can find it suspect, while Bosses often fail to appreciate anything for its true value. The Mother Hen may respond by making family members and friends feel guilty. She whines and complains, and she can become abusive of food, medication, or alcohol in an attempt to dull the pain of so much unrequited emotion. Hypochondria is another common pattern of behavior, as her subconscious calculates that, in order to win recognition for her talents, she must appear to be ill.

For your information

A Mother Hen in literature

The faithful friend of Sherlock Homes, Dr. John Watson, is a rare example of a male Mother Hen in literature. Far from the amiable buffoon of the Hollywood films, the Dr. Watson depicted in the books was loyal, brave, and concerned for his friend's health and mental well-being. Medicine was his natural metier—he was a caring, loving man, and a healer. However, Dr. Watson's emotions were often ungovernable, and Holmes was often amused by the doctor's weakness for beautiful women.

Their creator, Sir Arthur Conan Doyle, was a Mother Hen himself, with an Actor's wing. Keenly interested in Spiritualism and spirituality in general, he is generally thought to have drawn on his dominant Life Sign in the depiction of Watson and his flamboyant, ruthless streak in the peerless creation of Holmes.

Type Three, the Actor

The third Life Sign has an exciting and engaging personality that is often charming.

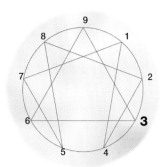

Some of the many names that can be applied to this Life Sign are the Motivator, the Succeeder, the Egotist, the Achiever, and the Get-Up-And-Goer. However, the Actor is the name that most aptly applies to the whole spectrum of this Sign, because he always needs an audience. Maroon an Actor on a desert island and he will believe that he has ceased to exist. His only hope will lie in the fantasy that the world is seeking him desperately, bereft at an irreplaceable loss.

Affectionate childhood

It is not surprising that many Actors are only children or first children who are the object of intense maternal affection in their early years—but the opposite can also apply, when a natural Actor finds a childhood starved of affection has intensified the need for attention and applause. That drive for affection inspires the Actor to great achievements, and he inspires everyone who applauds him. He understands instinctively the need for self-confidence, and holds himself in high esteem. Without these qualities no one, whatever their type, can enjoy sustained success, because the nagging sensation that the success is undeserved will spoil it.

The tragic and comedic faces of the Actor

Ambition and charm

The Actor's compulsion to be seen to do well translates itself into ambition, whether directed at a career or his social standing. When success is hardwon—or worse, unattainable—the ambition can coagulate into an obsession. But more often, the combination of energy and self-assurance carries the Actor to his goal. On the way, he will become efficient and competent—he is no faker, and you may be sure that the pinnacle he regards as his birthright was won on merit.

There is no such thing as an Actor without charm, but the charm can be switched off if aggression is required. An Actor's charm is not a veneer. He possesses many layers, like an onion, which express different levels of his personality. If success is easy, the charm can be replaced by arrogance and narcissism.

The Actor is in danger of being a brownnoser and backstabber, searching out successful, talented people to schmooze and flatter, while behaving with contemptuous disdain to anyone whose value is not apparent to him. The Actor does not believe that all people are equal. His motto might be, "All people are useful but some are more useful than others." The risk in brownnosing is hard for an Actor to understand—that some people actually do not like flattery. And the risk in backstabbing is even worse, because one day one of those underlings may be a rung above the Actor.

The Actor should remember a film star might imagine he was destined for fame, but no waiter supposes he was destined for obscurity. Everyone can dream—and the lowliest cleaner in a fast-food restaurant could have a dream come true. Backstabbing, in truth, is a cheap way for an Actor to bolster his ego. Subconsciously, he is telling himself that he doesn't deserve to be climbing the ladder and that he can defend his precarious position only by being offensive. Why not offer a helping hand to others lower down the ladder—they won't pull you off, and they might return the favor some time.

The Actor can become convinced of the importance of his every word, rudely uninterested in other people, full of self-love and selfishness. This type of pride comes before a hard fall, but to his credit, a fallen Actor will not lie on the ground for long. He will pick himself up and start planning a comeback.

Self-perception and judgment

When the Actor appreciates the value of what he has achieved—and this is particularly true when he has built a loving, stable family around himself—he is deeply grateful to God for his blessings. He knows he came into the world with exceptional gifts, and that he might just as probably have been born without them. When the things he values are threatened—by money problems, the emergence of rivals, or the fading of his talents—he frets and devises endless plans to stave off disaster. More often than not, he succeeds.

When others perceive an Actor very differently from how he expects to be perceived, he is confused. His sense of reality is shaken, and he doubts his own core identity. He is unlikely to realize that other people are pursuing their own agendas and not his, that their perceptions are guided by what they want to see. This essential piece of self-knowledge can act as bedrock in an Actor's life.

Because the Actor does not feel other people's pain too badly, he is often the best person to solve outside problems. Being detached and objective, emotions and sentiment do not intrude on his judgment as he identifies what needs to be done. The Actor can be an excellent politician, general, or business consultant when he exercises this quality.

Type Four, the Artist

Not all Artists are artistic, but this type typifies the popular conception of the artist in society.

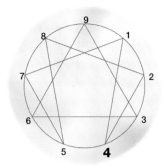

When it comes to determining their Life Sign, many great artistic people, including painters, sculptors, musicians, and writers, do not necessarily fit in the Artist personality—outstanding creativity is possible under all the Life Signs. However, the popular conception of "the artist" as a sensitive, introverted person moved by powerful feelings and emotions that are not given to easy expression best describes the type Four Life Sign named as the Artist.

If an Artist can find an outlet for her inner life, she will be happy and fulfilled. If she cannot, she will never be satisfied—she will always bottle up her emotions and yearn for self-expression. Artists are introverts, and they naturally turn to look within their hearts. They seek to understand their feelings, but this cannot be done by introspection alone—the heart must have a voice.

Finding a route for expression

An articulate Artist who can select the words to describe her emotions will turn naturally to writing, but what she writes does not necessarily need an audience. She might keep a diary, as Anne Frank did when her family was in hiding from the Nazis in an Amsterdam attic. The only people, it seemed, who could possibly read Anne's diary were the very people who should not—the prisoners who lived, slept, and ate beside her every day for almost two years. Anne's spirit was able to escape from that prison through her written words, and after her death—when her father returned after his liberation from a concentration camp and found her diary—Anne's writing found its way into many homes around the world.

From the heart

The singer Paul Simon laments on his neglected masterpiece, *Hearts And Bones,* that he often thinks too much. Paul's Life Sign is the Artist, and, like other Artists, he can benefit from switching off his mind. Deep meditation involves a long learning process, but even beginners can enjoy relaxation with a simple meditation. Breathe slowly and gently, counting each breath up to 50. Concentrate only on the breaths and the numbers; in a couple of minutes your head will be clear and your body relaxed.

An artist can find expression through long letters to friends, or simply in heartfelt conversations. But if she is more inarticulate, she can try to use pictures, objects, and music to express herself. She must overcome her inner censor, who fears other people will reproach and condemn her for the often shocking emotions she wants to release. She is sometimes frightened at the enormity of her own feelings.

If the censor wins, and the taboo remains unbroken, the Artist is prey to depression. Her outer life, always prone to untidiness, will become chaotic, and she may be destructive or even violent. Deep relationships become impossible when she cannot be true to herself. She will try to blot out the pain—which her insight recognizes clearly—with alcohol or drugs, deliberately seeking oblivion.

Natural sensitivity

The Artist's defenses are a sense of humor at her own eccentricities and failings, a mercurial temperament that switches unexpectedly to laughter in the middle of anger, and a fine sense of irony. She can learn to take herself not too seriously, although she is inclined to self-pity and enjoys her melancholy interludes, but she is also sensitive to others' pain. The Artist takes hard words personally, and she is capable of nursing a grudge all her life for an insult that may have been casually spoken and instantly forgotten by her enemy. The positive aspect of this is her natural tact and compassion.

When the Artist is loved and can accept that love, she will respond with gentleness. She is drawn to beauty and her love is always romantic. She wants to adore her children with a blissful blindness to their faults. If a child is careful with her delicate heart, an Artist can be a wonderful mother.

Spiritual intelligence

Of all the Life Signs, the Artist is most likely to recognize and nurture her spiritual intelligence. It is the equal of emotional and intellectual intelligence, and rarer to find. Some philosophers argue that it is the true moral sense that differentiates humans from beasts.

Spirituality is as far removed from intellect as birds are from trains. Birds have the freedom to soar, but they are delicate. Massive trains are hard to push off course from their established tracks. The Artist instinctively recoils from patterns of behavior that are set by convention—routines and modes of living that would suit most other people. For example, fashions are meaningless. The only habits she adopts are those that reflect her heart, which are idiosyncratic. If these habits strike the world as odd, and the world says so loudly, the Artist may shyly prefer to conform, for fear of drawing attention to herself. This fear evaporates when her inner confidence is strong—she may not be talkative, but she will let you know when she needs to be assertive.

This extract from the philosopher William James's book, *The Varieties Of Religious Experience,* sums up the Artist's spiritual potential: "I was in a state of quiet, even passive, enjoyment, not actually thinking, but letting ideas, images, and emotions flow of themselves through my mind. All at once, without warning of any kind, I found myself wrapped in a flame-colored cloud. For an instant I thought of fire, an immense conflagration somewhere close by; the next instant I knew that fire was in myself. Directly afterward there came upon me a sense of exaltation, of immense joyousness, accompanied by an intellectual illumination impossible to describe...I became conscious in myself of eternal life."

Writing is one form of expression available to an articulate Artist.

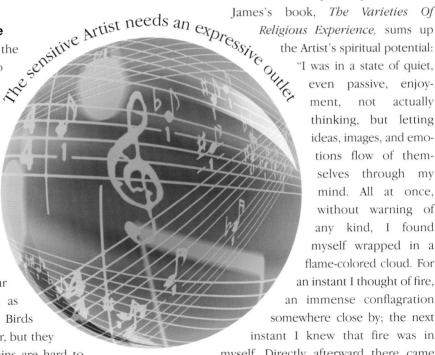

The sensitive Artist needs an expressive outlet

Type Five, the Intellectual

The Intellectual is a thinker, with a powerful capacity for concentration.

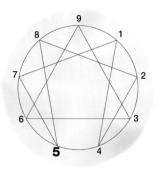

Those familiar with the television program *Star Trek* will recognize that Mr. Spock's incisive intelligence was unable to compute the meanings of emotions. "That is not logical, Captain," he remarked whenever the feelings of others puzzled his intellect. Mr. Spock is the caricature of the fifth of the Life Signs, the Intellectual. He has no emotional or spiritual intelligence, but believes his analytical ability will compensate.

Lost in thought

The Intellectual may not be "bright" in the conventional sense; for example, some are undiagnosed dyslexics who struggle to read and write, despite having an acute cognitive ability.

When he concentrates on his thoughts, they bore through ideas like a laser. This can create an aura of absentmindedness, but the mind is not actually absent, just fully engaged on an inner task. The result can be a poor short-term memory, coupled with an exceptional long-term memory. The Intellectual may remember the bones of a theory, plot, or plan from decades before, and be able to recall its strengths and weaknesses with ease, as though he had a computer database for a brain—yet he sometimes finds himself standing in a room, wondering what he was looking for.

The German philosopher Arthur Schopenhauer's friends related a story of how he was once wandering in a city park when a thought so gripped him that he forgot to walk and stood like a statue in a flowerbed. A gardener saw him and yelled out, "What do you think you're doing? Just who do you think you are?"

"Ah," replied Arthur, "if I only knew the answer to that."

Relating to others

The Intellectual does not relate well to others. He is often chaotic in personal affairs, committed to theorizing, endlessly creating concepts, yet indifferent to the reaction of the world. Nutrition, exercise, and physical health are often neglected, which leads to a reduced sex drive—but this may not be a bad thing for an Intellectual who prefers mental gymnastics to the physical kind (the writer Honoré de Balzac used to say that every time he had sex, he wasted an entire novel).

The Intellectual is capable of affection and love, but he needs to display it. The introverted pattern of thinking spreads to all aspects of life, so that social behavior is internalized. He might think of witty things to say or warm statements to proclaim, but the words come late or shyness keeps his lips sealed.

The analytical side of the Intellectual

A talented storyteller, the Intellectual also has the capacity to visualize in detail, to fantasize wildly, and to dream in vivid color, which makes him a natural psychic. He can be proficient at psychokinesis, affecting objects without touching them—proving the literal power of mind over matter. To an Intellectual, the brain is the sexiest muscle in the body. When words do not come readily, a pen (or a computer) solves the problem. The Intellectual is no 500-word-a-minute motormouth like the Busy Bee, but in an hour he might choose and commit to paper 500 words that will say more than a chatterbox manages in a lifetime. He prefers the literature of ideas to that of feelings—the best science fiction writers, who create emotionally thin characters in conceptually rich universes, are gifted Intellectuals.

Practical matters

The danger of over-reliance on thought is that practical matters are forgotten or treated with contempt. The Intellectual in a university who despises the way his ideas translate into action in the real world is a dangerous figure—for example, all the most murderous political movements of the 20th century began as concepts in ivory towers. Marx, Nietzsche, Lenin, and the architects of apartheid and the Holocaust are all horrific indicators of

From the heart

The ultimate Intellectual, Albert Einstein, was a pacifist, unable to see why people would want to kill each other. Intellectuals often avoid confrontation, not from cowardice but because it confuses them. They see it as being irrational, emotional, and uncontrolled—confrontation represents everything that repulses them.

what can happen when intellect is not balanced by spiritual and emotional intelligence.

The Intellectual who is thwarted by the outside world—the one, for example, who has two college degrees but is working in a fast-food chain—is prey to paranoia and a high-strung intensity that can spiral into madness. He needs outlets for his innovative, inventive, provocative, abrasive mind. He needs to be argumentative, to strut his cynicism and wit, to demonstrate his open-mindedness, and to embrace radical concepts.

The Intellectual can become so lost in thought and unresponsive to others, that she may seem like a static statue.

Type Six, the Believer

The sixth Life Sign, the Believer, has a strong need to belong to a group.

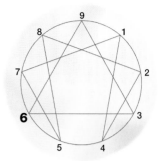

The Believer is often the glue that bonds society, bringing together the people whose sense of community defines their individuality. She knows she is a shadow of her real self if she is denied a network of friendships, recognition of her status, a role, a place of work. She brings dedication, commitment, and a relentless sense of duty.

How others see the Believer is how she sees herself. When the Believer takes a job, the job becomes part of her personality. This is true as much of the wife and mother who makes her role in the home as of the banker or lawyer whose friends are almost exclusively bankers or lawyers. She needs the respect her role supplies.

A belonger

To emphasize her commitment to her ideals and ambitions, the Believer will join with others. When attempting to get into shape, she will join a weight-loss club and a gym. When she needs to express her creativity she will join an amateur drama group or a choir. She is often a member of her local church, the parent-teacher organization, and the office coffee club. Wherever she joins, she aims to participate by being a committee member or acting as treasurer. The Believer believes in democracy and in sharing her opinion, unless she happens to have joined an autocratic society demanding obedience to the leader.

This passion for belonging can be dangerous, especially for adolescents. If the Believer's judgment is poor, she can commit herself to questionable societies—from a gang of unsavory friends to a brainwashing religious cult—that don't value her in return. Well-meaning attempts to pry her away will be met with defiance. Worse, they will increase her determination to keep the faith—those not with her must be against her. At its worst, this breeds fanaticism, racism, and religious hatred. Fed by prejudice, this type of thinking is contagious and is at the root of world-wide ethnic warfare.

Security and trust

The social respect the Believer craves is usually its own safeguard. Communities expect people to follow the rules, and the Believer will do this—and enforce them on others. She can be authoritarian and opinionated, and she is a stickler when in charge, but she is also a loyal follower.

The Believer's need for security leads her into a strong marriage, where she will be devotedly affectionate, loving as much as she is loved. Never a free thinker, she does not like to act on her own

Loyal to the ends of the Earth

The Believer has a strong need to participate in a group. She will rarely be seen in a solo activity.

impulses, although she can be flexible when offered change by a partner she loves. The Believer is loyal and will follow her spouse or her employer to the ends of the Earth.

The disappointed Believer is a pitiful figure. If her loyalty is rewarded with lies and tricks, she will retreat into a shell of suspicion, seeing a devious mind behind every pair of eyes. When questioned she will be evasive, never frank, using empty words and barricading herself behind jargon. If she is unsure of her own status within her group—for example, a manager unsure of her job or a mother who sees her children making their own friends for the first time—she will show hostility to outsiders.

When a Believer's trust has been well-placed, she will happily serve her whole community, helping to make it such a place to be proud of that everyone will share her Believer's zeal. She can be a wonderful teacher, a ferocious politician, an inspirational churchwoman, and, if she is blessed with the best of everything that life sometimes has to offer, the head of a loving family.

For your information

Forever loyal

Charles Dickens found ways to describe the nightmarish Victorian London in language that hints at the horror without spelling out the details. In *Oliver Twist* Nancy is one of Fagin's "girls." That is her life, and she is loyal to it. She loves her man, the brutal burglar Bill Sikes, and she sticks by him even through beatings and abuse. However, the affection she feels for Oliver is softer. She acts on her inner conviction that although her life is bad, it is good enough for her, but Oliver deserves better, and she risks her life to save him from Fagin. Nancy is a Believer. She has to belong to a community, even if it is a den of thieves. Betraying the people who have brought her so low is the hardest thing she could ever do.

Type Seven, the Busy Bee

Most other Life Signs get tired just watching the Busy Bee surge through life in a blaze of energy.

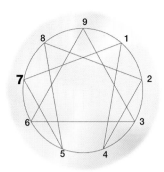

The Busy Bee will do everything that flutters within his range, afraid of tackling nothing. It may seem strange that all the great achievers in history don't fall under this Sign, or that so many Busy Bees buzz furiously through life and leave little to show for it at the end. Strange, until it is understood that the Busy Bee's sting is much more dangerous to himself than to anyone else.

The whirlwind of energy of a Busy Bee

He is his own worst enemy, which is the only piece of wisdom a Busy Bee needs in order to triple his efficiency. If he can watch out for his own sting, all that furious buzzing will create a noise that the whole world can hear.

On the move

The Busy Bee throws himself fearlessly at tasks. He hits the target, first time, so hard that his momentum carries everyone forward. Too often, however, he tires of that job almost immediately. Although he enjoyed himself immensely and got the project moving, he now wants to do it all over again. Of course, as soon as he ceases to apply pressure and his attention wanders, the momentum is quickly lost.

He is often moved to rage when what he started slows to a quick stop, but he hates to go backward and he won't be likely to return to get things going

again. The people around him know this and will make a pretence of helping him get started, knowing that they can ease off as soon as he loses interest.

A natural talker

The vivacious Busy Bee is full of spontaneous chatter, coming up with one-liners and telling stories. There is no such thing as a quiet, reflective Busy Bee. He will talk through anything. He may be flamboyant if this helps him gain attention when his ideas are in full stream. Or he may prefer the stripped-back, no-nonsense style.

He is not a natural listener, which is a simple lesson he needs to learn. The wise hear more than they say, but the unrestrained Busy Bee says so much that no one else has a chance to speak. When Busy Bees meet, they often captivate each other for the first few hours—after that, they cramp each other's style and a battle of egos develops.

Compulsive behavior

Shopping gives the Busy Bee a thrill, and it is something that can be done over and over—until the money runs out. A shopper's appetite is never sated, and the Busy Bee can sting himself by overspending.

He makes an enthusiastic connoisseur and an astute collector, but he is likely to drop his hobby before he acquires first-rate knowledge or taste. If his collector's instinct is thwarted (and he collects people as well as objects), he is at risk of dropping his scruples, lying, and breaking trust as he becomes more materialistic and acquisitive. Emotionally, this can lead to faithlessness and compulsive promiscuity. A Busy Bee who finds a good partner is well advised to constantly invoke his pledges of fidelity.

The Latin word for this easily bored type was *quidnunc*, which means "what now?" The Busy Bee is always on the alert for gossip, current affairs, and other people's misfortunes. If he can control and channel his energy, he is unstoppable. If he runs wild, he will burn out or be stuck in a cycle of manic activity and depressed inactivity.

The Busy Bee often rushes around in an attempt to get everything done all at the same time.

For your information

Meddling ways

Emma, the heroine of Jane Austen's novel of the same name, is vain and pleased with herself, but she is ignorant of her own emotions. Emma is bored, so she meddles. She is miserable unless she is plotting or creating mischief. She uses other people as playthings, and tosses them away when she has had enough. She is not bad, but irresponsible; not heartless, but blind to her own heart. Emma is a Busy Bee in a bottle, buzzing furiously against the glass walls. As others deal with the situations she creates and moves on, Emma is forced to grow up. She will always be a Busy Bee—our Life Signs don't change—but she won't be so silly.

Type Eight, the Boss

The Boss will know her Life Sign as soon as she glances at the list of the types.

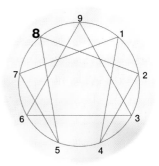

There is no competition—none of the other eight types seem remotely applicable to the Boss's personality and she is not inclined to waste any time thinking the issue over. In fact, the Boss scarcely sees the point of defining her Life Sign—she is who she is. If she has completed the questionnaire in this book, she probably did so as a friendly concession to a beloved partner—although the Boss is confident about herself, she does need practical support and love, and she will appreciate it when she gets it.

For your information

A literary hero

Lacking introspection and a capacity for torturing her own soul, the Boss rarely prospers in literature as a hero. One exception is found in Herman Melville's *Moby Dick*. Captain Ahab is an archetypal Boss, whose vendetta against a white whale becomes a crusade against the fickleness of Fate. His charisma and forceful speaking convince his crew to help him with his mission, to scour the seas for a single whale.

Ahab is a fighter. He regards any hint of insubordination as a challenge to his authority. He never seeks compromise and always crushes an opposing view. He forces men to see the world as he sees it, but he will sacrifice everything for those who make a great sacrifice for him. Because of this, he inspires undying loyalty.

No lack of confidence

The Boss believes that she is in charge based on her own merits, and she generally regards most other people as lazily weak. She is dominant, even overbearing, in every relationship. Even when the Boss is forced to make a concession to a superior force—for example, to a senior colleague, a parent, or a social heavyweight—there is no sense of inferiority in her deference. She believes that she is as good as the very best, and better than the rest.

Good at delegation and quick to seize every initiative, the Boss follows her ideas from start to finish. She is capable of making things happen, because she is not afraid to tell people to get busy. She can also be powerfully enthusiastic about new ideas, although her own innate creativity is often hampered by her reluctance to look into her own heart for inspiration.

The Boss is courageous, and she will stand up to be counted or stand up and fight. However, her courage can easily overspill into recklessness. Believing herself to be invincible and immortal, she will take on challenges even when the odds are stacked against her. This Life Sign will win the most outrageous gambles, but when she fails, she can lose everything. In Fact, the Boss is more at risk of bankruptcy than any other Life Sign.

Life for the Boss is a struggle for survival, a test of her will against the world. She will be ruthless, although she is always willing to bend the rules to make deals. She has a tendency to keep score of her success, using money for points, and she is no pushover for charities—after all, she has won her wealth the hard way and is not about to simply give it away.

However, if she does decide to back a charity, she is worth countless donations, because her organizational acumen and relentless energy will always get results. The Boss's favored causes are not for animals, but for people, such as sick children, who cannot help themselves.

A real life rise and fall

The disgraced tycoon Robert Maxwell lived a life that spanned the extremes of his Life Sign. From poor beginnings in Czechoslovakia, after fighting the Nazis in World War II, Maxwell used the sheer force of his personality to impose himself on Western business. He was never anything but a Boss—dynamic, dominant, and addicted to danger. After his mysterious death, the depth of his financial malpractice was revealed. He stole from the pension fund of his employees, leaving hundreds of people to face an old age of destitution. Yet the same man had created a business empire through decisive leadership and a strong strength of will.

To anyone whose Life Sign is type Eight, or who loves a Boss, Maxwell's spectacular rise and catastrophic self-destruction are not only a vivid illustration of this Life Sign's strongest potential but also a dire warning of its very worst aspects.

Heartbreaking

Although the Boss does need love, she is also a flirt. The thrill of sexual frisson, even in a chance encounter or an offhand remark, can be electrifying to her. The risk and the implied social importance make flirting irresistible to most Bosses, and their partners learn to take it in their stride. The employer who carries a friendly relationship with his

From the heart

Bosses are not introverts and tend to despise any self-absorption. However, you don't have to be moody and withdrawn to enjoy a little inner reflection, which, in moderation, is healthy for most people. To help you start the process, find a picture of yourself 20 years ago, and try to remember how you felt on that day. Compare your character then to how it is today. Look not only for changes, but also for elements that have remained unchanged.

The leading force of the guiding star

personal assistant into the realm of thoroughly inappropriate behavior is both a cliché and a staple of sensational reporting. A prime example can be seen in possibly the biggest Boss in the world, ex-President Bill Clinton, who was caught in a type of extreme flirting, and almost paid for his love of danger with the presidency itself. His wife, Hillary, notably, has long made allowances for his flirting.

For other types, it is easy to question why someone would risk his marriage and career for meaningless sexual encounters. In Clinton's case, his marriage was the envy of America; Hillary is beautiful and supportive, a great mother, and she possesses the political talent to become a senator herself. What more could a Boss desire? The answer is risk. To a Boss, risk will always be the ultimate temptation.

Type Nine, the Magician

In an ideal world, we would all be Magicians, reflecting this peace-loving, reasonable Sign.

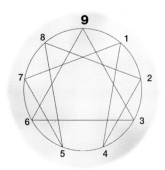

Blessed with an easygoing nature, the Magician has a talent for communicating clearly and a habit of seeing all sides of the argument. However, if the Magician had his say, maybe the pace of progress would be slowed. Instead of white-hot technological revolutions and digital change at the speed of light, we would have committee meetings that took all morning to reach an indecision. A planet peopled wholly by Magicians might not even have gotten around yet to inventing the internal combustion engine. Or the steam engine, for that matter.

To which the typical Nine will respond, "That doesn't sound like a bad thing." He can imagine a rural life—his idea of a vacation is to stretch out in the garden of a small country home with a glass of wine and a book, instead of strapping himself into a frightening roller-coaster ride (that will be the Busy Bee) or touring every sight recommended in the guidebook (that will be the Reformer).

Intuitive powers

Of all the Signs, the Magician is the one who can most easily accept and develop his powers of intuition, but this psychic element only partly explains the name for the type Nine Sign. It is the Magician because he can work magic between people,

bringing families together and healing rifts; building bridges between opposing departments and calming angry colleagues; learning to listen and becoming the therapists of the everyday. Anyone, any Sign, can take a problem to the Magician and watch it evaporate with a touch of his wand.

His secrets are few and simple. He hears what people say and balances their feelings against his own. He says what he means, tactfully, but articulately. And he doesn't grow a big head. He is a different type of Magician to the ones you will find in the Harry Potter stories that are captivating millions of children worldwide. Harry Potter is a wizard, of course, but his creator is a true Magician. Balancing fame with good parenting and public charm with a fierce regard for her own privacy, the author J. K. Rowling behaves with exemplary poise.

The healing hand of the Magician

Laid-back attitude

Actors and Busy Bees are often exasperated by the Magician. They see talent, but without the ambition to make something of it. The Magician can be lazy, both in his career and with his feelings. Presented with a golden opportunity, he can hold back indecisively for a few moments too long. Presented with a difficult emotional situation, he can hold back a little too far, wary of committing his feelings where he could be easily hurt. If he does not develop his emotional ties, he risks being labeled as a fairweather friend, someone who is only around when the going is easy.

The Magician has an idealized view of how the world should be. If he can beat his inertia, he will campaign effectively for good causes, especially targeting the arms trade, ecology, and world poverty. But he risks locking into a fantasy of the world, slipping away from reality, ignoring current affairs, and refusing to look at facts that don't fit his ideas.

He recoils from judging others, which can place him at risk of choosing the wrong partner. As a partner he is deeply loyal and loving, but his emotional self-awareness presents a risk to all his relationships, with friends as well as lovers. As he grows older, he will—like every Life Sign—mature and change, and he will be alert to those changes. If he feels that personality shift is putting him too often in conflict with his partner or friends, his instinct is to break the relationship and move on, instead of staying to confront the crisis and weather the changes.

For your information

A Victorian Magician

Charlotte Bronte's *Jane Eyre* scandalized Victorian readers with its story of a woman who would not marry a good man. Jane, a decent, honest woman, was betrayed by the man she loved, Edward Rochester. He had a wife—mad and locked up in an attic. Jane finds a home with St. John Rivers but cannot love him.

In an orphanage, a dying friend shows Jane that to keep her self-respect she must master her temper. Jane learns never to reveal her outrage, so she gains control of her life from people who would destroy her if they knew her true feelings. Jane is the consummate Magician, resolving her problems with cool wit and honesty.

The Magician will always prefer the tranquility of a quiet garden to a noisy, crowded vacation spot.

CHAPTER THREE

Understanding yourself

By now you should understand the basics of the Life Signs, but how can you use this knowledge to help yourself? In this chapter you will discover new ways of drawing on the intuitive wisdom of your subconscious and thought-provoking concepts about every aspect of self-development. You will also discover how your own type interacts with all other types, which will help you to develop your own far-ranging character.

Accepting yourself

Many people experience a sense of anticlimax and dissatisfaction after completing the questionnaire and establishing their dominant Life Sign and its wing.

This unease comes from a desire to be somebody different. It is natural to hope that a personality test will reveal a secret side that is dynamic and confident, always ready for action and powerfully charismatic. For example, when a young man picks up his girlfriend's magazine and fills out the answers in a feature titled "How Good are You as a Lover?" he wants to be told he has a combination of Warren Beatty's drive and Brad Pitt's looks. However, it is important to remember that no one is perfect, and, along with bad qualities, we all have good qualities.

Life-long pattern

One of the most essential lessons of the Life Signs is that your personality is well established by the time you reach adulthood. If you need to give love to establish a sense of purpose in your life, as Mother Hens do, you will always have that need. If you are a whirlwind of ideas and activity, a true Busy Bee, you will not grow out of it. Age may mellow you and enable you to take control of your character's more unruly aspects, but you will always be a Busy Bee.

Behavior can change. What you do is within your control, but the forces that drive you are in motion, and as long as you live and think, they cannot be stopped. Accepting this is like learning to breathe well—you can control your oxygen intake and maximize the capacity of your lungs, making yourself healthy and relaxed in a disciplined and natural way, but you cannot do without air itself. Some things can be changed, but the core things cannot.

Your inner critic

One element you can control is the critic inside your head. The cartoon character Jiminy Cricket called himself the "small clear voice of conscience," but that voice for many is raucous, rude, and destructive. Instead of saying, "You can do this right," it yells out, "You're doing this all wrong!"

The critic may be an echo of all the criticisms you have suffered. Sometimes, if you had good teachers and good parents, those criticisms were constructive and valuable. They taught you to recognize the

For your information

Establishing a category

Many incisive ways of classifying the Life Signs have been devised. British political columnist David Aaronovitch labeled himself an "herbivore," an animal that doesn't hunt or eat meat. "I am afraid to offend and terrified of hurting," he said. In contrast, most of the people he knows are "carnivores," predatory and unafraid to cause damage to others if it serves their purpose. There is a third category, the naturalists, who are camouflaged and observe from a safe distance.

This terminology throws an interesting light on the pattern of the enneagram. Herbivores are placed at alternate points: Nine, Two, Four, and Six, or the Magician, the Mother Hen, the Artist, and the Believer. Carnivores occupy four more points: Seven, Eight, One, and Three. These are the self-promoting types: the Busy Bee, the Boss, the Reformer, and the Actor. This leaves the aloof and observing, but cautious Intellectual.

proper course of action. But overlaid on those good voices were the attacks of snide colleagues, picky employers, envious friends, and cruel classmates. The subconscious mind absorbs everything it hears, and it is hard for anyone to dismiss a criticism so completely that it is forgotten, however meaningless and trivial it really was.

Tackle your internal critic head-on. It purports to be a voice of reason, so fight back with logic and reasoned argument. Remind yourself, "Yes, maybe I could have done that better. But I was doing it to the best of my ability, and it is working out pretty well. I don't need impossibly high standards that will condemn me to failure at everything I do. What I need is a good enough standard, a level where I get by. And frankly, looking at what I've achieved today, I've cleared that standard and excelled it. Can you criticize that?" This pragmatic attitude will always crush your inner critic. Apply it every time you catch yourself being too hard on your own self-esteem.

Whatever your Life Sign, you can do your best. Do not condemn yourself when you slip below this level—you can't change past performances by blaming yourself. It is better to accept that you did what you did, you gave it what you could, and you are doing okay. You are who you are, and you are doing well at it.

> " WE ALL HAVE POSSIBILITIES
> WE DON'T KNOW ABOUT. WE
> CAN DO THINGS WE DON'T
> EVEN DREAM WE CAN DO. "
>
> Dale Carnegie, American writer
> and lecturer (1888–1955)

Becoming more balanced and effective

The Life Signs system promotes a balanced personality because it recognizes that all of the nine types are equally valuable to society.

After you complete scoring your questionnaire, you may find that one or two Life Signs dominate the others. This does not mean that your personality is entirely devoid of other elements. There are many personality traits that may not come automatically to you but which you have acquired, perhaps to pro-tect and help your family, perhaps to improve your career performance—or perhaps as bad habits that you would be glad to lose.

Whichever Life Sign is your main type, it is a good one—but that does not mean you have to per-sonify that Sign to its extreme, or to the exclusion of all other typical behaviors in order to be your best. None of the Life Signs depends on a single trait. It is important to realize that we have other traits, but to a lesser extent. Recognizing these traits in ourselves will help us to relate to others.

The low-scoring Signs

Some Life Signs naturally assimilate the behaviors of other types. Believers can fit efficiently into the social machine, Actors can adopt the talents of others they admire. Other Signs recoil from imitat-ing other people. Intellectuals regard much social behavior as a waste of time at best and hypocritical at worst. Reformers instinctively see other people's habits as "wrong" if they clash with their own. Artists who have not broken the cycle of introspection will often assume that others see them as they see them-selves, forgetting to imagine life from other angles.

Take another look at your scores—which type scored lowest for you? If you are a Boss, perhaps you rarely chose the Artist. That does not mean you are low on creativity—remember, anyone can nurture their imaginative, artistic skills. (The Artist is not the sole artistic sign, just as the Mother Hen is not the only sign capable of good parenting.)

Look at that low-scoring Sign and ask yourself why you feel so little sympathy for that type. Perhaps

For your information

Eastern balance

In the ancient Hindu system of Kundalini yoga, there are seven energy points, or chakras, along the body. They are the Crown, Third Eye, Throat, Heart, Solar Plexus, Hara, and Root chakras, and they are found at the crown of the head, on the forehead, at the throat, over the heart, below the ribcage, above the sexual organs, and at the base of the spine. When a point is weak or too strong, the personality is out of balance—and the physical form suffers as a result. When the chakras are balanced, energy flows smoothly, bringing clear thought, improved emotional and spiritual awareness, and good health.

The Life Signs system also places emphasis on balance. When all your personality traits are in balance, you can function more effectively. Becoming unbalanced can lead to health problems; for example, being too demanding can cause stress, which affects your health.

the qualities it embodies are ones that are not relevant to you. A Busy Bee may feel threatened by the Mother Hen's capacity for quiet sacrifice; a Reformer may be infuriated by the Intellectual's habit of seeing all sides of an argument. Where opposite qualities strike you as antagonistic—when it makes you angry to even contemplate them—then it would be false and counterproductive to emulate them. Life Signs are about being happy with who you are, not striving to be who you are not.

Finding a balance

Think again about that opposite Sign, and try to find something in its makeup that you admire or that is typical of your own personality. It may help you to think about friends you have known and people you have admired. Find one in your memory who may have that Life Sign, then focus on a certain quality in that person.

Your memory has probably led you to someone you did not entirely like. You may admire that person, but feel some dislike. Perhaps you are thinking of a friend with whom you no longer associate or a relative whom you cannot bear to speak to often. Try to focus on the cause of the dislike or the rift. Was it provoked by something that typifies their Sign? Did a Busy Bee frustrate you with her restless changeability; did a Reformer infuriate you with his dogmatic persistence? Or—be honest with yourself—was your own behavior at the root of the problem? Looking back, was it unreasonable to expect anyone of that Life Sign to put up with your attitudes indefinitely?

Musings like this can be productive. When old disputes are seen in a nebulous swirl of emotions, the issues will never be understood. By seeing your actions as part of the patterns of the Life Signs wheel, you can begin to learn how to temper yourself and become more positive, and you can discover the best way to interact with other types. This is an early step toward achieving more balance and harmony in your life.

Something to think about

Your life is organized into efficient routines. You might not think so, but you would miss the daily patterns you follow without thinking if they were to suddenly change. This exercise will help you change some of the little things in life .

Remember when you once took a note from home to your teacher, excusing you from sports? Today, write a note to yourself and slip it into your wallet or purse. It should say "I have permission to do things differently." Now act on it. If you usually have lunch in the cafeteria, go for a walk. If you usually watch the news on the television, listen to the radio. If you phone a loved one on Tuesday, do it on Sunday.

Small experiments like these can set you thinking about your life in different ways, and that is a big step toward becoming more balanced between the Life Signs.

Playing to your strengths

One of the most liberating lessons of the Life Signs is learning that we cannot be perfect at everything. We are simply not designed that way.

Each person has her own individuality, with both strong and weak points.

This wisdom, the kind of comforting advice that a mother gives an anxious child, is often forgotten when we reach adolescence. Peer pressure sets in, and we aspire to be a synthesis of all the best things we see in all our friends and role models. Advertisers make sure that pressure never lets up—nothing sells like envy. Advertisers want you to want to be someone else. Life Signs teach you about being who you are, and being the best you can be.

To accept your Life Sign is to accept your individuality. Your personality is one of a type, but one of a kind as well—remember, there are 6 billion individuals. Just as you can be proud of sticking to a healthy diet when you happen to be 40 pounds heavier than the average supermodel, you can also be proud of working hard to achieve your best when others seem to be doing somewhat better at the cost of very little effort at all.

Establishing your own benchmarks

You can learn to measure your achievements by determining your own benchmarks, not someone else's. A thin model might be happy with her body, but many others would probably be uncomfortable to be as thin. Whether the issue is your body image or your abilities, it is up to you to establish what makes you feel comfortable, not peer pressure or the advertisers.

Think of your schooldays—maybe you struggled in one particular subject, such as mathematics. There would have been other pupils in the class who scored well in tests without struggling the way you did. They took the top marks and won the teacher's praise, while you were simply informed that you must try harder.

That kind of negative reinforcement is hard to break. It teaches that others are inherently better than you because you are lazy and stupid. You know that it was wrong to assume you weren't trying because you were—but this is outweighed by the authority wielded by the teacher. You subconsciously accepted the teacher's judgment, much in the same way that you probably subconsciously accept the truth of anything you read in a quality newspaper, even when you know some of the facts are wrong.

Another point to consider is establishing in which area your strengths lie. Continuing with the same example, you might struggle when it comes to mathematics, but you might excel in writing—just as those who excelled in mathematics might struggle when it comes to putting words onto paper. We each have our own talents, and it makes sense to make the most of what we can do best.

Achieving your potential

Recognizing your potential and then achieving it requires you to vest ultimate authority in yourself. You are your own teacher, so value your judgment. You are your own editor, so believe in yourself.

Some Life Signs will find this easier than others. The Reformer, the Boss, and the Busy Bee are authoritative types and will naturally put their own views first. The Intellectual can withdraw from others if she doesn't like what she hears, but she is determined enough to put herself first; however, she should be careful not to become too critical of others along the way.

An Actor is always willing to cast himself as his own guru. He loves the idea that somewhere in his brain is the voice of a proud parent who will praise him every time he does something well. It is no

> "SUCCESS IS A STATE OF MIND.
> IF YOU WANT SUCCESS,
> START THINKING OF YOURSELF
> AS A SUCCESS."
>
> Dr. Joyce Brothers,
> American psychologist (1928–)

coincidence that many Actors are their parents' only child. The inner praise comes unbidden. Sometimes there is too much of it and others will perceive the Actor as being smug, but no one can deny it is a powerful boost to him in everything he does.

Both the Mother Hen and the Magician are quite happy to help others instead of concentrating on their own needs. They need to put others aside to concentrate on themselves. The Artist is another type who will need to learn to reach her potential without relying on others.

At the other end of the spectrum, the Believer often lacks this built-in authority figure. He will look for it in others at work, in his community, or in his church. For many Believers, finding religious faith is a massive release; it enables them to move away from other people's envy or disapproval, and to accept a spiritual judgment that is more understanding. If you are a religious person, whatever your Life Sign, this higher judgment is fundamentally honest and compassionate—and radically different to the unfair criticism of your old teacher.

From the heart

What are you terrible at doing? Say aloud the first thing that comes to mind—is it cooking, or organizing, or debating? Now ask yourself how you know that you are talentless in this department. If you are like most people, it is because other people have told you so.

It is time for you to cast off their criticism; put it aside and take a close look at your real potential. Build up your resolve to try again—if you do even a little better than you expect, that is a massive success.

Knowing someone else's type

By now you are probably looking at the people around you and trying to assess their Life Signs. To enable you to practice your new skills on real people without the risk of giving offense to anyone, here are nine thumbnail portraits, all drawn from life. Personal details such as names have been changed. Can you identify the types?

◆ Karl

A mechanic with a motor racing team, Karl joined after high school, on a wage that barely paid to keep his motorcycle on the road. He rose before dawn at his parents' home to get to the team base, slept in a bed in a van when the team was at the racetrack, and now works long hours, seeing his wife and two children for a

few quality hours each week. He loves the job, and the team values him highly and pays him well. His ambition is to be head of engineering.

◆ Rita

A successful entrepreneur, Rita runs her own company, selling cosmetics by mail order. She started it when her children were in elementary school; her husband reduced his working hours to look after the young family. Now the children are grown, they both work for her, and she hopes to pass the business onto them when she retires. There is much to do before then.

◆ Edward

A grandfather, Edward cares for his three grandsons while his daughters are at work and also takes the boys on outings. His wife died when the first grandchild was a baby, and he reflects how cruel it is that she did not live to see her grandchildren grow up. He regrets that his own career prevented him from seeing enough of his own girls when they were young. That was a sacrifice that had to be made, but he is happy to live on a small pension now. Being with my family, he says, is what I call success.

◆ Simon

After two decades and three children, Simon's marriage is on the rocks. He married his first girlfriend when he was 19 and now feels he made too many binding decisions too early. When he tries to explain this to his wife, she calls him self-pitying. He suspects she has not been faithful but cannot bring himself to accuse her, because of the pain it would cause them both. He thinks it may be kindest to them both if he left, but he is scared of taking such a large step.

◆ Jo

Although Jo left school with poor grades, three years ago she began studying for an English Literature degree at night school. Her husband was supportive, but he was astonished when she told him that she now wants to train as a teacher. As she explained to him, she has grown and now, at 43 years old, she feels like a whole person—and, of course, her affection for her family has not changed. She is determined about this, and there is to be no argument.

◆ Muhamed

Converted to Islam in his 30s, Muhamed likes a religion that places the fate of individuals in the hands of Allah. He had run three businesses, which all crashed through a combination of bad management, bad judgment, and bad luck, and he suffered two nervous breakdowns. He still has difficulty in ceding control, however small, to other people, and he still launches himself into ambitious plans—he is currently raising funds for a new mosque. However, everyone says he is calmer since he found God.

◆ Doreen

Divorced at 36 years old, Doreen has never had children. She never felt the time was right, and her husband left when his lover became pregnant. Now Doreen wants children, but she is fearful of another bad marriage. Friends set up dates for her, but she pulls out at the last moment. The men she does meet are unsuitable, she says. She has almost finished redecorating her apartment; when it is finished she will feel better about inviting people to it.

◆ Emily

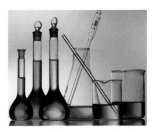

Despite frequent complaints from her mother, Emily is single. She has a responsible job in a large company as a research chemist. Many of her male colleagues are single or divorced, but she never meets any of them for drinks after work—she finds it emotionally confusing to socialize with them. She tells her mother that if her biological clock starts ticking loudly, she will be practical and find a husband through an agency.

◆ Lewis

A wealthy Porsche 911 driver, Lewis has a new girl every month. He likes to drop names of celebrity friends and wealthy business contacts. He wears his gray hair in a ponytail, and says he doesn't care that older friends still have dark locks—he suspects they dye them. He doesn't talk about his parents, school, or if he was ever married. Lewis talks well and listens badly.

ANSWERS

Some of these people are likable, some less so. Remember that each Life Sign is a spectrum and anyone can be happy if his or her true potential is realized. Did you recognize the types?

Hardworking, loyal **Karl** is a Believer
Risk-taking **Rita** is a Boss
Home-loving **Edward** is a Mother Hen
Miserable **Simon** is an Artist
Newly fulfilled **Jo** is a Magician
Energetic, controlling **Muhamed** is a Busy Bee

Fussy, perfectionist **Doreen** is a Reformer
Shy, practical **Emily** is an Intellectual
Show-off **Lewis** is an Actor

If you disagree with the answers, you are already coming to a personal interpretation of the Life Signs. In the sketches of each personality, several character traits are outlined. That means you may discern the "wings," as well as the main Signs. Based on the sketch, you might see Muhamed as a Believer, for example, with a Busy Bee wing.

Nine key ways to attract love

We all need to be loved, at every stage of our lives, whether we are young adults just reaching maturity and searching for a partner, or older people in the twilight years of life.

Loneliness can afflict anyone at any stage of life, whatever the Life Sign. Some people are taking longer to commit themselves to a permanent partnership—going from one relationship to another—and, with separation and divorce no longer a taboo in society, many people who have been in long-term relationships suddenly find themselves on their own and alone. The death of a life-long love partner also causes tremendous loneliness.

In these situations it is not only the Artist or the Mother Hen whose grown children have left home who will feel lonely; the outgoing Actor and Believer will feel painfully alone, too. Although you will need some time after the end of a relationship to regain your confidence, at some point you will be ready to find new love. However, this is usually not as easy as it sounds. These nine rules can help you find love, whether it is your first experience or one of several.

The Reformer

Dismiss your preconceptions of the type of person you want to meet. When you do meet the real partner of your dreams, you will not feel a thrill of recognition, because dreams do not work in that way. Superficial details, such as hair color, profession, and bank account, are less relevant than a shared capacity for love and trust. When you dream of a new love, the imaginary lover is not the important component of the dream; it is the relationship itself that your subconscious mind is seeking. So abandon your preconceived ideas of whom you want to meet, forget about the "tall, dark stranger" of your imagination, and concentrate on the loving relationship, not the lover.

The Mother Hen

Act as if you are a successful person because, actually, that is what you are. If loneliness is making you doubt your self-worth, make a list of the 10 greatest achievements in your whole life that make you the proudest. They may come to mind slowly, but, as you start to write them down, you will feel like an achiever, a success. And success will build your self-confidence, which will, in turn, make you more attractive to others.

The Actor

Be honest. If you present yourself as you are, without the varnish, you will win trust—and, more important, there will be no danger of breaching that trust by being caught telling lies. You have every reason to tell the truth, so why assume that anyone would like the false you better? Lies never fully impress your new acquaintances because some sixth sense will always alert them. So stop pretending to own a house on Martha's Vineyard, don't claim that your Mercedes is in for repairs, and stop dropping celebrity names like you know the people personally. All you need to do is just be yourself.

The Artist

Do not dwell on a previous lost love. The past cannot return, however much you yearn for it. The love you enjoyed is part of your life, but it is not part of the present. You should treasure your memories, not use them to torture yourself. If you use the ideals of your lost love as a measuring stick, one thing is certain—no one will measure up. Every new love will fail in some way because you are condemning the new relationship as soon as you compare it to your previous one. You are also making grief for other people—no one likes to be compared to an impossible memory.

The Intellectual

You need to look after yourself physically. By taking care of your health, you clothes, your diet, and your personal hygiene, you will make yourself far more attractive to others. Ask yourself what is more important—money or cleanliness? The answer is cleanliness. A man who dates a wealthy woman with greasy hair and bad breath is definitely after only one thing, and it is not romance. Many Intellectuals neglect their appearance, wearing old, threadbare clothes and taking a lax attitude to niceties, such as haircuts and deodorant. They expect others to overlook these superficial aspects and see the real character underneath. However, the reality is that most people take one look at you and decide there is no point in developing a relationship. They will reason that if you won't take care of yourself, you won't care for others. You need to show others that you are a great human being—and make sure it shows on the surface.

The Believer

Be ready to embrace a whole life, not just a lover. Even if you are in your early 20s, your ideal partner may be accompanied by children—or by elderly parents or physically disabled siblings. When you fall in love, you must shoulder a whole new set of responsibilities, or the love won't last. Anyone who expects a new partner to clean the slate of the past, abandoning all former ties, is certain to be abandoned in the future. Unfortunately, many people get married thinking they will be able to sideline those troublesome, sick parents or noisy stepchildren. That is a mistake.

The Busy Bee

When you search for a new love, be sure that you look beyond sexuality. Sex does not have to be the spark that ignites a love affair. You can fall in love with someone without falling into bed. Real, satisfying sexual attractiveness is often born from a deep desire to be with your partner forever. The electric charge between strangers may be exciting at the moment it occurs, but it is very fragile—a word or a look can shatter it, which is no basis for a relationship. After a short encounter, you may find yourself left only with regrets.

The Boss

You need to be patient and listen to others. A romance is not all about you, so do not hog the conversation from the moment you set eyes on each other. Of course, you should say something about yourself, but make sure you also ask questions and wait for responses. This is especially important if the new friend you would like to know better is shy. Silence can encourage conversation, but monologues will kill it. Be reassured that what you do say will make more of an impression if you keep it to a minimum. Speak a hundred words in an evening, and every one of them will hit home; speak ten thousand and they will all be forgotten.

The Magician

Take positive action when you are lonely. Do not wait for love to come and find you—get out there on the trail of love. You need to be bold. There is no limit to the number of clubs you can join, evening classes you can attend, hobbies you can discover, or trips you can make. Don't be afraid of seeming nervous—most of the world is more scared than you are. Widen your circle of friends away from employment and you will be amazed at how many ways you know of sharing common interests that have nothing to do with your job.

Life Signs compatibility in love

By becoming familiar with how the Life Signs interact with each other, you will better understand your own involvement with others, especially in the area of romance.

You'll find on these pages all the pairings of the Life Signs. The gender in these descriptions is neutral—either partner could be male or female. Although the combinations are affected by gender—in the same way they are affected by wealth, national culture, and education—the essential chemistry of each pairing is the same. For example, a match between a wealthy Artist and Actor who live in a large urban American city share the same dynamics of a rural Irish Artist-Actor partnership. Some matches may require more understanding than others for them to work, but any combination can enjoy a successful relationship.

These love matches are organized from the Reformer to the Magician, and there are four pairings listed under each type. If you don't find your particular match under one type, simply look for it under the second type in your match. For example, a Reformer-Actor match cannot be found under Reformer, but it is under Actor. If you and your partner have the same Life Sign, turn to pages 108–109.

Reformer-Mother Hen

Feelings of innate superiority can be lethal to any relationship, and in this combination it is the Reformer who must consciously drive out all suspicion that the Mother Hen's role is in any way inferior. The Mother Hen does not espouse a set of high principles or loudly declare one main ambition; however, that doesn't mean he or she is weak or incapable of making his or her own decisions about major issues. Indeed, it is far weaker to proclaim a lofty ideal and fail to reach it than it is to take life day by day and deal with every problem to the best of your ability. When the Reformer does strut and boast, the Mother Hen should chide but never condemn. Above all, both partners must nurture a regard for the contributions offered by the other—in both cases, they are unique and irreplaceable.

Reformer-Artist

A partnership formed between the Reformer and the Artist is a strongly complementary one. The Artist's belief system may be just as strong as the Reformer's, although not necessarily as well articulated. However, if the Artist lacks a strong system of beliefs, he or she will find the Reformer's world view enticing and may adapt it. Naturally, the Reformer will be delighted and flattered to influence another mind and will admire the Artist's good judgment and clear sight. Any relationship begun with mutual admiration will always have a strong basis, and the initial impression that each has met an exceptional human being will be strengthened over the years. Other people might wonder what these Signs find attractive in the other, but no explanations are necessary to the Reformer and the Artist.

Reformer-Intellectual

A possibly explosive combination, these two Life Signs may at times seem to have been born to undermine one another. The Reformer will be easily infuriated by the Intellectual's constantly shifting moral positions; the Intellectual will cause frustration and anger by submitting the Reformer's firmly held principles to logical dissection. However, logic is only one way of understanding an issue—emotional and spiritual interpretations are equally valid, and the Reformer is right to reject many of the attacks made by his or her partner. Nevertheless, the Intellectual is unlikely to submit to someone else's mindset. For this relationship to last, these two Signs will have to work together, agreeing to be a team, to respect each other's differences, and to celebrate all that they do have in common.

Reformer-Boss

These two Life Signs typically enjoy confrontation, and they will certainly get plenty of it in this combination. They will draw strength from each other's displays of will and obstinacy, and they often lock horns when it comes to different objectives. The Reformer will refuse to deviate from an established plan, while the Boss will want the power to change the plan at any time. Many of the arguments in themselves will be pointless, but they reflect a deeper antagonism in the relationship. When both of these partners recognize this warring trait affecting their relationship, they should address it and draw up ground rules—and stick to them. Beyond the fighting, there is real admiration for each other that helps strengthen the relationship.

Mother Hen-Actor

Yearning for a different type of life is often at the root of this relationship; however, it can be a successful combination. The Mother Hen envies the Actor's self-centered fun and flair, and he or she wishes for the confidence to live out the Actor's dictum that we get only one chance at life and, therefore, should take chances when they come. Conversely, the Actor painfully feels the absence of the fulfillment that is experienced by the Mother Hen, which only selfless sacrifice can bring. For both

Life Signs, change is an impossibility—they might as well try to fly to the moon by flapping their arms rather than attempting to switch their lifestyles. However, through each other, both of these Signs can enjoy their opposite mode of living. It is a vicarious thrill that encourages both of them to live up to their Life Sign's full potential, usually to the delight of their partner.

Mother Hen-Artist

The Mother Hen is a powerful role model to the Artist, who may feel strong urges to be emotionally generous but who cannot find an honest way to release his or her feelings. The key to the Mother Hen is the Sign's naturally cheerful refusal, or inability, to judge and hold grudges. When the Mother Hen is happy and fulfilled, all crises are quickly forgotten. The Artist, in contrast, is scarred by every confrontation and often needs to secretly examine his or her wounds. The Artist should learn to imitate the Mother Hen's unjudging love—and it can be learned, it does not have to be instinctive—which will allow the grudges to disappear and the floodgates to open with love pouring out. The Mother Hen will see the opening up of the Artist's heart as his or her mission.

Mother Hen-Intellectual

The Intellectual has never wanted to abandon the original mother figure, and the Mother Hen is especially protective toward those who lack toughness. This combination is frequently seen in the homes of successful scientists and writers. The Mother Hen's role is to establish a safe, orderly routine where the Intellectual's gifts can be fully developed. Although this can be achieved successfully, there is a danger that the relationship will settle into an infantile pattern, with the Intellectual happily consenting to be babied. This often precludes a healthy sexual element, which, in turn, makes the Mother Hen vulnerable to romantic predators.

Mother Hen-Boss

To both the Mother Hen and the Boss, this relationship represents a strong ideal. It will probably mirror the ones that both sets of their parents shared, although the gender roles may be reversed—it does not have to be "Poppa" Boss and "Momma" Hen. Either partner can be a breadwinner, while the other is a homemaker, and the equality lies in the simple understanding that this is "how their life should be." This pairing makes a strong team, which will be envied by some friends, but dismissed by others as old-fashioned. The truth is that this type of partnership will never go out of style—however, other types will resist copying it simply because it appears traditional and, therefore, "right."

Actor-Reformer

These two Life Signs have opposite personality traits. The Actor is adaptable, while the Reformer is not. The Actor will reject everything to do with aging, until it becomes an undeniable issue, then he or she will try to wear white hair and wrinkles as badges of dignity and wisdom. The Reformer, in contrast, will welcome any signs of aging, because its implied maturity and seniority lend gravitas to every statement. If the Actor sees the Reformer as a real token of aging, there is danger that the relationship may not last. The Reformer may be discarded by the Actor, who may deny his or her own encroaching years by seeking a younger partner. The issue of aging may seem trivial until it is too late, so both partners should make an effort early on to understand how it can strike their relationship. Frank discussion is a good place to start.

Actor-Intellectual

That an Actor-Intellectual combination have managed to find each other at all is a miracle, which suggests that their partnership was written in the stars. Who are they to balk at destiny? Come what may, they had better go along with the miracle. The Actor's flair and superficial style will make little impression on the Intellectual, who will probably take it all at face value and then dismiss it. The Intellectual's preoccupation and hesitation will strike the Actor as a weakness in his or her personality. On the rare occasions in which this match makes headway, both partners must see something exceptional and uniquely valuable in the other—and if they hold onto that, all the differences in the world can be overcome.

Actor-Believer

The confident Actor will carry the Believer to the ends of the Earth, and the Believer will go willingly. However, if the Actor falters and admits to self-doubt, the Believer will be horrified. The idea that things are not all they seemed to be is never a welcome one. True communication can be difficult between this couple, who both rely (in different ways) on comforting illusions. The key to success in this relationship is to establish vital constants that cannot be erased by changing circumstances. They need to reassure each other that come fire, floods, illness, or financial disasters, the love they share with their family will not be easily wiped away.

Actor-Boss

The Actor will have to adapt to fit the Boss's dominating style, but the Boss must be aware that the Actor's compliance can change if he or she feels that the relationship is becoming either boring or too oppressive. However, even the threat of change can be deeply unsettling to the Boss, who is flattered by the notion of possessing a personality so strong that others are compelled to bow down to him or her. When realization dawns that the Actor is consenting to be ruled, the Boss must resist the temptation to impose that rule all the harder. The result would be a series of bitter confrontations and an unstable relationship. Shared responsibility and open discussion are difficult concepts for both of these Life Signs; however, such valuable tools should not be left to rust forever if they want the partnership to be successful.

Artist-Actor

The Artist would love to be an Actor and possess the Actor's self-assured, charming manner; however, when the Artist sometimes tries, he or she simply appears more awkward than ever. The Actor envies the Artist's inner compass, the unchanging emotional certainties that help steer the couple through life's moral maze. But when the Actor attempts to adopt those certainties, they seem pretentious, even false. Both partners must understand that they are made up of opposites—the Actor is all surface, right down to the center, and the Artist is all core, right up to the tender skin. When they stop staring at the sometimes wide gulf between them, marveling at their differences, they can start taking into account everything they have in common and appreciate their relationship.

Artist-Believer

The Artist and the Believer are a common combination, a simple proof that opposites do attract, especially when it comes to love. The Believer is wary of making judgments about anything that defies his or her broad guidelines. For example, there might be a rule that "modern art is nonsense" or "watching sports is a good way to relax," but finer, individual preferences within those general boundaries are difficult to decide upon. Conversely, the Artist will not be chained by generalizations, but makes intense pronouncements on the individual merits of every case. The Believer will defend the Artist's right to rewrite the rules every time, while never attempting to understand them. The Artist will appreciate the Believer's general approach for what it is—a successful effort to impose some type of order on chaos.

Artist-Busy Bee

The Artist will sometimes find it despairing when it comes to a partnership with the Busy Bee, who switches so quickly from core values to irrelevant fringes and back again. The Busy Bee will proclaim one minute that "nothing matters except my family" and, the next moment, will set off with great fanfare on a money-consuming project that leaves no time for helping and playing with the children. The Artist will feel put out, taken for granted, and underestimated. The Artist's own talents may be great, but they are not anything to report about in comparison to the gusto that the Busy Bee can muster up. Tension and resentment may enter the relationship on occasion. Because neither partner is likely to change his or her attitudes, mutual understanding is essential for the relationship to continue. The Busy Bee, in particular, must guard against reaching an understanding for a few days and then forgetting about it.

Artist-Boss

These two Life Signs can make a complementary couple. The Boss can be deeply proud of and protective toward the Artist's gifts, while not needing to understand them in any depth. The Artist's reticence and introversion will lead him or her to hand the main stage to the Boss, to both their satisfaction. The Boss will willingly take control of their daily organization, finances, and vacations, and he or she may even decide who should be counted as a friend and who should not; the Artist will accept this control and be grateful for the spiritual freedom that is gained. However, if the Artist suffers from the bouts of depression that can afflict this Life Sign, the Boss will find it hard to sympathize or to cope. And if one of the Boss's gambles fails spectacularly, the Artist may be ill-equipped to pick up the pieces. Both partners must remember that life often brings hard times as well as good times, and that everything must be faced together.

Intellectual-Artist

The Intellectual is used to rationalizing every emotion that he or she has, so it will come as an intense shock to form a partnership with the Artist, who feels things so deeply that, although under a reserved surface, a heart may beat that is close to bursting. The Artist will mistrust the Intellectual's alien habit of dismantling a pain until it ceases to hurt and will suspect him or her of having no real emotions. The Intellectual's logic and the Artist's intuition are indeed different ways of interpreting the world, but they are not opposite and each can observe the other, learning and gaining insight. Talking is less reassuring to this couple than physical reassurance—in this partnership, silent but certain friendship can be worth a million words.

Intellectual-Busy Bee

In this partnership the essence of thinking meets the dynamo of doing. The Intellectual may be drawn into this relationship before the introductions have sunk in. However, by the time the Intellectual makes the first, tentative evaluation, the Busy Bee may have lost patience and powered off elsewhere. The Busy Bee will rarely allow the Intellectual the necessary space for reflection. Every decision made by the Busy Bee will come hurtling in at an impossible pace. However, there is a rhythm to the Busy Bee's buzzing, and if the Intellectual can latch onto it, the ride will be exhilarating. Other people will look at them and say "They are totally different—no wonder they seem so right for each other."

Intellectual-Believer

This can be a difficult partnership because the Intellectual will question everything that the Believer regards as certain. The Believer may interpret the Intellectual's constant quest for new ways of seeing the world as a personal attack on his or her own lifestyle, with its established values. The Believer must learn to respect the Intellectual's natural inquisitive probing and see that doubt is as necessary to one partner as security is to the other. The Believer is a social creature who needs status among peers; the Intellectual is indifferent to status and behaves awkwardly in social situations. For the relationship to flourish, the Intellectual must conquer this social reserve and try to be gregarious.

Intellectual-Magician

The idealism of the Magician and the innovation of the Intellectual are the perfect complement for a couple who want to inhabit a castle in the air. In combination these are two impractical signs, both unrealistically optimistic, both happy to pay the bills with next month's rent, confidently believing that "something will come up." When put under financial pressure, both partners will find it so distressing that their relationship will suffer. Shocked that they can argue about something as trivial as money, they will question the depth of their true feelings. For their relationship to survive, at least one member of this partnership will have to act more responsibly.

Believer-Reformer

The Believer must be in accord with the Reformer's view of life. If this single condition is met, the partnership between these two Signs is unbreakable; if not, it is doomed to fail. The Believer-Reformer combination is often found in religious families, one partner committed to the faith and the other simply loyal to his or her partner. The Believer often lacks the fire and fervor of the Reformer's thinking, but in moments of doubt the constancy of the Believer will offer a reassurance as comforting as a mother's love. With the backing of the Believer, the Reformer will gain the strength and confidence to achieve their goals fearlessly. Couples in this combination must learn flexibility toward their children, who may feel excluded at times by their parents' interlocking certainties.

Believer-Mother Hen

Where the Believer is the provider and the Mother Hen is the nurturer, this couple will form a strong core to establish a family. The Believer will gain strength and self-respect from the Mother Hen's reliance, and he or she will become confident and dominant without undermining the real source of power in the relationship—the deep, focused love of the homemaker. Where the Mother Hen is the provider, or where both partners share the responsibility of working, the Mother Hen may feel resentment, because sacrifices—especially if they affect the family—will have to be made on both sides. The Believer may take the relationship for granted as it matures. Talking problems over might seem weak, but it is essential and can save this partnership.

Believer-Busy Bee

The Believer and the Busy Bee can be compared to two halves of a wheel—when one half is on the ground, the other one is in the air, but together they keep rolling. These two will never truly understand each other, but by learning about each other's Sign both can appreciate what different forces drive them. Most of all, they offer each other support, which is priceless beyond words. During an argument, when the Believer wants time to make choices and decisions based on reason, the Busy Bee may be too impatient to listen. The Busy Bee might win many battles, but he or she will not win any wars when hurried decisions fall apart and reason comes into play. Unfortunately, there is always the danger that the Busy Bee will impatiently race away so fast that the ties of the partnership will be snapped.

Believer-Magician

The Believer's sense of how to do things—and how to keep on doing them—will be a source of inspiration to the Magician, who fears that the immensity of life will casually crush any individual

hopes and aspirations. The Magician may wonder what the Believer can admire in a character that is so much less solid and unsure, but The Magician's ephemeral beauty of spirit, and the charm with which it is presented, will hold the Believer's heart once it has been won. The Magician finds it easy to put into words what less poetic minds can only sense and cannot say—the first time the Believer encounters the Magician, it is like hearing a song with lyrics that unravel all of life's mysteries.

Busy Bee-Reformer

Like the fox and the tortoise, the two human types defined by philosopher Isaiah Berlin, these two Life Signs have different agendas. Berlin said the fox knows many small things and the tortoise knows one big one—the Busy Bee has a broad range of objectives, which are constantly changing within the relationship, while the Reformer has a fixed goal. By explaining themselves to each other, they can find plenty of common ground to build their partnership. A lifelong habit of open discussion must be maintained for this partnership to last.

Busy Bee-Mother Hen

A magical combination is formed between the Busy Bee and Mother Hen. These two Life Signs bring together every element in human nature, promising a combination that will be deeply satisfying and fulfilling to both. The Mother Hen creates stability, the Busy Bee generates excitement; the Mother Hen nurtures the family, the Busy Bee fills every day with stimulation and discovery. The children of this pair will be blessed with thrills and security, spontaneity and affection from both parents. However, a shadow threatens this partnership—the Busy Bee may be prone to destroy the most idyllic of families with wanton pleasure seeking or selfishness. Both partners should be grateful for all they have and never lose sight for a moment of the preciousness of their partnership.

Busy Bee-Actor

A couple consisting of a Busy Bee and an Actor are capable of every misunderstanding imaginable. They can be two wonderful people; however, if they are not on exactly the same wavelength, selfishness and thoughtlessness will cause chaos between the two. The Actor requires heaps of love and attention, but the Busy Bee's attention span will often be too short to be satisfying. The Busy Bee will be frustrated by the Actor's crises of confidence. They are two demanding people who need to learn how to give, but they will find life a joy in their partnership if they take time to look into each other's hearts as well as their own. Sexual attraction plays a significant part in the strength of their relationship.

Busy Bee-Magician

If the Busy Bee and the Magician appreciate even half of what they do to complement each other, they will be so full of praise for their partnership that their friends might grow sick of hearing about it. This couple inspire each other, the Magician with his or her ideals, the Busy Bee with can-do enthusiasm. When the Magician's self-belief is combined with the high energy from the Busy Bee, his or her principles will be heightened by the discovery that one human being can make a massive impact on humanity. The Busy Bee will be awed that the Magician's heart can hold so much purity, and he or she will seek that same purity within. The Magician must guard against becoming disillusioned at how many of the Busy Bee's projects—which are always begun in great earnest and fanfare—inevitably disappear before they are completed.

Boss-Intellectual

At first sight, the Boss and the Intellectual are two completely antagonistic types; however, their contradictions can give them strength if natural love preexists as a foundation for their relationship.

This partnership often arises from sheer physical attraction. There is much about each character that the other will never be able to understand. For example, the Intellectual cannot comprehend how the Boss can be so dismissive of abstract thought, and the Boss does not understand how the Intellectual can waste so much time on impractical ideas. However, when their personalities merge, the partnership is invincible. Mental acuity and thoroughness will combine with energy, forcefulness, and a willingness to take risks—and any outside obstacles will be easily swept aside.

Boss-Believer

Both the Boss and the Believer derive what they crave from this relationship—the Boss gets a follower and the Believer gets leadership. It is essential for both partners to value themselves equally. Although the Boss is usually responsible for setting the agenda and making decisions, it does not make the Believer's role any less important. The Believer will serve willingly and enthusiastically, but he or she does need a partner to tell him or her daily how much that contribution is appreciated. This praise does not have to be full of flattery and fancy words. A simple token of affection—a cup of coffee made without asking or a warm smile—is all that is needed to bond the partnership.

Boss-Busy Bee

If these two types are not working for a common goal, they should keep hard hats handy. They are the "immovable object" and the "irresistible force," and something has to give—even if it is the relationship. When they act in concert, success is guaranteed. The Busy Bee can direct all her energy to objectives behind the scenes, as the Boss maintains the public front and appears to take control. The reality may be that the Busy Bee's drive keeps the partnership moving forward, and the Boss's vision keeps them on target.

Boss-Magician

This relationship forces the Boss to grow and mature quickly, or to succumb to overwhelming frustration. The Boss may wish to deal with the Magician by using brute willpower, but this can often feel as frustrating as trying to grab a fistful of water. The Magician must learn to appreciate the Boss's qualities and submit to a dominant force rather than to try to instinctively side-step it. These adaptations require deep trust from both sides, a thing that cannot be willed into existence; however, as the partnership develops, the trust will grow. This will create an alliance that cannot be easily understood or invaded by outsiders; however, if the trust is broken, the relationship will not survive.

Magician-Reformer

A great combination for doing things, the Magician will smooth the path, while the Reformer will provide the drive. The Reformer may become frustrated by the Magician's willingness to accept compromises or changes to a plan, and this can lead to confrontation between the two. The Magician will be the first to back off, but trivial issues may become drawn-out wrangles. The Magician may be lazy about making decisions, allowing the Reformer to take all the responsibility. The Reformer will benefit from the Magician's loyalty and ability to intervene with others—in essence, the Magician is the Reformer's protective layer and safety net.

Magician-Mother Hen

These two Life Signs create a loving, close-knit household that others envy. The Mother Hen's nurturing instincts will be given full rein, with the Magician appreciative of the sacrifices demanded by family life. To outsiders, the Mother Hen appears to be dominant, but the Magician's tact and intuitive understanding will nudge and steer the relationship. The Magician will enjoy being smothered by affec-

tion and may be indolent, but a little encouragement from the Mother Hen will break any habits of laziness. A Magician-and-Mother-Hen combination will be supportive of each other in times of difficulty and illness, guaranteeing a long-lived partnership. The one area of friction may occur when it comes to the Magician's indifference to money—the Mother Hen requires financial security.

Magician-Actor

The Magician and the Actor make a good combination, with the Magician happy to make allowances for the Actor's exuberant personality. Others may wonder how the Magician puts up with the Actor, but the Magician basks in the Actor's glow. The Magician must not let the Actor become abusive when things are not going well, because this will quickly lead to an unbreakable pattern and a negative element in the relationship—even when outside factors improve. The Magician must learn to balance the Actor's constant need for praise and the less healthy tendency to self-pity—the Magician can flatter and praise the Actor, but he or she should not tolerate any whining.

Magician-Artist

The Magician and the Artist have similar personality types, which can lead to this combination becoming distant if both partners are sunk in introspection. The Artist must learn to rely on the Magician's gift for self-expression and never to resent her ability to communicate easily. The Magician must recognize that the Artist's feelings are often deeply felt, even if they are less openly articulated. Both of these Life Signs dislike a routine; however, the relationship will be healthier if a habit of regularly exchanging ideas is established. These two Life Signs should take time to sit down and talk every evening. Companionable silence will not be good enough—switch off the television and discuss the events of the day.

Sharing a Life Sign

Some people are reassured when they learn they have the same Life Sign as their partner, but others are alarmed.

The truth is that love has no rights and wrongs. Life does not come with a rule book. If a relationship is founded on strong attraction, physical or emotional, then it can be made to work. When similar characters are attracted to each other, there is a risk that narcissism is the driving force. Do these two people really admire and value each other, or are they reflecting their own self-love? But there is also a strong possibility that each will be able to bring out the best in the other—one partner will admire the qualities she sees and will seek to develop that same potential in herself.

Reformer-Reformer

This combination is almost certain to be a meeting of like minds. There may be shared political or religious ideals, and it is likely that a mutual enthusiasm brought the couple together and will continue to sustain them. However, if one partner develops significantly more than the other, the other one may feel betrayed by the change. This match is often made between two young people, whose strongly held principles may be molded as the character matures. Plenty of communication is essential, with firm ground rules in place. Keeping the discussions reasoned and calm will allow both partners to grow in understanding.

Mother Hen-Mother Hen

This partnership is more often seen between people who met at a mature age, perhaps both survivors of divorce with families to nurture. They will seek mutual benefit, as well as romantic love, and will pool their resources to make both their lives easier. Both must work hard to allay their suspicions that the other is more concerned about the original family unit than the new one—ex-spouses may threaten the stability of the bond. Reassurance will grow over time, but trust must be nurtured.

Actor-Actor

This combination is often found among career people who have little time to forge social networks outside their work or whose interest is limited for anything not directly connected with their everyday lives. Celebrities are a high profile example—many Hollywood marriages are literally Actor-Actor, but ballet dancers are another famous example of a type who almost invariably intermarry. Less visibly, teachers and journalists who are Actors will always be attracted to each other. The prime danger is that another Actor—younger, more dynamic, or simply more successful—may supplant one of the partners.

Artist-Artist

Two kindred spirits, close enough to touch but too often facing away from each other, a pair of Artists risk sinking into silence. Neither is confident enough to reach out, and neither has sufficient confidence to take a hand that is tentatively, warily extended. But the simple fact that they have found each other gives rise to great hope—they are both self-aware enough to recognize the similarity in their needs and aspirations. To help develop communication in the relationship, they need to take a sheet of paper, as large as they can find, and write on it in colorful, cartoonish letters, "We need to talk!" Their shared sense of absurdity will enjoy the joke—and the real message will make its point.

Intellectual-Intellectual

The natural "rightness" of this combination will be so apparent to both partners that they may never need to analyze their relationship, however odd it may appear to outsiders. The relationship can be put at risk if one partner enjoys success while the other battles with ideas that are never adequate to solve the problems that they are attempting to overcome; however, even a disparity in success, income, and acclaim can be ignored by both partners if they recognize each other's value. In this partnership infidelities may go unnoticed, but the same ability to overlook things can also mean that their children may be expected to fend for themselves. The couple must be prepared to deal with one difficulty that affects all people—old age. An Intellectual whose mental faculties weaken seems to become a different person to others, and shared values will not be enough to sustain both partners—this relationship demands unselfish love.

Believer-Believer

A common pairing from the workplace, this partnership is based on common interest and outlooks and, often, intense physical attraction. The relationship may be begun in secret, since most employers frown on romances among their employees. However, this couple must not turn their back on everything that brought them together—running away is not a solution, no matter how romantic it may seem at the time. These two Believers must take time to learn about their hearts, taking nothing for granted. Although characters rarely change, outside circumstances, such as jobs and finances, are constantly shifting, and it is important these two factors are not confused.

Busy Bee-Busy Bee

When a Busy Bee finds a partner who can keep pace with his or her own thousand-mile-an-hour chatter and electrifying stream of ideas, it can seem to be a revelation—as if God had placed on Earth a special human being specifically to grant the Busy Bee's prayers. However, disillusionment can set in just as quickly, as two congenitally unreliable people set about trying to establish a relationship. If each partner uses the other as a mirror, searching for faults as well as potential in their own souls, both of them will become immensely stronger. In any event, the greatest challenge for these Busy Bees will be to maintain a stable friendship that is deeper than any physical attraction.

Boss-Boss

For this combination to be successful, this pairing must combine forces, or they will run the risk of simply negating each other. If these Bosses share an aim, such as the building of a family business, and if they can learn to delegate work to each other—for example, so that one handles contractors and employees, while the other is responsible for dealing with clients and accountants—they will make a formidable team. If one of them weakens, the other can take up the strain. However, if one Boss is naturally much stronger and seeks to be the dominant partner, the other Boss may resent the loss of authority. Both partners must take the difficult step of examining their characters and their own motives, and accept the dynamic of the relationship instead of fighting it.

Magician-Magician

This relationship can be in danger of effacing itself to death, of offering so many concessions on both sides that neither partner really knows who stands where. A Magician's natural willingness to assess and improve a relationship will serve them both well. However, each partner should be unafraid of defining and stating what they expect and need from their partnership, which will help both of them to know where they stand. If one wins, they will both win. This couple will benefit from making formal pledges—for example, although a traditional marriage ceremony might seem outmoded and extravagant, it will give both of them a firmly stated set of promises to guide their relationship, which a live-in arrangement would lack.

CHAPTER FOUR

Relationships

We are children as well as parents, siblings as well as neighbors, friends as well as colleagues. Our relationships are part of a pattern, which, like the Life Signs wheel, is constantly assuming a new meaning. Life Signs can provide many helpful clues to happier relations, including those within stepfamilies. Knowledge of the differences in basic types of personality—our own and others—is essential if we are to understand relationships across generation gaps and among people of different backgrounds.

Friends

In times of trouble your friends will be there to support you, and at other times they may need to lean on you.

Friends can make the bad times better and the good times great.

From the heart

I was brought up in Israel, where Middle Eastern body language often prevails. I have noticed that Israelis who have emigrated to America use physical contact more than most Americans. Warm, reassuring gestures involving touch are easy to learn. They may feel unfamiliar for a few weeks, but they soon become instinctive.

The friendships that we make throughout our lives are some of the most important relationships we will ever experience, and it is important to our happiness and well-being that we nurture them. Friends can make joyful times more wonderful, and their comforting presence in times of crisis eases our pain. However, you should remember that your friends were once strangers to you. It took time for a bond to be made, from your first encounter to the moment you realized that you had found someone you could trust and who trusted you. Like any other relationship, a friendship needs to be worked on in order for it to strengthen and grow.

By giving you an insight into people's behavior and motivation, the Life Signs can help you to build and maintain these special relationships, and they will also enable you to become a more sensitive, understanding, and wiser friend to others. Gauging the Life Sign of a new acquaintance can be difficult, particularly during the first few months after you begin applying the theory, but it is well worth making the effort. It is not a matter of labeling someone the minute you are introduced; instead, it is about using Life Signs to work out what makes them tick, so that you can relate to them better and find the most effective way of getting closer to them. The Signs will also guide you when you need to second-guess how someone will react in any given situation.

One useful guideline that will steer you toward the right assessment and provide instant, valuable information about a person's character is to group the Signs into Doers, Thinkers, and Feelers (see pp. 14–17). These categories are very distinct and easy to apply, and they act as clear signposts. You will usually be able to recognize a new face as a Doer, Feeler, or Thinker within a minute or two, and from there it will be simpler to identify the Sign itself.

Understanding your friends

Once you have identified someone's Life Sign, you will be able to establish the key characteristics that will define your relationship.

Reformers are loyal and forthright when you need to hear some truths about yourself; however, if you anger a Reformer, the grudge could last for years. Mother Hens, on the other hand, rarely hold a grudge. They will defend you against anyone. All they ask for is your affection and appreciation.

Actors can be wonderfully entertaining company. They are usually successful, and their positive, can-do attitude rubs off on those they love. In contrast, Intellectuals can be difficult to draw out. If you share a common interest, conversation is easier—but don't be tempted to fill all the silences. You will need to be patient with Artists, too, but they reward friends who take the trouble to learn about their

hidden hearts. Don't judge an Artist by superficial traits because these are probably a smokescreen.

Believers need a peer group, and they forge powerful bonds with their community. They enjoy gossip and feel that talking about their friends is a way of showing love. Bosses like to dominate relationships. They make loyal friends to people who are happy to follow their lead, and their great strength of character is generously shared.

Busy Bees can be infuriating because they never seem to stand still long enough to listen. They will have a handful of close friends but tend to forget acquaintances if someone better sails into view. Magicians are different. Sometimes they will prolong relationships that they would prefer to terminate. They are sympathetic listeners who hate to hurt their friends.

Romantic love

One of the most powerful of all the human emotions is romantic love.

Whether it is the almost overwhelming surge of joy and excitement that comes with the beginning of a new romance or the warm, tender feelings of familiarity and trust that develop over the course of a long-term partnership, romantic love is important in most people's lives.

Keeping the spark alive

All relationships need to be nurtured, and it is unrealistic to expect everything to be perfect all the time. Tolerance and understanding are two of the most vital elements required to ensure a contented and supportive relationship, and to achieve these we have to recognize the inherent character traits that make our partners think and act the way they do. This does not mean that you should make excuses for your partner's inappropriate behavior—if you feel you have to do this, then you must ask if this person is right for you. Romantic love is about understanding what is in the heart and mind of your

From the heart

I feel every new relationship is like the beginning of a romance, even though it won't be sexual—my wife Hanna and I are happily and faithfully married. However, I love my close friends dearly, and love is always romantic because you never know how it will develop. A new friendship brings joy into my life, and the love of a friend can transcend the mundane and become something magical.

partner and accepting them for who they are. Each of the Life Signs has its own individual faults, but they are always balanced by strengths and virtues. The Reformer needs to bear this in mind. She may put her partner on a pedestal or regard him with suspicion. Neither may be justified, so her partner must be frank in revealing his true nature.

By using the Life Signs to reveal new aspects of your personalities and find fresh ways to relate to each other, you can avoid allowing your relationship to become stale. For some types, it is often easy to take a long-term partner for granted. Complacency can be one of the greatest threats to romance. The Busy Bee can be in love one day and bored the next—that is the danger of his whirlwind approach to everything, including romance. If you are in love with a Busy Bee, you may have to always work hard to keep him interested in a long-term relationship. Another Life Sign type to take note of is the Boss. With her love of risk, she may try to spice up her life with some extracurricular romance.

Understanding each other's needs

No two people are exactly alike, and sometimes new relationships flounder before they have a chance to blossom simply because one (or both) of the partners has ignored this fact. For example, while an Actor needs to feel that he is at the center of his lover's universe, demanding worship and devotion, a Mother Hen has so much love to give that she may overwhelm her lover with affection and demands for commitment. For an Artist, the core of the relationship is also the security and self-esteem it brings. His need for reassurance may sometimes seem self-pitying, but his partner should respond with love.

Sometimes you can look at a couple and think they are complete opposites and wonder how their relationship can possibly work. The answer is that they understand each other's emotional needs and do all they can to fulfill them. Conversely, you may wonder why two people who seem to be a match made in heaven cannot make a relationship work. Often, the reason is that they have put their own needs first—when two people are pulling in different directions, they tend to come unstuck.

Reading between the lines

It can sometimes be hard to read the signals that another person is sending out, which makes it difficult to know the right way to respond. The Intellectual, in particular, can be especially difficult to fathom. Don't be fooled by her airy declarations that romance should be a practical matter. She can feel love as strongly as anyone, but she is sometimes shocked by the strength of her feelings and will try to hide them from her partner. Intense feelings will also scare the Believer. When his emotions rush like a white-water river, the Believer fears that no one has ever felt love so powerfully before. Both of these Life Signs should be handled with care and sensitivity.

However, there is a flip side to all this selflessness that puts the Magician at risk. Her heart is vulnerable, because she tries so desperately to be fair to everyone. She should remember that love is never fair, and, in romance, she probably needs to learn a little ruthlessness.

For your information

Overcoming insecurity

Self-doubt can undermine all people, whatever their Life Sign. When we feel bad about ourselves, we feel bad about everyone else around us, too. Doubt yourself and you doubt the world. This kind of negative thinking is poisonous to all relationships but instantly fatal to blossoming romance. Self-doubt can undermine anyone, whatever the Life Sign.

● Introspection can make a Feeler's mind pick at a problem until a hole appears in the soul.

● A Thinker should remember that self-doubt is an emotional response to failure, not a rational choice.

● As a form of active denial, self-doubt can be an engine that drives a Doer to achieve.

Parents

To build and maintain a loving relationship with your parents, you need to accept them as they are.

Even if we did not grow up close to our parents, we know their characters with instinctive sureness. We can predict what they will do or say—perhaps more confidently than they could themselves—but we do not always know the reasons why. Instinct can guide us, but it does not teach us and it does not reveal. Only knowledge can do this.

Ask yourself what Life Signs your parents are, or were. You may be able to work through the questionnaire with them, an experiment that may bring you closer together. When you determine their Life Signs, you will gain valuable insights that will not only help you come to terms with any issues that may have troubled you, but will also help you gain

the knowledge you need to become closer to these people who have dedicated so much of themselves to your own life and helped form your personality.

Understanding your parents

Your parents' own childhood will have an effect on how they do as parents. For example, the Artist, who often has a difficult childhood, is a kind, conscientious parent, determined to avoid the mistakes of his own past. In this he is like the Intellectual, who will analyze his own upbringing and identify more efficient techniques. However, both types tend to be undemonstrative and can seem cold to children. Not so the Mother Hen. No detail is too small to escape her ministrations, from the state of a child's clothes to her eating habits—and this behavior does not stop even when the child becomes an adult.

The Actor is often an absent parent, chasing other goals; but childhood can be fun with an Actor parent, with plenty of games, stories, and make-believe. Like the Actor, the Busy Bee is seldom fully absorbed in parenting, but, as compensation, there will be plenty of spur-of-the-moment treats. The child of a Magician, however, may sometimes feel deprived of this kind of exuberance. The Magician expects his children to act in a grown-up manner at all times and is surprised at any displays of rampant childishness.

Although a loving and inspirational parent, the Believer may apply too much pressure on her child to conform to the parent's own standards. The Boss, too, may neglect the fact that a child needs room to make mistakes and learn from them. The Boss is guilty of only trying to give too much guidance.

Showing respect

No parent is perfect, and it is wrong to allow shortcomings to fuel resentment. We should expect to be treated by our children as we have treated our own parents. My mother told me this story when I was a child. I have never forgotten it:

Each generation is different but, as you become a parent yourself, you will appreciate your own parents' efforts.

For your information

Having a good talk

One of the most important elements in any parent-child relationship is to maintain open communication. If you can achieve this, you will achieve mutual understanding and respect, empathy, and honesty. It is all too easy to dwell on previous mistakes, but that is the biggest mistake of all.

- Feelers should let go of any grudges held against their parents for things said and done years ago.

- Speaking honestly to parents can be an emotional challenge for Thinkers—but silence is worse.

- Parents are part of the past and present. Doers should make time to allow their relationship to continue to grow.

A man was disgusted to see his wife's father drool as he ate at their table, so the old man was moved away from the table and banished to the barn. One dinnertime, the couple's youngest child was absent. They found her in the barn, trying to make a chair from bricks and pieces of wood. "Your Grandad can eat standing up," said her father. "Oh, no, Daddy" said the girl, "it's for you, because one day we'll have to make you eat in here and I want you to have a chair and table." The man embraced his daughter, then he embraced the old man and asked him to take his dinner with the rest of the family.

The message of this story was not lost upon me. My elderly mother lives in an apartment in our home, but the whole house is hers to enjoy when she wants. And I know that, wherever my son and daughter live, their homes will also be homes to my wife and me.

Your new baby

One of the greatest blessings of life is a new baby, but a baby changes life so radically that it may take time before the child is appreciated.

When my wife and I were waiting for our first child to be born, we, like so many young couples, made a promise to each other that "we won't let this change our lives." What were we thinking? There is no experience so destined to shake up your life as becoming a parent. I believe couples instinctively know this, and make a promise such as we did in an effort to stem the tide of panic. To create a new life is the greatest responsibility anyone can undertake and if young parents-to-be are not on the verge of panic, they have not grasped the enormity of what is about to hit them.

New baby, new emotions

The impact of a baby is not just in the amount of work involved or the expense. Nor it is the lack of sleep—although when you've been woken up five times during the night, you'll feel that you will never be young again. A baby's greatest impact is emotional.

New parents are wholly unprepared for the whirlwind of feelings whipped up by exhaustion and anxiety. Whatever they feel for the infant—and many parents are so shocked by this gigantic event that they cannot discern their own feelings of affection for weeks or even months—this love is unlike any they have known. It feels nothing like the love they remember feeling as children for their own parents, and it is completely unlike romantic love. If the bond forged between lovers could be as strong as the bond binding the hearts of parent and baby, the divorce rate would drop to almost zero. Emotion this intense creates a love that endures for all time.

New parents all experience this love, but there are other reactions to parenthood, too. For example, an Artist can feel overwhelmed. He will need to express whatever is in his heart when the baby arrives, perhaps to a confidant—not necessarily his spouse—who can share his emotional upheaval. For some Signs, especially the Reformer, it is the disruption to normal routine that causes the greatest turmoil. All the rules change when a new baby arrives—suddenly there is someone in the family who does not respond to reason. The Reformer must accept that her rational world will be chaotic for the foreseeable future. The Boss, too, may find the day-to-day demands of a new baby exasperating. But some things cannot be delegated, and a parent's love is one of them. Nursery care and babysitters let her get on with life, but she needs to make plenty of time every day for baby bonding.

Of course, although your own life may seem topsy-turvy, routine is of vital importance to an infant. This is anathema to the Busy Bee, forever flitting from one project to another, but the child comes first, and routine has to be the rule. Babies need basics such as warm clothes, regular food, and clean diapers. The Intellectual can too easily overlook these necessities. Make a list—it will help.

A Believer must resist the temptation to measure his own baby against everyone else's. Babies progress at different rates, and this doesn't make one smarter or better than another. Stop worrying and just enjoy. Take a leaf from the Actor's book. She just knows that her baby is perfect.

Finding time for others

For the Mother Hen, the baby is the most important person in the home, but she should remember that the baby is not the only important one. Other chil-

dren and especially her spouse will be hungry for her attention, too.

Everyone has a limit, and a baby will reveal yours. Don't sacrifice yourself to the point of exhaustion; this is not productive. The Magician should take note—don't suffer in silence; if you need help, ask for it.

From the heart

The comparative frailty of love may be revealed by the arrival of a new baby, especially when there are also toddlers in the household. The father may become jealous of the bond between the mother and baby. A type of rivalry erupts, with the father jockeying for attention, just as older brothers and sisters do. This is common when the mother is competent and seems to need less of her husband's attention. To avoid putting the relationship in danger, the father should be understanding of the demands placed on his wife and help with the other children.

Young children

A child's character is partly formed at birth, but the broad range of a child's personality develops over many years.

It is not until late in adolescence that we can clearly discern the Life Signs at work in a child. Before maturity, much of a child's character consists of imitating those around her. A part of this developing process typically involves a child's need to establish secure boundaries. She will want to know how far she can go before she is stopped—and she will constantly test those boundaries.

To help a young child achieve a positive outlook, give positive encouragement and reinforcement. This may seem an obvious statement, but some teaching styles are rooted in negative admonitions and discouragement. Most parents know how it feels to open their mouth and

> "WE CAN'T FORM OUR CHILDREN ON OUR OWN CONCEPTS; WE MUST TAKE THEM AND LOVE THEM AS GOD GIVES THEM TO US."
>
> Johann Wolfgang von Goethe
> German writer (1749–1832)

hear their own mother's voice speaking. I still hear myself saying, "Because I say so," which was one of my mother's favorite expressions when I, as a child, made her impatient. I vowed then never to use the same words to my own children, but somehow they still managed to come out. This type of no-nonsense approach is often used by the Busy Bee when dealing with a young child. "Leave it alone," "stop it," and "just do it" are well-worn phrases in a Busy Bee household.

By using positive communication (see "Something to think about," facing page), you are reassuring a child that he is loved. All children fear losing their parents' love, and when they are confident this cannot happen, their behavior tends to be better. Of course, this does not mean that you should cosset your child or tolerate unacceptable behavior.

Finding a balance

Rules must make sense, but you don't have to make them complicated. (The Intellectual should take note: This is a child he is bringing up, not a philosophy graduate student.) Keep any rules simple, and try to always explain the reasons behind them. The Reformer, in particular, needs to be patient and to remember that although a child likes firm limits, she does not usually have an instinctive understanding of why rules are made. Irrational rules are no use to anyone, least of all the person who sets them. The impulsive Actor, in particular, should guard against laying down laws on the spur of the moment and promptly forgetting them.

From the heart

Young children find wonder in everything. They are bewildered by people "inside" a television, believing their favorite characters live inside the box. I never laugh at their wonder; instead, I try to share it. After all, I have only the shakiest understanding of how my image can be projected from a television studio into millions of homes, or why that flickering picture can act as a catalyst to the psychic abilities of countless viewers. Most people feign understanding, but wonder is the truly positive response.

Parents will reap the rewards in years to come as they help their young children develop into adults.

Of all the Life Signs, it is the Mother Hen who finds it most difficult to impose rules. But over-indulgence will not help his child—it risks literally spoiling her. In the worst cases, other relatives and friends may be turned against the child when they see that a Mother Hen is being too soft on law and order. The easygoing Artist is also reluctant to curb her child's behavior, however wayward it may sometimes be. She tends to forget that firm rules can help a child express his emotions. Guidelines show how things should be, which helps him to set out an emotional map.

A Believer should bear in mind that by keeping to the rules he set for his child, he demonstrates a more clear example than is possible by merely demanding obedience. The Boss can also live by this principle. If she ever hears herself telling her child, "Do as I say, not as I do," she should slap herself across the wrist. The arts of negotiation and compromise are great talents that a Magician will enjoy teaching. He needs to make sure he doesn't let his child charm her way into everything she wants.

Something to think about

The challenge to parents is to impose rules in a positive way. Some Life Signs have a head start—Artists and Magicians often examine their own motives. Other Signs, such as Bosses and Reformers, may issue commands without stopping to question how they are phrased. Take stock of your own vocabulary and invent positive alternatives. Here are a few examples:

Negative: Don't do it like that.
Positive: Here's the best way to do it.

Negative: Stop moaning.
Positive: Here's a happy thought…

Negative: Wait your turn.
Positive: It is Ruth's turn now, then I'll make sure you have your turn.

Negative: You're in my way.
Positive: I have to get this done so I can play with you later.

Negative: You are a naughty girl and you are making me angry.
Positive: You were very good earlier, and that was wonderful. I'd like us to be like that now.

Teenagers

To a 14-year-old teenager, 40 seems beyond ancient. To the 40-something-year-old parent, 14 years of age seems barely past infancy.

Every parent finds himself saying, "When I was your age…," and we don't mean back in the Civil War; we mean recently, within emotional memory. A teen and his parent are like two people with their eyes glued to a single telescope. The adolescent is looking through the big lens, and adulthood appears almost invisibly far off; the grown-up is peering into the small lens, and the generation gap seems tiny.

For many parents, it is hard to take a step back as children grow, but everyone needs the space to make their own mistakes in safety. The challenge for parents is to provide that space, without abandoning the child. Remember when your baby first started to walk? You let go of his hands but hovered nearby, close enough to catch him when he stumbled. While he wanted you to let go, he also wanted you to stay close—and he wanted your approval.

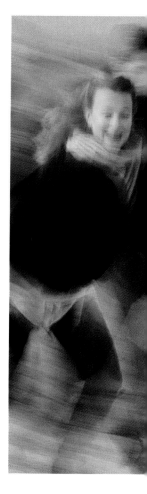

It is during the teenage years that we first establish our independence.

As that same baby grows into a teenager, nothing changes except the emphasis. He is still far from mature adulthood, no matter what he thinks—and he knows this, too. However, if you continue to hover nearby, you will be suffocatingly close.

Giving up control

Some Life Signs are better at ceding control than others. The Reformer is often accused of "control freak" tendencies, and this can certainly be true when the personality's selfish traits are not curbed; however, she has a strong instinct for good parenting, and she can will herself to offer the right levels of unobtrusive support. Life with teenagers is more of a challenge for the impatient Busy Bee and the Actor. Both are used to commanding exclusive attention, and adolescent egos can be seen as a threat to adult dominance.

For the Mother Hen and the Believer, the challenge is to let go at the right moment, but not too much. Teenagers need just enough freedom to start exploring their surroundings in safety. Deny them this, and they might fight back in dangerous directions. The Young Artist and the Intellectual are especially prone to rebellion, and they often lack the

From the heart

Evolutionary psychologists believe all human behavior is rooted in our caveman past, and the habits we developed then control us today. They believe that the animosity between teenagers and their families is a survival mechanism, forcing young adults away from hunting grounds where game might be scarce.

Personally, I regard evolutionary psychology as a kind of scientific superstition. Whenever you face problems in any relationship, search for causes and solutions here and now.

social skills to see the risks in what they are doing. As parents, they will be more aware than most of their own teenage protests against authority. Rebellion from their own teenagers will be a sharp wake-up call.

Of all the Life Signs, the Magician and the Boss have temperaments that are best suited to handing over control to their children in stages. Delegation and compromises are their natural talents.

Different perspectives

It is important to be aware that your children may not share your Life Sign and see the pacts and deals that you offer in a different light. By the time a child

> " THE BOND THAT
> LINKS YOUR TRUE
> FAMILY IS NOT ONE
> OF BLOOD, BUT OF
> RESPECT AND JOY IN
> EACH OTHER'S LIFE. "
>
> Richard Bach,
> American author (1936–)

is 14 or 15 years old, you should have a clear conception of what his Life Sign could be when his personality reaches full maturity in adulthood. By understanding his Life Sign personality, you may better understand how he will react to certain situations and should be able to use that knowledge constructively.

One useful advantage for parents, at the long end of the telescope, is perspective. If you have a 14-year-old who suddenly doesn't want to be treated as a child, think back to how he was at the age of 7, and how recent that seems to you. In only another short seven years that 14-year-old will be 21, and truly beginning adult life.

Adult children

Your relationship with your grown-up children will be different from the relationship you had with them as teenagers.

Your adult children will have more confidence in themselves and be more independent than they were as adolescents, but that does not mean that they won't at times turn to you for support or advice. However, remember that they now have their own lives—they may even be married with their own children. This is especially important advice for the Mother Hen—it is unreasonable to expect her adult son or daughter to run home for pampering.

You will find that you have a changing role with your children—perhaps you become closer friends or you become a confidant whom your children can trust. Many Artists parents have Artist children, and this Artist-Artist relationship can grow to a deep level of understanding. There may be times, however, when it may seem as if your children haven't grown up. Adult children don't always get on with each other. Old sibling rivalries can erupt, and it is the Magician parent who patches things up.

Be careful that you don't judge your children's ambitions by your own success and career choice, or you may find only disappointment. Your children may be as successful as you, but in ways you would never contemplate. It is important for your children that you accept their choices without criticism. The Actor should accept that his children may not follow his career path, but they still need to receive his applause. The Intellectual can experience similar feelings of disappointment and bewilderment if her children do not follow academic paths.

Becoming grandparents

One issue that can create battles—or solidarity—between parents and adult children are grandchildren. There can be a fine line between offering

For your information

Feelings of guilt

According to the British Psychological Society, guilt suppresses the immune system. In a study, after indulging in petty pleasures, such as eating chocolate, people were asked to rate how much pleasure and guilt they felt. Their saliva was tested for immunoglobulin A, which is present in a healthy immune system. Those who reported more pleasure had more immunoglobulin A than those who felt more guilt. Try to banish guilt from past experiences and build a positive relationship.

- Guilt, a powerful depressant, can cripple the emotions of Feelers. Try to keep busy and ignore old regrets.

- Analysis doesn't make guilt go away but helps the Thinkers to understand their personal situation.

- Doers can expunge old feelings of guilt by taking positive action now. What is done is done; what matters is still to come.

helpful advice and interfering. Being there for support and advice when it is asked for will be greatly appreciated, but spoiling a grandchild or going against her parent's wishes will only cause confrontation. Try to learn how to read your child's reaction when you offer your help.

Even in adulthood, your children can enjoy having your support on special occasions.

The joy of becoming a grandparent can change a Believer's life, because a new generation creates a clan feeling. Adult children should be quick to involve Believer grandparents in every aspect—their help will be invaluable.

It is difficult for any Reformer to cede the symbolic role of "head of the family" to the next generation. Many Reformers cling onto authority, even when they know they are driving their children away. The certainty of a Boss that she did a great job with her own children is prone to make her a stern critic when grandchildren arrive. Bosses must face facts—they cannot make the rules all the time.

Putting the past behind

Many parents carry a burden of guilt, which their grown-up children may not realize exists. This guilt may be rooted in relationship issues between an adolescent's parents; for example, if a marriage breaks up, the father may not be in the home and will miss the child's everyday activities. The father may feel guilty, and after the child has grown up, the guilt can be as strong as ever. A Busy Bee may not have put aside enough time for her teenagers, and this can lead to a deep resentment in later life. However, it is never too late for a Busy Bee to slow down and make room for her children.

A parent should discuss his guilt with his adult child, even if that means opening up a wide area of vulnerability. Set aside the invincibility that children confer on their parents and ask for forgiveness, which does not come painlessly. It is easier to talk about these problems with friends, colleagues, or professionals—easier with almost anyone but your child. In fact, sometimes people who approach me for an autograph will express their problems to me—a total stranger.

> "TO UNDERSTAND YOUR PARENTS' LOVE, YOU MUST RAISE CHILDREN YOURSELF."
>
> Chinese proverb

Stepfamilies

Forming a relationship with a new partner may also mean establishing a relationship with that person's children.

Fifty years ago divorce rarely occurred, but today divorce—or the breakup of a partnership—is common. It is also common to form new relationships that include children. As anyone who has tried it will testify, constructing a stable second family can be challenging. If it works out, it can be the happiest alliance ever made, not just for the adults but for the children, too. However, making it work can take every ounce of strength in your heart and soul.

For your information

Strange customs

One of the hardest aspects of accepting complete strangers as instant family is learning how different their habits and customs might be. Things you take for granted might strike them as strange—and vice versa. It sometimes helps to think of each other as visitors to a foreign land, becoming acclimatized to a different culture.

- You "think" with your emotions, so you may act on subconscious prejudices—challenge them.

- Try to be tolerant if others deal with life in different ways, even if they don't have logical behavior.

- Avoid rushing in and doing things "the way they should be done," without stopping first to think if you will give offense.

By the time we have been through a long-term relationship, established a career pattern, and begun to raise children, we know who we are. Our Life Signs have become fixed and our characters established. And as we reach our 30s, 40s, and beyond, we become less flexible. A young couple will readily sacrifice habits and routines. Their love outweighs such trivialities as who sleeps on the left side of the bed or who uses the bathroom first. For an older couple, tiny obstacles can become stumbling blocks. Patience is required for their relationship to work, especially if one of the partners is a Busy Bee. New relationships, like ancient Rome, cannot be built in a day, and a single heart-to-heart may not solve everything. A Reformer needs to remember that this is a new family—he should not try to replay old relationships, even if he tries to avoid the old mistakes.

The stepchild's viewpoint

Tougher still is the impact on those who had little say in the new relationship—the children. The erosion of previously established family traditions, such as watching a favorite television show together or visiting Grandma for Sunday lunch, becomes symbolic of the upheaval in their lives. Logical explanations may only make them more upset.

Some Life Signs deal better with radical change than others, but don't take anything for granted. A young Reformer can be very resistant, and an Artist may be harboring deep pain that won't show for months or years. An Intellectual son may appear to be dealing sensibly with all the changes, and a Mother Hen daughter might seem happy to take charge of her younger stepbrothers or half-sisters. However, these types need just as much care and

With patience, establishing a stepfamily can be a truly rewarding experience.

Communication is essential to form bonds. An Artist will have to open up. In new relationships, especially with young people whose emotions are in turmoil, no one will guess what the Artist is feeling unless he speaks from his heart. A Boss will need to be willing to listen when others need to talk.

The absent parent is often still in the children's life. A Mother Hen may have some reservations about looking after someone else's children when there is an ongoing relationship with the absent parent, but giving her own love will be appreciated. The Intellectual should be ready to put up with any chaos and avoid losing his temper over superficial things.

empathy—they could be denying or hiding their pain. Keep a watch out for danger signs such as sudden, unexpected bursts of rage, nightmares, bedwetting, moody periods of silence, and lethargy. Never ignore sudden changes in a child's behavior. He needs support if he is to stop hiding from his pain.

Bonding with stepchildren

It often takes time for children to accept a new stepparent, but it is important that you be patient. True success in family life means selflessness. If the Actor is tolerant when a child expresses anger that isn't really meant for her, she may eventually break through any barriers. A Believer is always willing to embrace his new role robustly, but he needs to be patient if the children are not yet ready for his commitment. A Magician will work overtime at healing rifts and building bridges. She may feel unappreciated, but her support will be missed if it is removed.

From the heart

Tackling a fresh relationship takes energy, especially if it comes with children. You have to greet this new situation with a spring in your step, not dragging your feet. Keeping a relationship going is a dance. Start dancing, even if the effort may wear you out at first. Your emotions and your spirits need to be kept fit to be buoyant, just as your body needs exercise to stay healthy.

Coping with serious illness

Nothing is more devastating than learning that you or a loved one has a serious illness, but there are ways to help you deal with the situation.

Whether it is a chronic, disabling condition or a potentially terminal illness, your whole world will seem to be turned upside down and your focus will change completely. Nothing will seem to matter any more except the illness and its inevitable effects. Happiness and optimism will be replaced by fear and uncertainty.

The oncologist Jeremy Geffen, who began specializing in the treatment of cancer shortly before his own father died from the disease, put together a five-step strategy for patients to follow when cancer is diagnosed. However, his advice is just as relevant for anyone diagnosed with a serious illness, and it can help those supporting someone who is seriously ill.

Geffen's five-step strategy was carefully formulated to minimize the disruption caused by shock,

and he emphasizes that every patient faces a unique challenge. He does not offer a cure-all formula, but his suggestions have helped many.

Five steps to handling illness

First, accept that you are afraid. Fear is totally natural. What faces you seems vast and unknown, and, of course, it is daunting, but fear is not invincible. You can conquer it. It is fine to be afraid, but you don't have to be afraid of your fear. Avoid over-analyzing the illness. Some Life Signs, such as the Artist and the Intellectual, risk paralyzing themselves by doing so.

Second, slow down. You will feel as if you have to have all the information right now. You will want to know about diets, vitamins, and alternative therapies; you will want to hear about other people's experiences; you will want to read everything you can find. But this doesn't all have to be done today. If you are the patient, you risk making yourself weaker through panic; if the patient is someone you love, then remember that the most important gift you can give is unwavering support. This is especially hard for the Boss and the Busy Bee, who desperately want to regain control over the disease, and the Reformer, who is liable to react with anger. This attitude can help them summon the energy to fight the sickness, but it also puts their families under increased strain.

Third, be sure you trust your doctor. Don't be afraid to ask for a second opinion—and a third and fourth if that is what you need to feel at ease. The Magician and the Believer may be awed by the doctor's status, but they need to build up a strong relationship with their doctor. If this fails, consider turning to another, equally qualified person.

From the heart

The news that someone close and dear to us is seriously ill and may die is always shattering. Often, I believe, our unconscious minds warn us of the shock to come. For years I had a recurring dream of a body lying beneath a window in a tiny apartment. The body rolled over, and my own face stared up at me. I was afraid that this was a premonition of my own death, but when my father died I realized that I had been psychically preparing myself for the shock. He had suffered a fatal angina attack and fallen beneath the window of his apartment.

Fourth, pay attention to your spiritual needs. The body has a sickness, but malaise can easily spread to the soul. This condition can hop between people much more easily than most physical ailments—depression and anxiety are swiftly transmitted. Treat your mind and spirit with the same care and attention that is being lavished on the body. The Actor and the Boss are the most prone to forgetting this—they are so shocked that anything can strike them physically, threatening to sweep away their aura of immortality, that all their other defenses become doubly vulnerable. For a Mother Hen, feelings of self-pity can become overwhelming. She has spent her life looking after others and is liable to feel neglected and become depressed if she is not treated with a similar standard of care.

Discovering that you or a loved one has a serious illness can be a traumatic event; for your emotional well-being, it is important to still make time to enjoy yourself.

Finally, try to understand that life flows like a river. It does not stop for anything or anyone. Whatever your past has been, whatever you miss or regret or recall fondly, life has brought you to this present moment. And tomorrow, this moment, too, will have been left behind in the flow. Everyone passes through moments of deep fear, of illness, of grieving. This is universal. Your troubles are not unique, and they are not vengeful. Everyone suffers, and you share your troubles with the world. You will find there are many caring individuals and organizations ready to help you bear the burden.

Aggressive people

Using aggression to get what you want often means losing what is most precious—your relationship.

A. E. van Vogt, a best-selling writer of science fiction, formulated a theory about violent men. He called them "Right men," because they have to be right in every situation. A Right man cannot bear to submit to authority and can never accept that any opinion except his own is right. He cannot use reason to prove he is right, so he will bully his family instead.

The Right man represents the very worst aspect of a problem that affects us all—aggression. Occasionally a situation demands a vigorous verbal response, but too often hostility and rage erupt at the slightest provocation. Many times these outbursts are triggered by frustration and exhaustion—feelings that are too common in our fast-paced,

competitive world. But outbursts can and must be controlled; they are damaging to both the aggressor and the victim, and they will eventually destroy even the most stable relationship.

Aggressive tendencies

Of course, aggression is not an exclusively male behavior, and it is a trait seen in all the Life Signs—but it is more prevalent in some types. The Reformer, like the Busy Bee, will fly off the handle if things are not exactly right—both may regret it later, but caution is not a characteristic of either Sign. Remember the golden rule: Before you blow your top, count to 10; then, if necessary, count to 10 again.

The Actor and the Boss will resort to bullying tactics simply to get what they want. The Actor knows how to use physical presence, but she is in danger of generating a violent response from adversaries. The Boss often assumes that everyone around him is as thick-skinned as himself and is unaware of how much hurt he may cause. Surprisingly, a Mother Hen may also underestimate the impact of her anger. She knows that underneath she is still her soft old self, but others don't see that.

Although rarely aggressive, the Artist, when convinced of the necessity, can use extreme violence. The most merciless soldiers are not the extroverts but the quiet men. Brains, not brawn, are the Intellectual's way. She rarely displays aggression, and, when she does, she is unconvincing. The Believer is also unlikely to let his temper get the better of him. Staying put and showing a brave face is intrinsic to his nature. Similarly, the Magician will resort to force only if all attempts at moderation have been abandoned.

For your information

Domestic violence

If physical violence in the home is affecting you now, or has affected you in the past, you are not alone. There are a lot of people going through it and many who have found ways to survive it through organizations and support groups (look for one in the Yellow Pages of your telephone book under "Social and Human Services").

Many of the lessons in this book teach self-esteem. The first of them is this: You do not deserve to suffer violence. Act, don't endure.

 Feelers desperately want things to be right but, if they don't take action, nothing will change.

 Thinkers should believe in their right to be loved without threats. They shouldn't listen to excuses.

 Doers should resist the urge to fight back; instead, they should seek a way out of the situation, knowing that they are not at fault.

Animals and pets

The bond between pet and owner can be very beneficial, especially for the young, the lonely, and the sick.

All my life I have owned dogs, and I know that the unconditional love I receive from them is like a healing energy. Being with my canine friends fills me with vitality and high spirits. Animals are reservoirs of love into which you can pour an infinite amount of affection to be drawn on whenever it is needed.

Dr. Rupert Sheldrake, an internationally respected biologist, has studied the bond between human and pet. One example is Jaytee, a dog who knows when his owner, Pamela, is coming home, even if she arrives at odd hours. Videotapes show that Jaytee spends 4 percent of his day at the window, but he is there more than half the time when Pamela arrives.

Reaping the benefits

Owning a pet provides a deep sense of security for the old and the lonely. Studies have found that simply petting an animal can help reduce stress, and some hospitals routinely arrange for animals to visit their patients, both adults and children.

Owning a pet teaches a child responsibility; for example, she must feed the animal, and walk a dog, brush a cat, or clean out a rabbit's hutch. It also teaches an essential lesson about death. A youngster who loses a beloved pet does suffer, but it is not helpful for parents to protect their children against that pain. We all need to learn about grief. In this, as in so many things, animals are wonderful teachers. For children, who may feel they are facing an uncertain world where love comes sporadically, a pet offers solid, unquestioning love. The Reformer will form a strong bond with her childhood pet, who will always be fondly remembered as the perfect dog or cat.

The Artist and the Mother Hen can both become devoted to their pets. Often it will be a cat, and the lucky animal will be treated as a surrogate child, fed

Something to do

Have you got a psychic pet? It is difficult to make people believe you when you explain that your dog or cat can read your mind; however, if you can record some real evidence, you might find you have got a celebrity pet on your hands.

Use a video camera and a notebook to keep track of times when your pet seems to be reacting to your unspoken thoughts. Try these experiments:

Experiment one: On the first day, call your pet for its dinner and time its response. The next day, at about the same time, open the food and put it down without calling the pet; time this response.

On the third day—at a different time—do not touch the food or the dish, but summon your pet with mental messages. Say the words that you would usually call out in your mind, "Come and get it! Food! Dinnertime!" Does your pet respond to the telepathic summons?

Experiment two: When your pet is resting, with its eyes closed, try calling its name in your head. Watch its face—it may not wake up, but you may see the shadows of dreams flitting over its closed eyelids. Is it dreaming of games it enjoys playing with you?

on the best tidbits and treated to the best bed in the house. The pet can be an extension of the Actor's personality. When you see a cat in a gem-studded collar or a dog that does tricks, you can be sure that it is an Actor's pet.

For the Believer, pets offer a route into a community. Whether it is the simple camaraderie that exists between dog walkers—you are never alone in the park when carrying a leash—or the rivalries between cat-show enthusiasts, animals help humans connect. Breeding budgerigars or keeping tropical fish can be an absorbing hobby for someone who is stressed, a kind of living meditation. This is especially true for the Boss.

Not for everyone

Owning a pet is not a natural choice for everyone. Before acquiring a pet, the Busy Bee should ask himself, "Do you really want that puppy? Or is it a whim that will be forgotten tomorrow?" Only a human can be a Busy Bee. All other animals, especially pets, demand long-term commitment.

An objection to a pet might also be due to the type of pet. Much to her mother's dismay, the Magician will often choose an eccentric pet, such as a rat, snake, or iguana, to emphasize her individuality. The Intellectual may say that he does not see the point of deliberately committing himself to the demands of an animal, but he often finds himself becoming inexplicably attached to his friends' pets when he cares for them while they are on vacation.

The Mother Hen often feels uneasy at the closeness between a family member and pet, whether it is a child's terrier or an elderly aunt's bird. He should not be tempted to control the relationship, even if plenty of objections occur to her: "Who is going to look after the animal if you are not here? How will you feel if it dies?" The truth is that logic has nothing to do with her anxiety. Ask instead, "Do I need to control this relationship? If I do, why is that?"

Having a pet is a rewarding experience, one that is beneficial to both the owner and the animal.

From the heart

Pet telepathy once saved my life. I was 14 years old and I got lost in the hillside caves above my school in Cyprus. After two hours of hunting for a way out, I curled into a ball and prayed for help. I had left my dog, Joker, 4 miles away, at my stepfather's hotel, but in the darkness I heard him barking, and suddenly he was licking my face. Joker knew the way out. Since that day, one of my dogs always has been named Joker.

God and spirituality

There is a growing body of scientific evidence suggesting that religious belief can prolong your life.

Although the media regularly proclaims "the death of God," religious belief is, in fact, on the rise. In the United States 85 percent of Americans believe in life after death, which is up from 76 percent in the 1950s. Only 2 percent of the American population are genuine atheists—and most of them are probably Intellectuals. There will always be cynics, but claims about the positive health benefits of prayer and meditation, regardless of the type of religion, have been widely publicized in recent years.

Quiet, reflective thought acts as a stress buster, and stress can have negative effects on your mental and physical well-being (see pp. 138–143). Dr. Mike Money, a staff member at the Centre for Health,

> " MAY FAITH MAKE YOUR LIFE SERENE
> AND HOPE HELP KEEP IT BRIGHT...."
>
> Kahlil Gibran
> Lebanese poet and artist (1883–1931)

Healing and Human Development at John Moores University in England, has a fascinating theory about a link between the brain and the body's natural immunity generators. When spiritual thoughts reach the thymus, a gland at the base of the neck that regulates defenses against infection, the functions of the immune system are strengthened.

A research study at Duke University, involving 4,000 people over the age of 65, found that those who regularly attend services at a church, synagogue, or mosque are more likely to have lower blood pressure levels than their non-service-attending neighbors. Whether you reach a level of tranquility through religious prayer or quiet meditation, you will reap the benefits.

Seeking comfort

Religion is a comfort to many people. The realization that none of us is immortal is frightening, and none is more affected by that thought than the Actor, who may turn to religion to cope with her anxiety. She is likely to have a great interest in the idea of life after death. For the Mother Hen, too, belief helps him to cope. His most fervent prayer is for spiritual strength, and this is one prayer that will always be answered—simply focusing on the request renews his energy. The Artist tends to have an uncompromising faith. Similarly, when a Believer has faith, it is strong—and he is unlikely to keep it to himself. The Believer will be evangelistic, wanting to spread the word and convert others to her ideas.

For some, spiritual certainty is almost a matter of convenience. The Boss finds the idea of questioning

From the heart

I have always believed that God is everywhere, especially in our own hearts. When you need to pray, a church, synagogue, or mosque is a wonderful aid to calmness and concentration; however, you can create that atmosphere even in the busiest places—in a traffic jam, in a doctor's waiting room, or at the supermarket. Take a deep, slow breath, and let it out—that simple action prepares you for prayer as fully as a monk's chant or a priest's blessing. Visualize in your mind a bright light, and watch it glow for a few moments. Begin your prayer now.

a religious belief contradictory and a waste of time—if God had meant the Boss to ask theological questions, He would have made him a priest. For others, questioning is an intrinsic element of their faith. The Busy Bee may wrestle with her conscience and question her faith every day. The Magician is also willing to explore the limits of faith. For both, enquiry makes their devotion stronger—their spiritual awareness is ceaselessly alive and vibrant.

Not all the Life Signs are as accepting of religion. When his faith is tested by grief or illness, the Reformer may abandon it to the detriment of his health. The Intellectual has difficulty accepting something that she can't explain logically.

All of the Signs are open to the benefits of prayer. There are no limits. Whatever you feel, however you believe, when your mind is filled with positive images, you will feel strong. When your thoughts are sad, your body will feel sad, too. You would not pray fervently for something you did not want—by the same token, be sure to let your thoughts lead you in the direction you wish to travel.

Something to think about

I want you to try this experiment. Buy two inexpensive plants, such as ivy or spider plants. Place one of them at each end of a shelf, and put aside a quiet moment every day to tend them. As you water one, pray for it silently. Request of God, "This is only a tiny plant, but it is part of your creation, as deserving of divine love and energy as any living thing. Please fill this plant with health and power to grow. Make it strong. And as I am no more significant in this great scheme than a tiny plant, may I, too, be blessed with your love and energy."

Go to the other plant and tell it telepathically, "I pray that you do not grow. This is a scientific experiment. I can only pray positively for the other plant. For you my prayer is that God will freeze your growth. For six weeks you must not grow. Just stop, stay still. Don't grow for six weeks, and then I will help you grow."

This experiment is a re-creation of a serious piece of science, first conducted over 40 years ago by a congregational minister with a master's degree in chemistry. The Reverend Franklin Loehr instructed 150 volunteers used to daily prayer to focus their spiritual thoughts on 27,000 seeds. Two major effects emerged: plant growth could be enhanced by prayer, and it could be held back.

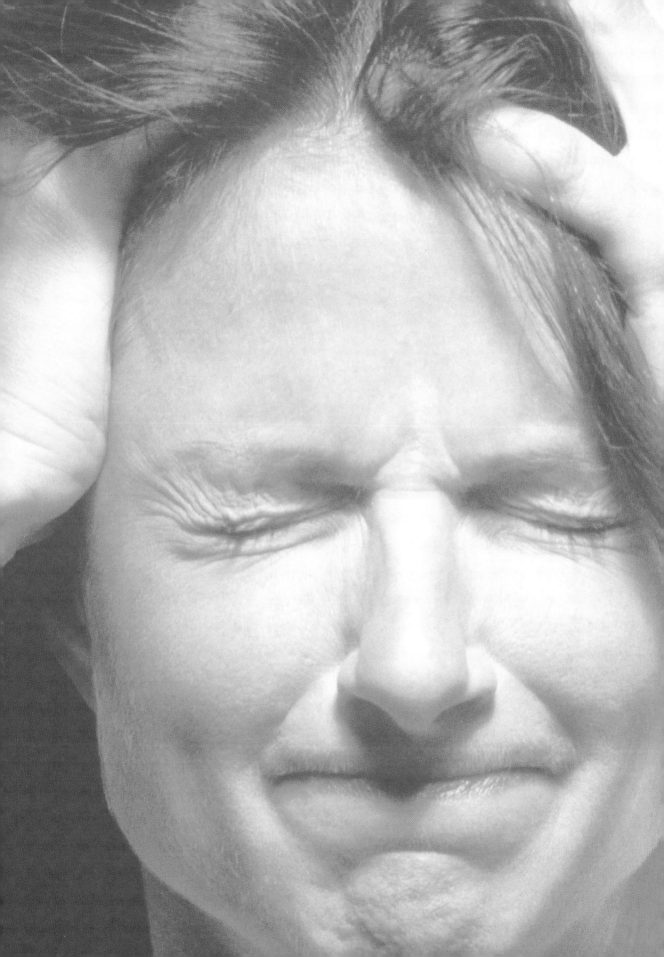

Coping with stress

You may feel that the world is spinning too fast and you are besieged by too many problems. In this chapter you will learn about stress and how it affects the mind and the body. You will also learn to control stress by maximizing the potential of your own Life Sign and to cope with some of the most debilitating stress factors, such as divorce, bereavement, illness, aging, money, and work.

Understanding stress

The feeling of being under stress is part of our "fight or flight" response, which helped our ancestors survive danger, such as an attack from a wild animal.

The Viennese endocrinologist Dr. Hans Selye (see box below) pioneered in the study of stress. After emigrating to Canada, he experimented with rats, subjecting them to environmental stresses—confusion, noise, and sudden shocks—until they induced breakdowns. Selye believed that humans in many ways react to stress just as rats do. Despite our intelligence and rational minds, which enable us to think our way through trauma, our bodies, like those of rats, are prone to break down under stress. Diseases of adaptation to stress in humans, as Selye described them, include heart problems, hypertension, and stroke.

The three stages

Our bodies react to stress in three stages. First, we are alarmed—alert, tense, our minds racing. Second, we resist, which is the "fight or flight" stage. Last, when the danger is over, we collapse, overwhelmed by a tiredness that is greater than we might expect from a few seconds of physical activity.

The symptoms of the first stage of stress are well documented. The stress hormones adrenaline, noradrenaline, and cortisol are released, giving the body a rapid boost of strength and confidence, with an underlying painkiller. The heart beats faster, and blood flows away from the skin—causing the "white with fear" look—to the muscles, which contract, ready for action. Kidney function slows, and digestion stops. The sphincter may tighten or dilate, which in the latter instance can cause vomiting. The liver releases fat and sugar to power leg and arm muscles. Muscles demand more oxygen so breathing becomes fast and shallow. The pupils of the eyes dilate, saliva glands dry up (causing a dry mouth), and sweating increases, which may have made the hairless human body harder for predators to grip.

When the threat is physical and brief, all of these changes are positive, enabling us to run away or fight back. When the threat is emotional or long-term, these changes in the body are harmful. Thrill-seekers often enjoy excellent health, perhaps because adrenaline in short bursts stimulates the

For your information

Keeping eustress in control

According to Dr. Hans Selye, stress is the body's response to new situations that demand adaptation, whether pleasurable or painful. He called this the General Adaptation Syndrome. Some stress can be good—this he named "eustress." It keys us up, sharpens our minds, and gives us a thrill. But for eustress to be truly beneficial, we have to remain in control.

● Feelers should not try to deal with stress on a wholly emotional level. Strategies are essential.

● Thinkers often refuse to acknowledge the stress they are under. Face it, and take action.

● Doers tend to continue working even under impossible burdens. They need to stop and evaluate the situation.

immune system. Longer bouts of stress run down the system, leading to general fatigue and sickness. One solution is obvious. If you have a high stress lifestyle and love it, you must still plan for plenty of breaks to give your body time to recover.

The addictive element for people who thrive on stress is noradrenaline, a naturally secreted chemical that produces a sensation of elation and confidence. If your body habitually creates too much noradrenaline, your mind will race constantly, even during sleep, provoking vivid, tumultuous dreams that will detract from your rest. You will be hyperactive, and you may turn to such stimulants as caffeine and tobacco to maintain the "high" when your body is too tired to make its own noradrenaline.

From the heart

Maybe you are an adrenaline junkie—I know I am. Like many Actors and Busy Bees, I need excitement and seek it out. The adventurer who launches himself into a bungee jump or heads off on a white water raft is seeking "eustress," the good stress that keeps us alert. However, even a hardened adrenaline fiend will find other forms of stress, such as a fire or car accident, debilitating and traumatic.

Holmes-Rahe stress test

In 1967 two Americans, Dr. Thomas Holmes and Dr. Richard Rahe, formulated a "social readjustment rating" chart to gauge the stress factors affecting an individual. Their findings were that people suffering abnormally high stress levels were four times more likely than normally stressed individuals to suffer an accident or illness. The test has evolved. For example, in 1967 the test was addressed to heterosexual working males. Now it is designed to include the experiences of all contemporary men and women.

Today's updated test will give you an idea of your current stress levels. Check the boxes indicating situations that apply to you now or have affected you during the past 12 months. If you feel you are still suffering stress from events that occurred more than a year ago, include them but reduce the score by 50 percent. Add up your score to evaluate your stress rating.

1. Death of a partner or spouse . . . . . . **100** ☐
2. Death of a child . . . . **80** ☐
3. Divorce . . . . **60** ☐
4. Separation from partner or spouse due to arguments . . . . **50** ☐
5. Separation from partner or spouse due to work or similar problems . . . . **40** ☐
6. Serious personal injury or illness . . . . **50** ☐
7. Major change in physical condition; for example, menopause or pregnancy . . **40** ☐
8. Onset of severe health problems; for example, impotence or migraines . . . **40** ☐
9. Jail sentence . . . . **80** ☐
10. Suspended sentence . . . . **50** ☐
11. Court case . . . . **35** ☐
12. Death of a parent . . . . **60** ☐
13. Death of other close relative or friend . . . . **40** ☐
14. Termination of employment contract **40** ☐

15. Marital reconciliation . . . . **40** ☐
16. Retirement . . . . **40** ☐
17. Serious health changes in an immediate family member . . . . **40** ☐
18. Ongoing serious health problems for a family member . . . . **35** ☐
19. Working more than 40 hours per week . . . . **35** ☐
20. Birth of a child . . . . **35** ☐
21. Change in work role; for example, promotion, demotion, or reorganization . . . . **30** ☐
22. Change in financial situation . . . . . . **30** ☐
23. Ongoing financial difficulties . . . . . . **35** ☐
24. Bankruptcy . . . . **50** ☐
25. Increase in marital disputes . . . . . . **30** ☐
26. Major financial commitment; for example, mortgage or big loan . . . . **30** ☐
27. Repossession of home . . . . **50** ☐
28. Less than seven hours of sleep regularly . . . . **25** ☐
29. Less than five-and-a-half hours of sleep regularly . . . . **35** ☐
30. Conflict with in-laws or children . . . . **25** ☐
31. Accomplishment of major ambition . . **25** ☐
32. Change in spouse's work pattern . . . **20** ☐
33. Child begins or completes education **20** ☐
34. Child marries . . . . **25** ☐
35. Parent remarries . . . . **25** ☐
36. Major change to living arrangements; for example, apartment-mate moves, lodger arrives, addition built . . . . . . **20** ☐
37. Change in personal habits; for example, quitting smoking . . . . **20** ☐
38. Disagreements at work . . . . **20** ☐
39. Disagreements with neighbors . . . . . **20** ☐
40. Disturbance from neighbors; for example, loud music or noise . . . . . **20** ☐
41. Change in working hours . . . . **20** ☐
42. Moving home . . . . **30** ☐
43. Child changes school . . . . **15** ☐

44. Change in religious commitments . . .**15** ☐

45. Change in social pattern . . . .**15** ☐

46. Minor financial loan . . . .**10** ☐

47. Change in social activities
with the family . . . .**15** ☐

48. Minor infringement of the law . . . . . .**10** ☐

49. End of minor relationship
or friendship . . . .**10** ☐

50. Engagement for marriage . . . .**20** ☐

51. Engagement of a child . . . .**10** ☐

52. Drug abuse by a family member . . . .**25** ☐

53. Sexual identity confusion for a family
member . . . .**20** ☐

54. Taking vacation of seven days
or more . . . .**10** ☐

Additional scores

You should add in stressful factors that have not already been included in the test. There will certainly be personal elements that are unique to your own situation.

Where scores do not appear to reflect the severity of the stress you are suffering, you can increase the points, using the benchmark of 100 points for the death of a partner or spouse as an indicator of a truly catastrophic event. Do not discount any event listed, even where it was wholly happy, such as the engagement of a child or the attainment of an ambition—even good events make demands on the human nervous system and cause stress.

ANSWERS

If you scored **over 400** points, your body is at risk of serious health problems related to stress. You should talk to your doctor. If tranquilizers or antidepressants are recommended, give this suggestion serious consideration—chemical aids can be hugely beneficial to some people, but they can exacerbate problems or create new ones for others. You might want to seek a second opinion.

If you scored **over 300** points, you are weathering a period of severe stress. Do not recoil from discussing the situation with your doctor. Health problems will probably be caused by the trauma your body and mind are suffering. Take time to care for yourself.

If you scored **over 200** points, you are under a great deal of stress, although how well you handle it depends on your personality type. For example, the Busy Bee will find this burden lighter than the Artist will. Do not judge yourself—your ability to deal with stress is largely physiological and says nothing about your moral strength. Some types,

such as the Believer, can use prayer to calm their minds—religious faith is a powerful gift.

If you scored **over 150** points, you are on the edge of the danger area. Take action to reduce stressful factors wherever possible. In particular, you should aim to get eight hours of sleep a night—this will bolster your physical defenses.

If you scored **over 100** points, you have a stress burden that will probably be well under control. If it seems hard to handle, look at the stress checklist again. Are you honestly facing up to all of your problems? You can guard against future increases in stress by eating well, getting plenty of exercise, and practicing open-minded thinking and tolerance.

If you scored **under 100** points, you may not be living your life as fully as you could. Do not be afraid of responsibility, and be willing to extend your social circle. Stress is not all bad—it can impart vital energy, reminding the mind that the body is still alive.

Overwhelmed by stress

Everybody suffers from stress—it is impossible to imagine a modern life untouched by it—and everyone responds to it in different ways. Some people thrive on it, using it to create a sense of pressure that allows them to pack more into each day. Others have a lower tolerance and may become overwhelmed if too many demands are placed on them. No matter what your tolerance is, stress becomes a problem when it gets out of control—even for those who thrive on it—and you feel overwhelmed by pressure at home or at work.

Few people are naturally equipped to deal with stress, and even fewer have been properly taught. No wonder Oxford University psychologists Dr. Gillian Butler and Dr. Tony Hope believe stress management techniques should be taught to every child at school. They feel that the first positive stage in combating stress lies in recognizing your own symptoms.

From the heart

 My life is not always perfect. In the 1970s I found myself under so much stress that I developed a serious eating problem called bulimia. I was becoming weak, but it was not until I struggled to get out of a car before I realized that my eating disorder had to stop. I managed to use my own strong will power to return to normal eating patterns. However, others may need to seek professional help, and no one should be embarrassed to do so. The important point is to get better.

Since that time I have learned how to cope with stress to avoid letting it take over my life. The first step is to learn how to recognize when stress affects you. You can then use breathing, relaxation, and meditation techniques to keep you calm as you cope with a stressful situation.

The symptoms of stress differ from Life Sign to Life Sign, but they fall into four basic categories: behavioral patterns, thinking habits, emotions, and physical sensations.

Reactions to stress

The types in the Feeling group are most likely to have emotional reactions to stress. The Mother Hen may become irritable, and the Reformer may be seized with irrational fears, feeling that he has lost control. The Magician is often prey to health worries and hypochondria, and her stress sometimes erupts as physical symptoms of phantom illnesses. All three Signs are prone to low self-esteem and blame themselves for being unable to cope. If you are one of these types, it is important to remember that you can cope—and everyone can suffer from stress.

When stress strikes, the Thinking group will be rocked by deteriorating mental habits, and the greatest enemy will be depression. Actors, Artists, and Intellectuals will try to reason their way out of the blues, but depression is like a knot that gets tighter as you try to unravel it. You cannot untie it, so you have to slice through it. An Actor under stress may become indecisive. The Artist will avoid making decisions, too, and he will also worry endlessly about problems instead of tackling them. The Intellectual will be confused, forgetting and losing things, and her concentration levels will slip.

The Doing group will be beset by the physical symptoms of stress. The Busy Bee may have insomnia, and impotence is common. The Believer is prone to a loss of sex drive, which in turn can have a catastrophic effect on relationships, causing more stress. The Boss may suffer back, neck, and muscular pain, accompanied by headaches and stomach disorders, including ulcers.

All of the nine Life Signs will see a deterioration in their behavioral patterns. If you think stress is affecting you, write down the changes in your daily patterns since the onset of stress. Have you started drinking or smoking more, or have you resorted to taking tranquilizers or painkillers? Has your social life been put on hold? Do you make more short journeys every day, even if they are not all necessary? Are you side-stepping the difficult tasks and letting them mount up? Are you taking on too many responsibilities and setting yourself up to fail? Are you working longer at the office and still bringing work home on weekends? If you are stressed, some of these descriptions will hit home. However, once you recognize the symptoms, you can take steps to reduce your levels of stress.

Stress relief

There are two main ways to cope with stress. You can either eliminate the causes or increase your tolerance for it. It is no good becoming better able to tolerate stress through meditation or other

For your information

Trigger words

You can train yourself to calm down when you hear a certain word or phrase, triggering a state of mental peace. Choose a phrase that you can slip into conversation. The Olympic keelboat team uses the phrase, "Only half way through," which their coach, Bill Edgerton, explains tells them: "It's not over yet, there's plenty of time to come back." Once you chose your words, put yourself into a relaxed state (see pp. 160–161). When relaxed, repeat your trigger word over and over. Relax again. Alternate relaxing and thinking of your trigger words for a few minutes every day for a week. You'll soon find yourself de-stressing. For best use of trigger words:

 ● Feelers should choose an emotionally neutral phrase that will not stir up unwanted feelings.

 ● Thinkers should focus on the trigger words and avoid getting lost in meditation.

 ● Doers are likely to think that trigger words won't work; however, they work for others and can work for them, too.

techniques, however, when what is needed is practical action against what is causing your stress.

When you are faced with too much stress, first determine the cause. For example, if money problems are causing you stress, take positive action such as talking to your bank or your credit card company. If it is difficult to pinpoint the causes, keep a diary when you become anxious. If there are several causes, deal with each one separately.

When a relationship ends

Whether you are ending a marriage or a long-term partnership, the breakup of a relationship is often a difficult, stressful, and painful time.

When a loving relationship that you had hoped would last forever ends, your world falls apart. There are countless reasons why people fall out of love, but in the majority of cases, one or the other—or both—of the people involved will be left deeply wounded emotionally.

It is especially hard when you desperately want the relationship to continue but your partner does not, and the pain is even greater when another person is involved. In this situation, both the Mother Hen and the Busy Bee can be overwhelmed by feelings of abandonment that are often rooted in basic insecurity. They can emphasize their own self-worth by giving generously of their feelings to others—making those around them feel good will enhance their own self-image. Conversely, emotional distress is not the sole preserve of the rejected partner. Often the person who has ended the relationship will suffer deeply from feelings of guilt.

Adjusting to your new situation

Even if the relationship has been characterized by conflict, hurt, and unhappiness for some time, when the inevitable parting of the ways comes, there will be feelings of loneliness and emptiness. You have lost the comfort, closeness, and companionship that you enjoyed for so long and it can be very difficult to adjust to a new life alone.

If you become obsessed with trying to find someone to replace your lost love, you are unlikely to make wise choices. Work on being independent for a while—you may find that you enjoy it. The Actor is at risk of over-compensating for what she has lost by flinging herself into instant love affairs, which is ultimately damaging to everyone involved. Breaking up is a double-edged sword for the Intellectual. Although it hurts, he will welcome more time for himself. He can now be selfish and indulge in a passion that has been sidelined lately.

Dealing with anger

When trust is broken through infidelity or abuse, seething anger and bitterness rear their ugly heads. These feelings may be more than justified—you

---

For your information

Making a clean break

If the relationship no longer works, there are hard choices ahead and decisions must be made—who should move out and the division of property are just two examples. Make them, without worrying about them endlessly. You both have to make decisions to regain some type of control, and they should be made fairly.

- Feelers put the needs of others above their own, but they should avoid emotional blackmail.

- Dithering is dangerous. Thinkers shouldn't spend too much time analyzing; instead, move on.

- Doers will want to make a clean break quickly, but they shouldn't ignore the feelings of the other people involved.

gave so much time, energy, and love to make this relationship work, and look how you have been repaid—but these feelings can only be destructive. Obsessional anger will damage your mental and physical health, may harm your relationships with friends and family (who wants to be around someone who is projecting so much hate?), and, if you have children together, it will certainly place an enormous and unfair burden on them. When your soul is tormented, your heart is broken, and your mind is in turmoil, it is extremely difficult to be rational. But it is vitally important to avoid openly criticizing or accusing your ex-partner in front of the children. This is not their fight—they need to feel loved by, and be permitted to love, both of their parents. Do not neglect their emotional health.

The Reformer, in particular, is likely to seek revenge on the person who has caused so much pain, but it is pointless. She can get back at her ex-partner by going on with life, not by deliberately destroying her health or her career in a public display.

Moving on

No matter how destructive a relationship has become or how unhappy they feel, some people find it almost impossible to make the break. For example, because the Believer has such a strong sense of loyalty, he is often reluctant to admit a relationship has broken down. Similarly, the Boss may struggle in vain with an unrewarding relationship, feeling that to end it would be to concede defeat. Invest some energy in finding a positive way to say "Enough!"

The Magician will find it difficult to cope with the practicalities of the breakup. She will need a framework to help her move on; she should take small steps, such as making lists of things that need to be done, then ticking off each item as it is accomplished. Stay socially active and seek out old friends. The Artist tends to waste time and emotional energy yearning for a love that won't return. Stop living in the past—make plans for the future. He can enhance his self-worth by devoting some leisure time to an adult-education class.

Stress and bereavement

The loss of a loved one is traumatic. It drains the emotions and the mind and leaves us incapable of acting coherently.

As with all forms of stress, bereavement follows patterns that are common to everyone, regardless of your Life Sign. Grief counselors know that the agony of loss passes through four phases: shock and numbness, yearning and protest, disorganization, and reorganization.

First shock, then anger

The first stage brings disbelief, where it is impossible to adjust to the enormity of what has happened. Some Life Signs, particularly the Boss, may be able to accept the news quickly, but even she will be shocked by the numbness of her own reaction. This is the body's greatest defense mechanism—all feeling is placed in suspended animation. If you are numb, you cannot hurt. Many people, especially the Artist and the Actor, castigate themselves for this numbness. They call themselves heartless and callous because their first reaction is not deep sadness. Do not be self-critical—almost everyone feels this way at the onset of grief. It is a natural, involuntary defense.

For many people, religious faith can be a great support and comfort in times of bereavement. The Believer, in particular, may stay calm and composed when others expect her to fall to pieces.

The second stage brings anger, pain, rage, and conflict. Some Signs are shocked by the ferocity of their anger. At this time the Magician and the Believer may despise themselves because they feel such fury. Again, this is a natural mechanism. Their lives have been plunged into pain and turmoil—would it be natural to greet this with equanimity?

Once the numbness has worn off, the Actor and the Boss will also feel anger and rejection. The Actor sometimes feels as if death has been sent to spite her personally. The Boss must avoid bitterness by sharing his emotions.

> " LEARN TO GET IN TOUCH WITH SILENCE WITHIN YOURSELF AND KNOW THAT EVERYTHING IN LIFE HAS A PURPOSE. "
>
> Elisabeth Kübler-Ross, Psychiatrist (1926–)

When reality sets in

The third stage is hardest on the people around you, but you should not allow this to bring one moment

Putting your life back on track

The fourth stage is also filled with guilt. You begin to put your life back together, but that does not mean forgetting the loved one. You will always have special memories of the one you lost, but it is natural to live again, and no one who ever loved you would want you to live all your days in mourning. Take some positive action and find a focus. This advice is good for everybody, but is especially relevant to the Reformer and the Busy Bee. If an organization, such as a hospice, was especially kind when your loved one was ill, show gratitude by raising funds.

Grief can cripple you if you hold it inside without letting go. The Artist can work through his feelings by writing them down. As he works through grief, he will find effective ways to cope. As he comes to terms with his memories of the person who died, his self-esteem will come back and he will return to other relationships.

From the heart

I believe, without question, in life after death. When I work with people who are terminally ill, I always promise them that they will survive, in some form, after their souls have parted from their bodies. I do not make this promise lightly, and I know that it has brought comfort to some I have loved dearly.

Whenever someone close to me passes into the next life, I always receive a specific sign. On one occasion a bird flew into my conservatory, the glass-roofed room where my family dines each evening. The appearance of a bird is a rare occurrence—my dogs would normally be enough to keep any daring sparrows away—and its appearance coincided with a recent death. There is no doubt in my mind that the departed spirit of my friend was in that bird.

of self-criticism. This stage is the phase of falling apart. Depression and intense sadness will be with you every day from the moment of waking up, and it will prevent you from getting sleep. Other people find such deep grief too hard to countenance. It is a rare friend who gives support through all of these days. A Magician, however, will try to buoy everyone up, but she must make time for her own grief. A Mother Hen will not be deterred either, no matter how painful his own emotions are; but if a Mother Hen is coping with grief, he may be disappointed in the weakness of his friends. Do not judge them harshly—not everyone can look into the abyss.

Bereavement causes such pain that even the expert at denying emotions, the Intellectual, is forced to acknowledge her feelings. She needs to allow her spirit to grow with her emotions.

Moving house

Moving to a new home involves more than planning, paperwork, and packing; it often means pulling up roots from a secure community.

"Home" does not mean only bricks and lumber, it also means friends, neighbors, and familiar surroundings. It is about belonging. Home is where the heart is, which is why relocating can be an emotional upheaval for many people.

The move is often precipitated by other stressful events—a new job, the break up of a relationship, the arrival of a baby, or retirement. With the financial pressure and the paperwork involved, it is no wonder moving is one of the most stressful projects anyone can undertake. Even if the advantages of the move are plain, some people need a push to set the change in motion. Careful consideration is good, but

the Artist, in particular, must be careful not to over-analyze everything. She is likely to weigh up the pros and cons of a move in such minute detail that she will find it impossible to make a decision.

Making a move easier for yourself

Most moving companies will do your packing for you. If you have a family, it is almost certainly worth paying someone else to put everything in boxes. Your time will be better spent helping your family, particularly your children, to cope. Some children deal with a move better than others. Make sure their feelings do not get overlooked during the frenzy.

Something to do

The key to beating moving stress is planning. A successful general relies on maps, and you, too, can chart out every detail of your home-moving campaign to be assured of an easy transition.

- Be bold in your planning. Draw up a map of your new house before the big day and plot where every piece of furniture will go. Stick to the plan until the move has been completed. This will also help you decide whether you need to get rid of things before you go.
- No one cares about your possessions as much as you do, so be sure you have good insurance.
- Take care of the paperwork. Transfer your bank account to your new area; get copies of your medical, dental, and optical records;

arrange a cancellation date for services and utilities at your current address and establish a start date for the new location; inform credit companies of your change of address.

- If necessary, hire an electrician and plumber to do repair work or upgrading right away.
- Number all your boxes and make a list of what is in each one. Pack a box with things that you may need immediately. This could include a first aid kit, medication, toiletries, snacks and drinks, paper cups and plates, garbage bags, toilet paper and, importantly, one or two of the children's favorite toys. It is also a good idea to put together a small emergency toolkit with a flashlight, candles and matches, scissors, screwdrivers, and pliers.

The Busy Bee and the Magician tend to think they should be doing all the work themselves. Partly it is guilt, partly it is the work ethic, and partly it is the latent control freak in both of these Signs. They should learn to delegate and trust others to do the job properly, or stress will mount sky-high. A tendency to deny himself the simple things in life gives the Mother Hen more time to burden himself with the difficult tasks. Just for once, he should take

From the heart

The ancient Chinese art of feng shui can help beat stress in a new home. It emphasizes harmony and the calm flow of energy from the landscape and through the home. It is often thought that if you were to apply the principles of feng shui you would have to rearrange everything, but you can many times reap the benefits with subtle changes, such as moving a bed or mirror.

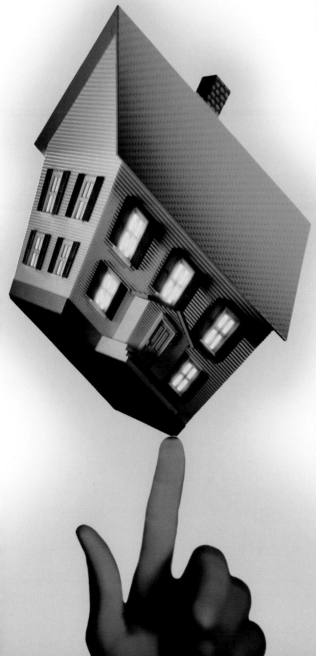

the easy option. He already has enough to do. If he finds a few moments of free time on the day of the move, he can use them to quietly gather his thoughts and calm his nerves.

Settling in

For some, starting over in a new location is an exciting adventure; for others, the fear of the unknown causes great anxiety. The Actor thrives on new situations and challenges. If there is anything better than being a big fish in a small pond, it is being a big new fish with a reason to show off. A love of risk and new situations makes the Boss an ideal adapter, but the Intellectual harbors a fear of the unknown, and a leap in the dark is not appealing. If possible, she should explore her new neighborhood before the move and introduce herself to her neighbors-to-be. For the Believer, the sadness at what he leaves behind will fade. He will move house or job, taking with him a list of people he intends to call regularly, but the past is soon forgotten.

It takes time for a new place to become home. The best way to create new ties is to make new friends. Once you have settled in, why not have a party to get to know your new neighbors.

Addiction

Anyone can be prone to a self-destructive cycle of addiction, where a drug or behavioral pattern that initially helps to cope with stress turns into a driving force in the person's life.

The most common addictive substances are tobacco and alcohol, but the increasing social tolerance for drug abuse makes this a growing problem for thousands of families. In the long term, dependency on these substances can have devastating effects on the body. While alcohol in moderation is acceptable and may provide some health benefits, too much can damage the liver and the brain. Smoking cigarettes can lead to several types of cancers and emphysema; an overdose of some drugs can be fatal.

The use of tobacco and alcohol, as well as certain drugs, is hard to give up because the body depends on chemicals that those substances provide, and it becomes physically and emotionally addicted to them. When the body is deprived of these chemicals, it has "withdrawal symptoms," signs of illness that last until the body adapts to life without them.

When we become addicted to a substance—even chocolate is an example—it contains a chemical that causes our craving.

Avoiding addiction

At times of stress, it can be tempting to reach for a drink, cigarette, or soothing drug to try to relax; but no one needs a drug to beat stress. The only requirement is your mind and positive thinking.

Any of the Life Signs can fall into an addictive cycle, but understanding your Life Sign type can help you to avoid the trap. The Reformer is a perfectionist who likes to do everything thoroughly, including drinking to excess. When she feels underappreciated by those around her, the Mother Hen may sink into self-indulgence, which may lead to overindulgence and turn into addiction.

Peer pressure is dominant among the younger age group. An adolescent with a Believer personality, or a Believer wing, may find it hard to resist emulating the drug abuse behavior of friends. Parents and teachers need to talk openly with this type. The Busy Bee may feel he needs all the turbochargers he can get, but it is a mistake to resort to chemical assistance. The Boss may also dabble in illegal drugs when her career is hitting overdrive, but this often leads to losing everything.

The Actor, who is obsessed with his health and cannot bear to see signs of aging in herself, may take too many tablets, such as vitamins, in compensation. Prescription drugs, including some antidepressants, can be addictive or lethal if taken in an overdose. The Artist who wants to combat depression with drugs should discuss the dangers with her doctor.

Treating addiction

Self-control is vital to beating addiction. Most addiction-busting programs emphasize the one-day-at-a-time approach. For an addict, the thought of a lifetime of craving can be difficult to handle, but the concept of a few more minutes, or even a few hours, of self-denial may be feasible. I would advise anyone who is giving up cigarettes, for example, to forget the financial calculations that show how much you will save by abstaining for 10 years. Instead, when you have a craving, focus on the thought of keeping your lungs free of toxins; the average nicotine craving lasts for three minutes. You will have to conquer this battle again and again, but once you have proved you can do it once, victory will progressively become easier.

For all the Life Signs, counseling or another type of professional help may be necessary to overcome addiction. The Magician responds well to counseling and alternative techniques such as acupuncture and biofeedback therapy. The Intellectual should not resist seeking outside help; she cannot reason her way out of addiction.

> "OUR GREATEST GLORY IS NOT IN NEVER FAILING BUT IN RISING UP EVERY TIME WE FAIL."
>
> Ralph Waldo Emerson
> American poet (1803–1882)

Something to do

Before lighting another cigarette, try this simple exercise to conquer your addiction. Straighten your spine and throw back your shoulders. Take in a long, cool breath and feel the smokeless air expand your lungs. Imagine the space inside your ribs filling with cold, crystal clear water, cleansing every fiber and washing away toxins.

This visualization is important, because it can ease the mind into a relaxed alpha-wave state of daydreaming. The alpha waves signify a calmer brain, less in need of the physical prop of nicotine. Tell yourself you will enjoy five minutes without the black, bilious toxins to poison your body. Within a few minutes, the craving will recede.

Job-related stress

A change in your job situation—whether by your own choice or due to other circumstances—can be a traumatic experience.

It was once common for people to remain working in the same company for a lifetime. However, most people now hold jobs with several employers over the course of their working lives. Many people move from one company to another to gain new opportunities. However, a volatile market in recent decades has caused many companies take on employees during their prosperous times, only to let them go during the bad times.

When you lose your job

If you are forced to leave your job through layoffs, it is only natural that you will feel stress. After all, you were not actively looking for new work and you do not know what the future will be. It is not unusual to be upset, even resentful, particularly if the news was unexpected. You may be shocked and disoriented. However, it is important to remain positive. Remember that thousands of people are laid off every year—you are not alone.

You should not let losing a job numb you. Your mind may be churning over all the possible negative implications, but you must keep a rational head. Those in the Doers group—the Believers, Busy Bees, and Bosses—should take immediate action. If your old position has disappeared, you will not get it back. Do not waste energy trying to keep in touch with former colleagues—you need to put your energy into your next challenge. The Feelers—the Mother Hens, Magicians, and Reformers—need to remember that losing a job does not mean losing their identity. They should resist the temptation to bore people endlessly with anecdotes from the "old days." They need to look to the future rather than dwelling on the past.

Being laid off is not the end of your career, and it is not a personal statement about your self-worth. The Thinkers—the Artists, Actors, and Intellectuals—should look on it as a springboard; losing their job could be the best thing to happen to them.

Something to do

Sometimes the idea of going to a job interview or starting a new job triggers extreme anxiety. Sweaty hands, a thumping heart, and feeling breathless and faint are all symptoms.

If you experience these symptoms, remember that you are most unlikely to black out. Try to breathe your way through it. Force yourself to take longer, deeper breaths and to hold onto them. If you can do so without making your situation worse, breathe into a paper bag. After a few gasps, you will have used up some of the oxygen. As less oxygen reaches your lungs, less is pumped into your brain, and your racing mind will slow down. Concentrate on breathing slowly and deeply. This exercise has the added benefit of forcing your mind to focus on something other than the anxiety itself—another sure method of imposing mental control.

Going on a job interview can seem like clinging to a rope to keep from falling into an abyss.

Moving on

Tackling job applications and interviews for jobs can be exhausting and unnerving. You may not be used to having to prove yourself to anyone, but others cannot know what is best about you unless you tell them. Doers should not be afraid to blow their own trumpets, but they should not expect everyone to snap to attention when they walk by—they will have to fight for a new share of the limelight.

If you are one of the Feelers group, you need to keep your emotions in check when you apply for a job. In a way, this is not about the real you—it is about the prospective employer and the imaginary person who would best fill the vacant role. Turn yourself into that ideal.

If you are a Thinker, your self-esteem may be at a low ebb. Give it a boost by acting as if you are the hottest property on the market. Sell yourself hard—there are plenty of buyers out there.

> " TRY NOT TO BECOME A PERSON
> OF SUCCESS, BUT RATHER
> A PERSON OF VALUE. "
>
> Albert Einstein, German physicist (1879–1955)

Adjusting to your new job

For many people, the workplace is like a second home and colleagues are like extensions of the family, so it is natural that starting over in a new place with new people is daunting. You need to get used to new routines and ways of doing things. Give yourself time to settle in and get to know the ropes. The Doers can appear overconfident in a new job, so they should try to keep their heads down for the first few weeks. No one likes a show-off who breezes into a job and tries to turn it into something different. They need to find their feet before taking bold steps.

The onrush of information when starting a new job can be overwhelming for the Feelers, but they are up to the task. They should look at their new colleagues—they survived their first weeks and the Feelers will, too. Thinkers must remember that they do not have to understand everything at once. Things that are confusing at first will soon be second nature.

Age-related stress

For some people, the idea of giving up work for retirement can be stressful; others may find changes in their health contribute toward stress.

Stress can be an enemy as we get older for many reasons. The stereotypical image of an older person as a victim of ill health, endlessly reminiscing about better times, and unable to cope with the modern world is a powerful one in a Western culture that values youthful vigor and competitiveness above all else. However, this image is wrong. Aging is a highly individual experience, and it is foolish to dismiss the elderly in this way. As you enter your senior years, do not let negative attitudes get you down. You still have much to contribute to the people close to you and to the wider community.

Coping with change

There are bound to be changes as you get older, just as there were when you moved from childhood to maturity, and these are often positive. For some, the pace of change can be stressful. The Reformer, for example, should not try to fight the world. She cannot stop society from evolving, so she should commit herself to keeping up. Conversely, the Mother Hen is more likely to look inward at himself. As his role changes, he should grow with it, instead of staying in the past. Now is the time for him to extend the love that he has always given to others to himself.

Retirement

Some people are particularly vulnerable to stress when their working lives come to an end. The Busy Bee needs a lot to fill her days. She needs to beat boredom by packing her days with interests, such as community work, hobbies, education, and her family. The more she does, the greater her energy will be. For the Boss, the loss of status causes the most

Something to think about

This easy meditation can calm and free your mind. Sit quietly with your hands resting lightly in your lap, the fingertips barely touching. Imagine in your mind a heavy, empty glass cylinder floating in the air before you. As you stare at it, concentrate on your breathing. Every breath you draw in is deep and clear, filled with pure air that penetrates every fiber of your lungs.

As you breathe, the glass begins to fill with white light. The light dazzles with raw energy as it pours into the glass and splashes down its sides in rivulets. It slowly fills the glass with an energy so dazzling it is almost too brilliant to look at. You feel your body fill with a corresponding vitality. Light burns in every artery, floods every muscle, and blazes in your bones. Tension evaporates as the light pours into you—you are almost weightless with light. It cascades through your brain and your heart. Your eyes shine with pure energy. Your body is afire with a power even more dazzling than the blazing light in the glass. The light overflows and cascades down the glass, splashing through the room—and the energy in you overflows, too. You are brimming with pure, positive energy.

For many people, retirement brings the best years of their lives, with plenty of time to enjoy vacations, hobbies, and family.

anxiety. Status is not about being in an important job as much as acting in a commanding fashion. He does not give up his status when he retires; his seniority and character mean that others will still respect him.

You are as old as you feel

You may not be as physically capable as you once were, but do not allow that to dominate your mind. Think positively, and try to keep as fit as possible. The Believer can stay feeling young by meeting new people. By joining clubs and taking up hobbies, she will make friends and gain a positive self-image. The Actor, who may worry about fading looks and loss of libido, should step up his fitness program. He has pampered himself all his life—why stop now?

In later life the Magician may be prey to disillusionment about unfulfilled goals, but she is a late bloomer, and it is never too late to set new goals. Wisdom comes with age, and it is great being an older Artist. He feels mellower as he learns to deal with the demands of his heart. The Intellectual also comes into her own with increasing age. The mind can be forever young, and there is no need to worry about boring things, such as other people's opinions.

From the heart

However old you are, you can help to heal yourself—and you do not need deep medical knowledge to start feeling better right away. All you need to do is smile. Smiling has been shown to generate endorphins—our bodies' own natural pain relievers.

Financial pressures

Stress often occurs when personal finances get out of control—which is all too easy with today's spending practices and reliance on credit cards.

"Where did it all go?" Unless you are extremely disciplined (or rich), you will have asked yourself that question on more than one occasion when you looked at your bank statement at the end of the month. By the time you have finished paying regular bills, such as housing, telephone, electricity, and insurance, there is often little of your hard-earned income left to spend on life's pleasures. Indeed, for many people, monthly expenses exceed monthly income—a situation that is bound to cause enormous stress and anxiety. If you feel that your personal finances are out of control, you need to develop a personal budget, and the first step toward doing that is to look at your spending habits. You cannot manage your money if you do not know where it goes every month.

Curbing your spending

Keep a record of your monthly expenses and note down those that could have been avoided. Look at the pattern—are you eating out too often? Buying too many bottles of wine? Shopping for clothes you do not really need? For most people, it is actually easy to reduce spending—but only if they really want to.

Lavish and extravagant are two words coined especially for the Actor. An Actor who is not in debt will probably start spending immediately to redress the situation. Vacations, clothes, and gifts for others are the favorite pitfalls for both the Actor and the Magician. A burst of high spending can always be justified with the words, "Because I'm worth it!" The Magician should be particularly wary of getting hooked on Internet shopping—remember it is not virtual spending, but 100 percent real.

The Busy Bee has so much energy that he is often a great earner—but he is also a great spender. He is also a dreamer, always on the lookout for the quick deal that will relieve him of money worries for the rest of his life.

Creating savings

While some people seem to be unable—or unwilling—to spend less than they earn, others are more cautious. The natural good sense of the Mother Hen

---

For your information

Avoiding credit card debt

When used wisely, credit cards are a useful way of spreading the cost of a large, necessary purchase; but using a card for nonessential, impulse buying often leads to overspending. All of those must-have bargains and special treats can build up to an unmanageable debt, which is increased by interest charges.

 ● Care and caution mark the Feelers, but the Magician does love an occasional spending spree.

 ● Thinkers overspend with credit cards too easily; they should use their cards more wisely.

 ● Staying in control of credit card spending is a practical matter for Doers, although over-exuberance can get the Busy Bee into trouble.

encourages her to always do the right thing, and, with finances, that means good housekeeping and sensible saving. The Mother Hen is unlikely to live outside her means, but she is often tempted to over-spend on friends and family.

Control matters to the Reformer, and spending is one area where he can maintain absolute control, through good accounting and filing. However, keeping finances in good order does not just mean keeping track of incomings and outgoings. The Reformer may be spending more than he should on credit card payments and loans.

Attitudes to money

The Artist often despises money, and frequently gets herself into financial difficulties. If an Artist enjoys her job, she probably does not place too high a value on monetary reward. However, she must make sure

that she gets paid properly, no matter how much she loves the work. She may think that money is the root of all evil, but she can use it in many positive ways.

Dismissive of money's power, the Intellectual sometimes rushes to make bad investments in the unrealistic hope of getting rich quickly. His finances are often in chaos, because his mind is always on more important matters. He simply cannot afford to be so blasé—his money has a nasty habit of disappearing if he does not keep an eye on it. To the Boss, it is more important to make money, not spend it. She is also fond of taking financial gambles. However, if disaster strikes, the Boss usually bounces back.

Although a naturally moderate type, the Believer often runs up debts in a bid to stay abreast of his peers. This is harmful to his health, as well as his bank balance. More than any other Life Sign, the Believer lies awake at night worrying about debt.

Test-related tensions

Preparing for any type of important test is a stressful time for many people.

Whether preparing for a work- or college-related exam or a driving test, almost everyone has experienced test-related nerves. For some people, the feelings of tension and apprehension become overwhelming and can seriously affect both their ability to study effectively and their performance on the day of the test.

Getting started

You should never allow fear of the task ahead to paralyze you into inaction. If you keep putting off what you know you have to do, you will only feel worse. It is a vicious cycle. As the time for studying gets shorter, the task becomes more and more daunting. The Magician will find it particularly hard to get started. She will spend hours procrastinating

From the heart

Why not celebrate the end of your exams with a spoon-bending party? Invite some friends—and children, who make great spoon-benders, and their happy energy is infectious.

Let everyone choose a spoon, hold it up and yell, "Bend!" The atmosphere will be relaxed, which is ideal for parascientific phenomena. Holding your spoon by the bowl, rub the stem between your thumb and index finger and tell it to bend; you may have to apply gentle pressure. Often, nothing will happen for a few minutes, then one spoon will bend, starting a chain reaction. Soon you will all be bending spoons. Have fun!

Something to think about

When you are facing an intensely stressful time, you can help your mind to fight back with color. Paint an orange circle on a white sheet of paper, and tape it to your bedroom wall. When you get out of bed tomorrow, spend a few moments gazing at the dot. Stand about two feet (30 cm.) from it, with your shoulders back and your chin up. Let your facial muscles relax and breathe in slowly.

Stare at the beautiful, blazing orb of orange. You will start to see a blue, flickering haze like an aura around the circle—it is caused by the reaction of the orange on your retina. Imagine the energy from that brilliant color suffusing your whole mind. Just the thought of it makes you smile and raise your head. Keep that energy in mind all day. When you need to concentrate with all your power, feel the orange luster in your brain. When the going gets gruelling, as the minutes tick away, you can tap into that dazzling orange brain of yours.

This is the power of color. With a few seconds of focus and imagination, you have charged yourself up with positive energy for the entire day. Your brain has been transformed into a pulsating power source—and you have done it all yourself.

when she could be making progress. Focusing on the smaller goals, instead of the intimidating whole, will make the task seem easier. Draw up a schedule, set a time to start, and just do it.

The Mother Hen needs to avoid the distractions created by the needs of others. He matters, too, so he needs to put himself first. He should find a good study area that is comfortable and quiet—and put a "do not disturb" sign on the door.

Distraction can also be the downfall of the Busy Bee, who loves to dart from project to project and finds it difficult to apply herself to a single task. She should ensure that she has everything that she needs before she begins; otherwise, she will be jumping up every five minutes to fetch things. The mantra of a Busy Bee must be "Stick to it!"

Fear of failure

Negative thinking is the enemy of success. The Artist never feels that he has done enough, which leads to low self-confidence. He should be rational—the Artist might be surprised at how much others admire his diligence. When his mind is distracted with worry, he should visualize a plain surface, clear of obstacles, and see himself racing across it.

The Reformer can beat anxiety by using positive affirmations. She can repeat again and again "I am successful. I will succeed." A Believer's greatest fear is that he will be left behind by his peers. He must stop worrying about what others are doing and take heart—if he works hard, he will always do well.

Avoiding complacency

Some people seem able to remain calm—even nonchalant—when everyone around them is in a frenzy with pre-test nerves. Others may envy their relaxed attitude but, just as excessive stress can adversely affect results, so, too, can over-confidence.

The Actor has trouble taking tests seriously. She is used to getting by on charm alone, but she must face up to the fact that sometimes success means making a real effort. The Intellectual tends to assume that brainpower alone will secure a victory. However, others can do as well—or even better—than the Intellectual by sheer hard work. He must work hard, too, but, if he does, he will always succeed.

The Boss loves to be stretched and to show off her stamina and prowess. The important issue for her is to cover all her bases with methodical practice—and to beware of over-ambition.

Avoiding stress

No matter the cause of your stress, you can follow the same techniques to beat it.

To regain control of your life and beat stress, you have to be able to relax. Relaxation is the best feeling in the world. The most effective tools for regaining control and learning to relax are organization and planning.

Planning ahead

Good planning will prevent you from committing yourself to more than you can do. It will also help you identify the events that are stressful to you so that you can cope with them early on. Don't store up problems in the hope that they will go away.

Those in the Doers group—the Believer, the Busy Bee, and the Boss—are prone to saying yes to projects that overtax them. When presented with a new commitment, instead of automatically saying yes, they should take time to think about it and make calculations. Is the schedule acceptable, and how will it affect other commitments? They should only say yes if they are convinced that they will have things under control. If someone wants an instant answer, alarm bells should ring. Why are they not allowing you to think about this properly? This may be a hard lesson for the Busy Bee to absorb, but she has to take things one at a time.

If you are in the Feeling group—a Reformer, Mother Hen, or Magician—you are used to efficient planning. However, when the workload mounts, one of the most stressing aspects will be the way your plans unravel. Keep telling yourself, "I can be flexible." Your plans are guidelines to help you—they are not written in stone. The Reformer should step back and study the wider picture. Even the most devoted Mother Hen cannot handle everything on his own. Instead of rushing to tackle every crisis, let someone else take responsibility. Another Life Sign who can follow similar advice is the Actor—she, too, should learn to delegate.

Taking a break

Relaxation techniques, such as yoga, self-hypnosis, and deep breathing, can help to reduce stress; and exercise, even a short, quick walk, helps to dissipate

---

Something to do

Self-hypnosis is a great technique to master to induce calmness and alertness in your mind, and all it involves is reciting a few trigger words silently to yourself. It does not have to include deep sleep or unconsciousness. The natural hypnotic state is much lighter, a feeling of being wide awake but untroubled by the usual stresses of daily life. Brain scans show it is characterized by alpha waves, the mental frequency common in daydreams.

To get started, recite these gentle, repetitive words in your mind. Or ask a partner to read them to you or record them onto a cassette tape:

"You are feeling calm. Your mind is clear. You are filled with calmness. Your mind is bright and sharp. You feel yourself draw a deep, cool breath. It floods your body with calmness. You breathe out and blow away all confusion. All that remains is calm. Your mind is focused. Now you can succeed."

stress hormones. You should also make time each week to do something you enjoy—go to a movie, read a book, or have dinner with friends.

If the Artist feels that stress is about to overwhelm him, he should take deep breaths and count to 10 before returning to the fray. The Magician should finish work on time at least once a week. Getting home in time to eat properly and relax will be a major release. Sleep is vital to the Intellectual's thinking processes, so she should force herself to sleep eight hours a night. The Boss should take time each day to treat himself. It may be as simple as a cup of coffee, but small things are great for relaxation.

From the heart

To relax in a hurry, let your head drop, so your chin rests on your chest. Take a long, deep breath, and as you inhale raise your head. When your lungs are filled, you will be looking straight ahead. Now breathe out, emptying your lungs and raising your face to the sky. Drop your chin to your chest; repeat the cycle eight times.

Yoga is ideal for beating stress. It combines physical, mental, and spiritual training and can be practiced by anyone—young or old.

CHAPTER SIX

Developing your personality

The key to achievement lies in your ability to exude confidence in yourself. When you trust yourself, others will trust you. For some lucky people, self-assurance was instilled in childhood. For many more—and I am among them—self-confidence has to be acquired.

In this chapter you will learn how to build up your self-confidence. You will also discover a new perspective on the Life Signs through the ideas of the psychologist Carl Jung. His teachings on personality types fit perfectly with the wisdom of the enneagram.

Understanding self-confidence

Most people go through a time in their lives in which they experience a lack of confidence in their own worth.

Your confidence is affected by the value you place on yourself, your self-esteem. Confidence does not rely on one single factor. There are several aspects involved, including positive thinking and high expectations, stress levels, decisive behavior and speech, and a healthy display of self-respect. Feeling that you are loved by friends and family will make you feel better about yourself; feeling that you are on your own and unloved will lower your confidence.

When your self-confidence is low, it is proclaimed through body language. You will stoop, avoid eye contact, and fidget with clothes or objects. You will move slowly and respond sluggishly to any instruction. Tension and nervousness will clearly be written on your face, and your standards of personal hygiene will slip—there is never time for a haircut and rarely time for a shower.

> " LIFE IS A SERIES OF COLLISIONS WITH THE FUTURE; IT IS NOT THE SUM OF WHAT WE HAVE BEEN, BUT WHAT WE YEARN TO BE. "
>
> José Ortega y Gasset
> Spanish essayist and philosopher
> (1883–1955)

Boosting your confidence

Everyone experiences times when they feel incapable of handling a situation. This is most common when stepping away from familiar paths. For example, the teacher who can control 30 rowdy 15-year-old teenagers may feel lost and inadequate when it comes to making a complaint at a hotel. However, if he can summon the same bravado that carries him through history classes, then he should be able to win an apology from the hotel manager. How we cope with these situations often depends on our Life Sign type.

When confidence is at a low level, those in the Doing group will step into the background, leaving others to take over any tasks. The Boss's naturally active personality will be overwhelmed by the passive mode. The Believer sometimes struggles to make herself heard in group situations, but she may keep silent for fear of ridicule. She will also be reluctant to start new projects or make changes. An uncertain Busy Bee will not be afraid to start a project, but he won't be capable of finishing it.

Negative mantras, reinforcing the belief that other people are inherently better, are common among the Thinkers—the Actor, the Artist, and the Intellectual. "I will never manage." "I have no talent." "I am too old." These refrains are reverse affirmations, and they carry more weight every time they are made. Because Thinkers have always striven for approval, they are often held back by their own fears that their best will not be good enough.

The Feeling group will be overwhelmed with anxiety when self-confidence drains away. Fear of what could happen, embarrassment at past failures, worries about current problems, frustration and anger—these all typify the Magician, the Reformer, and the Mother Hen at a low ebb. Resentment builds up, because the things that seem so difficult when confidence is missing are apparently easy for others.

The best approach to rebuilding your self-confidence is to forget about others and concentrate on yourself. Start with a small task and build yourself up to the important ones. Just giving yourself a pep talk will do wonders. Tell yourself "I think I can, I know I can, I will do it."

Something to do

Even if your self-confidence is currently at a low ebb, you don't have to make it obvious to others. You can appear certain of yourself by adopting these simple rules of body language:

● Speak clearly. If you want people to listen to you, you have to be audible. Why would anyone have faith in a speaker who mumbles? Unclear speech that is barely audible betrays poor self-respect.

● Look people in the eye. When speaking to someone, be certain that you make eye contact. Life is not a staring contest, but you need to display enough confidence that you can face others. This shows that you have nothing to hide.

● Keep your body open. Instead of standing in a closed, defensive position, as if you are about to fend off a blow, keep your arms apart, your back straight, and your shoulders back.

Self-esteem and depression

The greatest enemy of self-esteem is depression, which—like an acid—can eat into everything, including your confidence and enthusiasm.

Depression affects your ability to experience life's joy, your capability to work, and your relationships with family and friends. It saps psychic energy, too. When I feel down, it is much harder for me to bend a spoon or pick up images telepathically.

Everyone feels fed up and miserable at times; this type of transient depression is common and natural. Usually there is an obvious reason and the feeling fades or something snaps you out of it. However, an intensely low mood, affecting body and mind, that persists for weeks or months, is clinical depression. This is an illness—often with a physical cause—and there should be no embarrassment about it.

The four Life Signs rules

There are four Life Signs rules for beating transient depression: the Feeling rule, the Thinking rule, the Doing rule, and the Relationships rule. These rules work with all the Life Signs, but if you think you may have clinical depression, then seek professional help.

The Feeling rule says put as much fun in your life as possible. You only live once, and you deserve to treat yourself without feeling guilty. Have a piece of cake with your coffee, and don't count the calories. Listen to music you like. If you enjoy a good detective story or a romance, give yourself a few minutes to plunder the shelves of your library or bookstore. Let yourself escape into the book—there is no moral superiority in struggling with a French classic. This is important advice for the Reformer, who needs to permit himself to relax now and then.

Sometimes it is hard for the Mother Hen to feel positive about life, but the truth is that there are still good things around her, and she should try to make the most of them. When life is hard for the Actor, he should try to smile—it could be worse. The Artist's perception of the world is colored by her moods. When she feels down, everything and everyone seems to conspire against her. She must try to see the world as it really is—a lighter, happier place.

For your information

Talking away the blues

In a 1978 study, researchers Tirrel Harris and George Brown interviewed nearly 1,000 women about the factors influencing their moods. They found that women with at least one friendship based on total trust and openness—with a sister, mother, long-time friend, or partner—suffered least from depression. By talking honestly, they put their troubles in perspective. By listening to their friend's problems, they could feel valued, and knew that they were not alone—everyone goes through bad patches.

● Feelers should choose the incisive mind of a Thinker when they want to talk.

● A Thinker's best friend will be a Doer, who will give practical advice when the Thinker is lost in thought.

● The Doer's best friend is a Feeler, who will supply that instant link to emotions that the Doer sometimes lacks.

From the heart

If you need to unburden yourself, but you do not feel comfortable or sincere about telling your troubles to a friend, you can use a "worry doll," a custom from Guatemala. This can be a soft toy from childhood, or one you buy for the purpose. You can even make a worry doll from a clothes pin and a piece of cloth.

At bedtime, holding your doll in one hand, tell her you want her to look after your worries, because you do not want to carry them around any longer. Then pour out your heart.

To invoke the Thinking rule, eat well, sleep well, and maintain yourself. Hygiene is important. It affects other people's opinions of you, and their opinions feed back into your self-esteem. Thinking types, especially the Intellectual and the Artist, are prone to self-neglect. Neglecting yourself will only make you feel worse. There is nothing that seems so bad after a few nights of good sleep. If the Busy Bee gets some rest, his brain will function better, perhaps lighting the way to a solution for the problem at hand.

For the Doing rule, work out what you want to do and where you want to be. Write down your tar-gets—putting ideas on paper always clarifies issues. Identify the things that make you sad. If you are tired all the time, make that issue your target—your ambition must be to generate more energy. Do not overstretch yourself by planning all the changes you will make when you have that energy; for now, focus on one attainable objective. Write down strategies for staving off exhaustion, such as reducing stress, freeing yourself from draining relationships, or sleeping more. For the Boss, the target may be to give up a crutch, such as alcohol, coffee, or cigarettes, which only feeds depression.

The Relationships rule follows the principle that the best defense against depression is a close friend to whom you can tell anything. Many emotional problems are focused on relationships in the home, so confide in a friend who does not live with you. This also has the psychological benefit of disconnecting problems from their source. It is easier to feel objective about marital difficulties when you are sitting in a coffee bar than it is in your own kitchen. The Believer, in particular, should seek out friends and talk over whatever is troubling her. By using his skills at listening to the burdens of others, the Magician will make his own burdens seem lighter.

Believing in yourself

When you understand what motivates you and value your unique personality, you can recognize your true potential.

One of the benefits of modern psychological science is the validation it brings to individual human lives. Psychologists Sigmund Freud, Carl Jung, and others developed theories of personality that shed light on many aspects of human behavior. If you understand these insights, then you can understand your own motivation. With self-belief, anything is possible.

The most complete system of psychological typing was developed by Jung, who was steeped in the unwritten knowledge of the East. One of the founders of psychoanalysis, Jung transformed the ancient systems of wisdom into modern scientific tools. Along with Freud, he published Psychological Types

From the heart

According to Carl Jung, everybody has a second type, a fallback position, for dealing with life when it is not appropriate to use the predominant part of the personality. The quiet type, when pressed to go out with friends, may become a raucous party animal—the Intellectual makes way for the Boss. This concept of a second type is akin to the "wing" in Life Signs. My own main Life Sign type is the ambitious Actor, but it is sometimes superseded by my wing, the always active Busy Bee.

in 1921. This scientific approach has many similarities to the spiritual wisdom of the enneagram, the core of Life Signs. Jung's own analysis of personality types divides people into Thinkers, Feelers, and Sensualists (the Doers of Life Signs), with an added category, Intuitives.

The Life Signs may react differently to psychoanalysis. It appeals to the Magician, who believes everything can be solved once it is understood, but the open-ended style of Jung's thinking may not appeal to the Reformer. The emphasis on sexual imagery that runs through Jung's work may frighten the Mother Hen away. The Busy Bee expands her mind by following new modes of thinking, but one day it may be Jungian, the next day something else.

The extroverts and introverts

Jung also separated people into extroverts (represented by the Actor and the Boss) and introverts (such as the Artist and the Intellectual). We are outgoing, or we are inward-looking. We need other people, or we are self-reliant. We get involved, or we watch. Jung's theory has two vital rules built in:

1. There are all types of introverts and extroverts. Two people can be different in their culture, education, interests, and pleasures, yet they may have similar approaches to life. Introverts are introverts the world over, and extroverts are extroverts.

2. Natural introverts can learn to enjoy a little extroversion at times. Extroverts can train themselves to be more reflective, less reliant on others. Nobody is all one type all of the time, and everybody can change. But we all tend to be one or the other, according to our upbringing and our instinct.

The natural extrovert signs include the Actor, the Believer, and the Boss. They embrace the world, and they are sociable and confident of having the right social attitudes. Their surroundings include the notable address, the best furnishings, the right friends. If an extrovert does not have them, she aspires to them. An extrovert is usually on good terms with the world. An unhappy extrovert argues and quarrels, but she still engages with everything around her.

For your information

Jung's types of perception

According to Jung, we experience the world through four types of perception: thinking, feeling, sensing, and intuition. By thinking, he meant using our intellects to extract meaning; by feeling, engaging our emotions and morals to make judgments and gauge values; by sensing, absorbing the world through touch, taste, smell, sight, and sound; by intuition, perceiving through our unconscious minds. These parallel the three basic Life Sign groups, with a fourth element— the psychic skills—that can be developed by any of the Life Signs. Each of Jung's groups are further divided by being introverted or extroverted.

- Reformers, Busy Bees, and Believers are extroverted Thinkers; Intellectuals and Magicians are introverted Thinkers.

- Mother Hens and Magicians are extroverted Feelers, while Artists and Reformers are introverted Reformers.

- Actors, Believers, and Bosses are extroverted Doers, while Artists and Believers are introverted Doers.

The introvert draws back from the world, at least until he has time to decide if he wants to come out of his shell and start engaging with people around him. He is not sociable—possibly articulate, but not fond of the sound of his own voice. Natural introverts include the Artist and the Intellectual. He is independent. If you do not like him, he does not care. What others perceive as daydreaming may be productive reflection. Happy introverts are at peace with their own natures and enjoy solitary pleasures. Unhappy introverts sulk and avoid confrontation.

Enhancing the Thinking mind

All of the Life Signs can benefit from learning the best ways to use their thinking powers.

The ability to think enables us to make sense of the world around us. But if we think too much, we are in danger of feeling too little. Our calculations cut us off from our emotions. These observations are relevant to the Life Signs. Out-and-out Thinkers, such as the Intellectual, dislike their feelings because they believe emotions are irrational. Thinkers who repress their feelings often have disastrous love affairs. Unable to process the chaotic emotional information generated by bad marriages and unsuitable romances, they may react violently out of frustration. This pattern is especially true of the Artist.

The extroverted Thinker

An extroverted thinking type deals with facts, looks on the world as an external system to be handled systematically, and uses logic to establish order and define categories. He may favor traditional ideas or accept the mood of the times. Extroverted Thinkers believe in common sense. They have ideals, and stand by them. Of course, this attitude sums up the Reformer. It can also be typified by the Believer, especially if he has found his place in life.

The best extroverted Thinkers use creativity to establish new patterns to make sense of the world. One inspirational example is Charles Darwin, who was adventurous and humble as he sought a theory that would fit all the known facts. He saw the question of evolution as an external problem, something which dealt with objective realities. His theory upset many extroverted Thinkers whose systems of facts and categories (a world created by God in seven days) were not compatible with Darwinism.

Creativity gives power to the extroverted Thinker. After many fans asked Charlie Chaplin where he got his ideas, he decided to analyze the process. He

---

Something to think about

You can follow these three steps to develop your mind's creative thinking power:

- Find a fascinating stone, perhaps as you walk on the beach or by a field in the country. I have a Stone Age knife that I found near my home; 10,000 years ago, a man honed this knife to fit the palm of his hand. When I hold the flint knife, still sharp enough to cut paper, my mind becomes focused and clear. A beautiful rock crystal from a store is also effective, especially if it was bought by a friend as a present for you.

- Set aside some time to find a quiet corner and sit with the stone or crystal in your hand. A warm bath is ideal. Now relax your mind, perhaps by listening to some peaceful music.
- As you begin to relax, ideas will come into your head; take whatever they are and run with them. Maybe the bath or music will set off a train of thoughts; follow this train wherever it leads. You need not be afraid of silly thoughts—no one else can see into your mind. There is nothing to be embarrassed about, so let your thoughts run wild. You will be amazed where they take you.

discovered that his subconscious was always evaluating everything he encountered to see if the seed of an idea was there. Chaplin was a Busy Bee, and his method of drawing inspiration from every waking moment will resonate with all Busy Bees, who hate to see a minute pass without getting some advantage from it.

Without creativity, the extroverted Thinker is impeded by too much information. With modern technology bombarding us with global media, especially through television and the Internet, a creative system of processing information is essential. Any Thinker who tries to meet the flood of data will soon drown. The Boss who cannot protect herself from information overload will lose her grip—a canny Boss will use other people to filter out the mass of meaningless noise, leaving only the valuable data.

Suffering from information overload, the extroverted Thinker must stand back from facts and exercise imagination to survive. The alternative is to shut out all new data, and become fossilized. This negative response leads to intolerance. The Mother Hen will feel left behind by a world he cannot understand, and he will dismiss every innovation.

The introverted Thinker

Almost all the greatest writing, music, and art has been created by the introverted Thinker. She also can make a selfless teacher, inspiring pupils to be more rounded, sociable, and able to cope with emotions. A beloved university professor, for example, is likely to be an Actor with introverted habits.

Anyone who is an introverted Thinker, like the Intellectual, will not care enough about other people's opinions to compel them to think as she thinks. She is at risk of shutting out her other functions: sensing, feeling, and intuition. She must work to listen to her emotions. If the feeling function does not work, other people's needs will be ignored or misunderstood, and the Thinker could end up lonely and friendless.

The introverted Thinker can withdraw into her mind, ignoring all the noise around her. The absent-minded professor, the daydreaming schoolgirl, and the blank-faced office worker are all introverted Thinkers. The ability to shut out interference when a project must be completed is a valuable skill, but the Thinker must keep the other functions switched on. Any Thinker absorbed in her thoughts makes a poor companion. Friends drift away, marriages decay, and children grow up alienated.

Introverted thinkers need to adopt some of the techniques of the extroverted type to make their social relationships easier. If the basics of nutrition are being forgotten (look at any busy student, especially an Artist), lists can be stuck on the refrigerator. If punctuality is a problem, time management is a must; employers have no patience with gifted Thinkers who fail to turn up. Other Life Signs should emulate the Actor, who is concerned with making a good impression. Do not worry if it feels "false" to wear a suit and tie, or to tap along to other people's tastes in music—at times, everyone has to do what is convenient. The Magician will find this easier to accept than the Reformer or the Intellectual, which is why the Magician has the reputation of being the easiest, most amiable of people.

> "MAN'S MIND, STRETCHED BY A NEW IDEA, NEVER GOES BACK TO ITS ORIGINAL DIMENSIONS."
>
> Oliver Wendell Holmes, American writer
> (1809–1894)

Enhancing the Feeling mind

Of all the functions, the ability to feel is the most essential, and the least respected.

Feeling is more than emotion. Jung explained that other functions, such as happy thoughts, frightening premonitions, and sad music, affect emotion. However, the Feeling function is the closest to pure emotion, and it deals with the feedback from emotions. If the Feeling function is atrophied or bypassed, emotion will spill into areas that are ill-equipped to deal with it. In the worst situations, stressful emotions might lead to alcoholism, nightmares, and phobias.

When the Mother Hen, the Reformer, and the Magician respond easily to their emotions, they are berated as silly and too emotional. However, without this function, we cannot operate as social creatures. It is the bedrock of our humanity. We sum up the value of people through our feelings. Subtle judges of personality make good use of this function—the best politicians and managers are fine Feeling types.

The instant emotional hit the Busy Bee experiences feels good, but it is shallow. He needs to allow time for deeper feelings to develop. The Intellectual also needs time for her feelings to percolate through. She needs to slow down her instant reactions and learn to listen with her heart. If the Actor enhances his empathy, others will love him for it, but he must be sincere.

Extroverted Feelers

Jung found that most of the people who understood their feelings were women. Emotional intelligence is an attribute discouraged among men in the West. He praised these women as being well adjusted, clear-sighted about the world as it is seen by others, and having a wide social circle.

The less palatable aspect is that others take advantage of extroverted Feeling types. They know what they believe and what they like, but they do not know how to control those who do not care about other people's feelings. (The Believer, for example, should trust her own feelings. She knows when the empathy from other people is wrong.) Unless they have the argumentative nature of the Reformer, they shrink back from confrontation. They need assertiveness to build up self-confidence and determination to win in social situations.

When extroverted Feeling types are awed by more ruthless personalities, they become hollow. A "trophy wife," chosen only for her looks, who knew what she wanted but did not understand what she would have to pay to get it, is the archetype. She might keep her Magician's charm, but it will become insincere and superficial. If her partner and her children do not demonstrate their love, if she feels unneeded, she will be unhappy. Although she will suffer, the callous Sensing and Thinking types around her will assume she is trivial and incapable of any significant emotional experience. She needs to build self-esteem, expand her interests, and create a new network of friends to change her life.

Introverted Feelers

The gulf between extrovert and introvert is not as marked in the Feeling function. Feelings are projected onto the world, or they are not. Others may dismiss the introverted Feeling type as quiet or stupid. In fact, emotional intelligence is the equivalent of its intellectual counterpart. Daniel Goleman coined the term EQ, or emotional quotient, in a book that popularized research from neuroscientists and psychologists that showed we lose cognitive ability when our feelings wither. In order to think effectively, we need compassion, empathy, and the ability to respond appropriately to pleasure as well as pain.

The good news is that it is easier for people with a strong Feeling function to learn to think effectively,

> " THE GREATEST HAPPINESS OF LIFE IS THE CONVICTION THAT WE ARE LOVED. "
>
> Victor Hugo,
> French poet and author (1802–1885)

than it is for thinkers to start paying attention to their feelings. The bad news is that introverted Feeling types may suffer from low self-esteem. They do not help themselves by turning their feelings inward, which makes them seem unfriendly and cold.

Unspoken feelings can increase in potency and become overwhelming. It is essential for an introverted Feeling type to express her emotions. The Artist should learn to share her feelings. If she feels uncomfortable doing this verbally, then she must find other ways to express herself. An introverted Boss should let his feelings out and discuss his buried emotions.

It might also be helpful to learn to lie a little; no matter how much the introverted Feeler dislikes dishonesty, a little dissembling can make life easier. Why not try a few exercises in telling white lies: "It looks lovely" and "of course, nobody noticed." If an introverted Feeling type does not put on this protective cloak, she will feel naked when others ask questions or make criticisms. But if these safeguards are in place, she can enjoy a passionate, fun-filled life.

Something to do

Any of the Life Signs can learn to be more assertive by following the following exercises:

Thinkers: Stop saying "sorry." It becomes an automatic reaction, inviting others to blame you instead of blaming the real culprit. You are willing to accept blame when the fault is truly yours, but many Thinkers take the blame for everything. Try to get through the day without apologizing, and force yourself to respond in different ways.

Doers: Take command of your body language by watching the gestures of others. Try to mirror other people's body movements, without making it so obvious that it might seem odd. When you find your body instinctively moves in opposition to another human being—for example, you fold your arms or cover your mouth, both classic defensive gestures—try to make your signals more open.

Feelers: Your emotions will not be clear to others unless you make them clear. You cannot expect other people to be telepathic. Always speak clearly and boldly. If you whisper or mumble when you answer the telephone in a busy office, for example, challenge yourself to speak out.

Enhancing the Doing mind

The Doing mind is the least complex of Jung's types, and the most readily understood.

All of us have developed the Doing, or sensing, function at some time. The danger is that we too easily accept what we see and taste and offer no criticism. Sensing comes easily, but intelligent sensation is difficult to acquire.

The worst human dysfunction is ennui, the dissatisfied laziness that afflicts the Doing type. All the pleasures are there to be enjoyed, the personality is ready to indulge in life, but the only reaction is one of boredom. People who never learn to use their other functions—to think, to feel, to trust their intuition—will always take the coarsest type of sensate pleasure; and those pleasures quickly become stale.

Thinking about doing something is not the same as doing it—this is a lesson for the Intellectual. If she thinks she has a novel inside her, she should remember that she also possesses the energy, application, and vision to get that novel written. By starting to put down words, any words, on an empty sheet of paper, she will soon make progress. If the Artist wants to act but is hitting a mental block, he can break through it by taking action regardless.

Another lesson is that it is not the action that counts, but the achievement. It is better to do one thing well than many things halfheartedly. For the Busy Bee to improve her achievements, she needs to set goals and be methodical. The Reformer can be organized without being a perfectionist; he needs to realize when something is "good enough." Doing also involves compromise, but the means must be justified, which is something for the Magician to remember; she must judge herself by what she ultimately achieves. Past misjudgments are no guarantee of future failure. The Actor should judge his own actions, without waiting for others to pass their opinions. The Believer should remember that to try and try again is not failure but a growing process.

Extroverted Doing types

Because he reacts to external stimuli, the extroverted Doing type prides himself on being rational. When it rains, he gets wet; when the sun shines, he gets a tan. The key motivators are imagination and creativity. Without these, his senses become dull. At

---

Something to do

If your energy levels are flagging and you start every day ready to go straight back to bed, there is an easy, positive step you can take to restore your stamina—get some exercise. Physical fitness generates energy, not only muscular, but spiritual and mental energy, too. This is age-old wisdom. The Romans summed it up in the words "a healthy mind in a healthy body."

You should speak to your doctor before embarking on any new exercise routine. The first and best thing to do is take a first step—literally! Just put one foot in front of the other and keep doing it. Walking is the best exercise for your whole body. It can also save you money and help the environment if you walk when you might otherwise use the car for short journeys.

his best, the extroverted Doer is fiery and sensual. Casanova was a wonderful example. Energetic and romantic, enthusiastic and ravenous for experience, this is the most exciting of the human conditions.

It is the sensations that often provoke nonsensical reactions. Without a coherent system of values, implemented by the Feeling function, or a cogent view of the world and its categories, supplied by the Thinking function, the Doing type is prey to every shift in the world's mood. Tell him often enough that cardboard tastes good, and he will start to believe it. In the same way, others are great at getting the Mother Hen to put her own needs aside so that she can do things for them, but it is time for her to do something for herself. Tell an extroverted Doer that it is fun to get drunk, and he will drink until he is ill. The Boss, for example, has achieved much, but he has a tendency to throw it all away. He should not take any gambles that he cannot afford to lose.

Introverted Doing types

For anyone whose primary function is extroverted, the introverted Doing type is a marvelous secondary function. It offers the pleasures of solitude and indulgence. It is easy to imagine that a film star on a yacht, with a cognac in hand, Mozart drifting from a stereo, and a lover belowdecks, could be completely contented—even if these pleasures are far removed from the extroverted whirl of feelings that underpin most of the star's Hollywood personality. Introverted sensation—doing nothing, but doing it with great style—is best as a retreat, not a lifestyle.

As a primary type, introverted Doers are inarticulate, anxious, and prey to depression. Some great artists—Vincent van Gogh, for example—were introverted Doing types. They cannot express their deep experiences, and may suffer mentally. Because they take their pleasures seriously, with no regard for what others think of them, they risk being outcasts.

Intuitive types

Because intuition is so rarely developed, many people will deny that it exists—but not everyone is a skeptic.

Jung calls intuition the opposite of sensation, but as every psychic knows, an intuition can be as strong as anything experienced through the five senses. However, many people deny their own intuition and refuse to believe anyone can possess it. Even by definition, intuition is not tangible. According to Jung, "Intuition is a perception of realities which are not known to consciousness, and which go via the unconscious." You do not see these realities, you do not hear them, and when they reach the brain, you

do not know they are there. Yet successful intuitives wonder why anyone questions their abilities. After all, we do not all know the same things.

Skepticism is natural, but we should learn to be open-minded, especially the Intellectual and the Reformer. The psychic Daniel Dunglas Home, a Reformer, believed that all psychics who claimed to do anything that his own powers could not match were frauds—yet he could not bend spoons. The title "Magician" suggests that this Life Sign should be

excellent at discovering the brain's hidden powers—and she is. Her open mind, allied with her practical nature, makes her a natural psychic. The Boss can be even better at his job by getting the intuitive part of his mind to work.

The extroverted Intuitive

A hate of the familiar and commonplace and a love of sudden change and risk characterizes the extroverted Intuitive. This type loves people and needs people constantly, but she is never prepared to stop for a moment while a friend rests.

Tradition is scorned and religion is out. Often, rebellion is reason enough to do anything. This is not a destructive impulse but a liberating one. It is one type that is impossible to fake, but no one needs to, because the flame of reckless freedom is burning inside every human being. Everyone admires the risk-taker. That admiration, often grudging, is born of vicarious longing: "I could live like that, if I had the nerve." The people who have the nerve, and the talent to stay airborne in defiance of every law, become media superhumans, such as Ted Turner, Margaret Thatcher, Oprah Winfrey, Richard Branson, and Steven Spielberg.

For every success, there are a dozen failures. Many people began as extroverted Intuitives and crashed. They had rejected their old ways, with regret, and fallen into their secondary personality—inevitably the extroverted Doing type. They need confidence to reignite the flame that has been doused, perhaps in childhood.

Any of the Life Signs can be a successful Intuitive. The Actor's instinct about people is usually right, which is why she usually says the right thing and makes herself liked. The Artist intuitively knows when he is right. This gift comes to him naturally. The Mother Hen should excel in one particular type of intuition—telepathy, which is about trust between human minds. It occurs spontaneously with those we love, especially our children.

The Intuitive type often needs help in balancing her life, learning to value friends and family above the craving for change, learning to take pleasure in the moment, learning to reflect. A vital lesson, even for the Believer, is that intuition does not work alone. The Busy Bee will instinctively seek out the right people, but all too often he lets them go.

> " THE ONLY REAL, VALUABLE THING IS INTUITION. "
>
> **Albert Einstein, Physicist (1879–1955)**

Introverted Intuitive types

The inward-looking Intuitive is a mystic, a seer, a hermit. This type is not to be emulated. Encourage your psychic senses by all means, but use them to connect to other people. These powers have evolved to link people's minds and should be exercised in an outward-looking way. Turned in upon themselves, they find expression in visions, revelations, and religious epiphanies. This type of introversion is self-destructive. At its worst, it becomes a lightning rod for the spiritual cravings of people sated on extroverted sensation. Hitler is an example of an introverted Intuitive who developed his introverted thinking powers and became an object of unspeakable malignity.

This type is very rare. Society simply does not tolerate such people. We love Intuitive types, but only when they love us back. The wisdom of Life Signs concentrates on helping people to gain confidence and self-knowledge by developing extroverted Intuitive powers, as well as helping them to find a balance between all their personality types.

Something to think about

We all have telepathic power. When you sense someone staring at the back of your head or you do not want to answer the phone because you know it is your mother—that is telepathy.

To try to receive an image from someone else through telepathy, close your eyes and imagine a television screen broadcasting bright, vivid pictures—gold or silver lines blazing on a dark background. When you receive a telepathic image, you will see it on this screen.

It is best to work with someone you love—you are already on each other's wavelength, and you will be happy to spend some time together, even if the experiment fails. Ask your image-sender to choose exciting images—not dull circles and stars, but emotive words and symbols.

Balancing the introvert and extrovert

Most people are naturally extroverts. True introverts are rare in Western society.

People who are happy to exist in isolation from the good opinion of others—the true introverts—are extremely uncommon. In fact, they are so unusual that those who dedicate their lives to the inner existence are regarded by the rest of us as saints, hermits, or oddballs. Although Jung's classification of personalities is useful (see pp. 168–169), it is less complete than the ancient system underlying Life Signs, because the majority of people fall into one of three extroverted groups: Thinkers, Doers, and Feelers. While the pure Intuitive is a rare type, the pure introverted Intuitive is the rarest. William Blake is the example given in most books, but St. Francis of Assisi is another; it is unlikely that you will come across either of these personality types.

Changes to the balance

Introverted behavior is often forced upon extroverts when they are unable to maintain as much contact with other people as they wish. This can be for many reasons: a change in environment, such as moving to a different city; a change in work or education patterns, leaving college, for example, changing jobs, or retiring; a change in social roles, such as getting married or being widowed; illness; and countless other circumstances. These problems are common to us all, but they will seem unique to each individual. When there is no one around to help share the weight simply by listening and sympathizing, any difficulty can seem unbearable.

For an extrovert locked in an introvert's world, thinking becomes a source of danger. The same ideas begin to go around and around, trapped in a whirlpool. There are nine basic types of "bad"

thinking, and each tends to afflict one of the nine Life Signs. This is not a hard and fast rule, however, if you feel that negative thinking is holding you back or causing you unhappiness, consider all these examples of how perspective can become distorted.

The Reformer indulges in wishful thinking. "If that had not happened, I could make everything perfect." He does not have to like what he sees or approve of it, but he should try to understand things from someone else's viewpoint.

The Mother Hen will blame herself for things not in her control. "My mother wouldn't be so ill if I visited her every day." Instead of taking blame, she should find a positive way to turn things around.

The Actor makes a melodrama of every crisis. "After this no one will work with me." However, he should remember that one simple action can transform a negative situation into a positive one.

The Artist takes everything personally. "What did she mean by that?" When she thinks she has reached a dead end, she should confront the situation. She may discover a more positive response.

The Intellectual assumes everyone thinks as he does. "I find her difficult, and she probably finds everyone difficult." Negativity is contagious, so stay away from negative people.

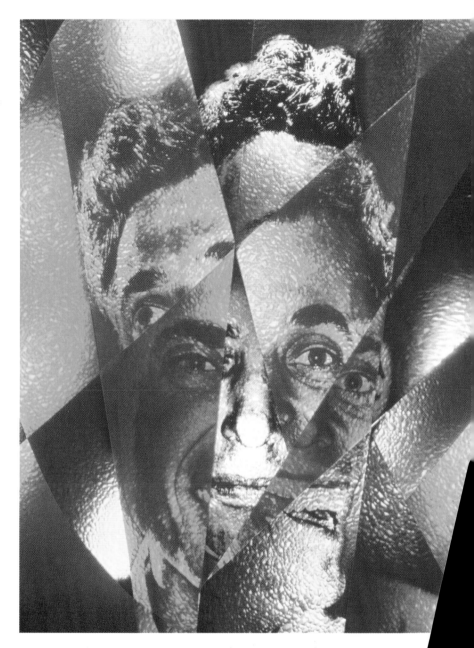

The Believer makes sweeping generalizations. "Everybody knows this is the way to do it." "Had a tough time lately? Thank God for the lesson—you will find value in the experience." She should remember that each situation is different and needs a different response

The Busy Bee will suddenly switch his opinion. "I used to love my work, but now I hate it." He should remember that he is the only true judge of his success; no one else has a true perspective or cares enough about his career to have a valid opinion.

The Boss filters out positive thoughts. "She only said she liked me because she has some agenda." Perhaps the problem is that he is looking at things upside down. Imagine a battery with its negative end where the positive point should be. It will not work, but turn it around and the energy flows.

The Magician mixes up feelings and facts. "I feel anxious, so something is about to go wrong." "I never liked her boyfriend, so I bet he's the one who did it." He needs to be careful and take a closer look at the situation to make sure that his facts are correct.

CHAPTER SEVEN

Improving your performance at work

There is no limit to the success you can achieve at work—whatever your age. If you are truly ambitious, energy counts for as much as experience, and neither of these factors matters as much as enthusiasm. Using Life Signs, you will be able to improve every aspect of your performance at work, whether you are starting a new career or making fresh strides in your current job.

Getting ahead in business

Your attitude and how you approach others will have a great effect on your career.

Whoever you are and whatever your Life Sign, there are several aspects of your personality that have to be understood and mastered if you want to maximize your potential in the workplace.

The art of successful delegation

Learning the correct balance between doing work yourself and assigning tasks to others is essential for good business practices. Unfortunately, the Artist is one of the worst delegators. She rarely believes that anyone will do the job as well as she can. This is not due to arrogance—it comes from having been let down sometime in the past. The Artist takes defeat personally, and she remembers instances when coworkers were less than trustworthy. The Artist's solution is drastic: "I'll do it all myself." Find a one-person business, where the product is made, marketed, delivered, and invoiced by the same person, and you will find an Artist. I know a pine furniture store that is run this way. The owner is a wonderful carpenter, a smart salesman, and a tireless delivery-man; but I wonder how much more successful his business would be if he trusted others to help.

Something to think about

There are nine key rules for ensuring business success. Keep these rules in mind as you deal with people and situations at work:

1. Move on every day. Business does not stand still.
2. Let others learn from their mistakes.
3. Do it for happiness, not cash.
4. Trust others; delegate some of your workload.
5. Put great ideas into practice.
6. Take a leap in the dark.
7. Be honest with yourself and those around you.
8. Demand a lot from others, but only if you make the same demands on yourself.
9. Use your ambition and energy to compete.

From the heart

Robin Hood, the mythical English outlaw, was an exemplary leader—and a Boss. He was famed for joining every attack and putting himself in the forefront of danger, always demonstrating to his Merry Men that whatever he asked of them, he also asked of himself. Result: the Merry Men were inspired to match Robin blow for blow and even outdo him. To get the most from your employees, follow Robin's example by pitching in with enthusiasm.

The Boss is great at delegation, but sometimes he is too great at it. For example, he will give managers impossible deadlines while calling on his cell phone from a golf course—how motivating is that?

The Mother Hen does not often launch or run a company, but she can be an important component in the corporate machine, holding everything together—as the secretary, assistant, or deputy. However, the Mother Hen sometimes protects her coworkers and boss so efficiently that the same mistakes are made repeatedly, which does not help anyone. There are good times to be overprotective—for example, when looking after a roomful of three-year-olds. However, there are also bad times when the Mother Hen has to control her instincts and let others discover their own errors.

Winning with the right attitude

Whether the issue is money or the prestige of having the "right" job title, it is important to remember that life is not a competition, where the winners go to heaven. The Actor loves to win, and he loves others to see him winning. However, in the process, many Actors lose sight of their original goal, which was to have plenty of fun while making a good living. The Actor should remember to avoid letting greed get in the way if he wants to continue to enjoy his job.

It is important to make sure that your desire to win does not overwhelm your compunction to be truthful. A Busy Bee gets so impatient with the world that she will sometimes change the facts to suit her agenda. However, the facts that she fabricates can be difficult to keep straight. It is bad enough that she is trying to kid herself, but when she starts trying to fool others, she must realize that she is simply lying.

The Magician wants everyone to win, but this attitude is a luxury in business. The Magician needs ambition and competition. He should remember that winning is not about crushing the other guy but about making sure no one finishes ahead of him.

Making things happen

Business is about achievement, not abstract concepts. The Intellectual, who sees the whole international pattern of business as an interwoven tapestry of theories and statistics, is prone to easing off at the crucial moment. She sees how to improve a product, but she does not see how important it is to get that product to the market.

You have to keep moving ahead. For example, there is a danger that a Reformer's dynamism will dry up after he achieves his first set of ambitions. He will blame everyone else for abandoning a perfect system—this is ambition in reverse, working backward toward a target that has already been passed.

The Believer is easily scared of what she does not know, but sometimes she must go into unknown territory. She has to learn to lead as well as to follow, to strike out on her own as well as to hunt with the pack. If fear holds her back, she should try to analyze it. And remember, if the business world bites, there is an antidote available—it is called "the rest of your life." Take courage from the things that really count.

> " I'M A FIRM BELIEVER IN LUCK, AND I'VE FOUND THE HARDER I WORK, THE LUCKIER I GET. "
>
> Thomas Jefferson, American President (1743–1826)

Nine key ways to get motivated

We all have phases in our lives when we struggle with motivation, whether at work or in our personal lives.

You may suffer a temporary loss of concentration for an hour or so, or you may feel an underlying restlessness that can last for weeks or even months. To increase your motivation, you first need to try to figure out why it is low. It may be due to one or more causes, such as boredom, overwhelming stress, fatigue, or depression. Being in the same job with the same responsibilities and little chance of change can make it difficult to feel motivated about your work. Your motivation can also be affected by unstable job security.

Sometimes you can resolve these problems, but not always. One way to come to terms with the situation is to put the problem aside and do the best work you can—for your own personal satisfaction. Balthasar Gracian, in *The Art Of Worldly Wisdom* (translated by Christopher Maurer) suggests, "Reach perfection. No one is born that way. Perfect yourself daily, both personally and professionally, until you become a consummate being, rounding off your gifts and reaching eminence." But how can you attain such perfection? You must renew your motivation daily. Different techniques work best for each of the Life Signs, but all of these tips may be used by any of the Life Signs.

The Reformer

You are trying to juggle too many things at the same time. Are you using your mind like a lighthouse beam, sweeping around and around, illuminating everything on the whole horizon for a moment or two before moving on? That is guaranteed to keep sending you around in circles. You

need to narrow your focus. Identify your targets and home in on them. Switch into laser mode and focus steadily on one point until the job is done. To put it another way—in the language of fighting instead of lighting—when one victory is achieved, move on to the next battle. Battle by battle, you will eventually win the war.

The Mother Hen

You need to overcome depression, perhaps with inspirational and beautiful words. Poetry has been proven to raise the spirits. Dr. Robin Phillips, of Bristol University, England, conducted studies to show that a daily dose of verse could be as effective against depression as a handful of pills. If you do not enjoy poems, you can try listening to inspirational speeches by such exhilarating figures as Winston Churchill and Martin Luther King, Jr. I keep a tape of King's most glorious moments in my car, and a burst of his magnificent language will supercharge my energy levels during long journeys.

The Actor

"Do it now!" The musician Paul McCartney says this brief slogan was his father's favorite exhortation whenever he faced a tough task. This is a great piece of positive advice, a burst of instant motivation to be taken literally. Whatever you need to do, you should simply do it now. You will waste more energy by procrastinating than you would spend in getting the job done. In fact, not doing something can be far more draining—and the job will still need to be done. There is no sense of achievement in doing nothing, which only causes any motivation you do have to ebb away. Do it now, and your motivation will only increase.

The Artist

Boost your spirits by making positive statements. If you are the only person who can hear them, that is fine. Tell yourself, "I feel great," "I am a strong personality," "I am unbeatable," "I'm a survivor," "I can endure," "I'll never quit," "I'm going to win," "I can succeed," "This is my life right now," "I feel healthy." Say your favorite phrase more than once—say it so many times that your subconscious begins to accept the truth of it without question.

The Intellectual

To motivate yourself, you need to take care of your body. Most important, get plenty of sleep, so that you can replenish your low energy levels or get rid of your depressed mood. When you are rested, you will naturally invest more energy into your personal appearance, taking the trouble to keep your clothes clean and tidy and your hair neat. These are minor personal details that some Life Signs take care of effortlessly; however, for you, they are too easily ignored. When you look good, other people treat you well and you will feel better about yourself—which will make you feel more motivated.

The Believer

Keep pictures in sight to remind you of your goals. If you are motivating yourself to go to the gym, find a snapshot of yourself as you were a few years ago when your body was at your ideal level of fitness. Or find a picture of someone else who will inspire you to emulate their achievements. I keep a newspaper picture of Lance Armstrong, who beat cancer to come back as a cycling superstar, on top of a pile of papers by my exercise bike.

The Busy Bee

You should keep a journal of your daily activities. Perhaps you think that you are not methodical enough or that you do not have the time. However, you would make time for a personal coach if you needed psyching up, so make time in your schedule for your most effective coach—your own mind. A journal will reveal, over a few months of analysis, where your most profitable hours are being spent and where you are wasting time. You will then know where to concentrate your efforts. You invest a lot of energy in living, so you can afford a little time to record it.

The Boss

Learn about the great people in history. Meditate a little on someone whose life could be your inspiration. Think big, and do not be afraid to compare yourself to the world's most successful and influential figures. Hemingway, Picasso, Einstein, John F. Kennedy, and Bogart were human beings as you are, and they suffered the same petty irritations that bother all of us. If you are not attracted to these particular greats, find biographies of the leading figures in your own field—whether it is teaching, childcare, business, retail, technology, or health, there have been giants. By learning about them, you can learn from them.

The Magician

In order to achieve, you must overcome fear and inertia, and these are not problems to be beaten with soft arguments and careful reasoning. You need to be aggressive with yourself. Force yourself to fight—shout and be physical. Be merciless, be ruthless, be a slave driver to yourself. Raw inspiration will motivate you, and raw inspiration is loud, close-up, and hard-hitting, like a drill sergeant in the marines. Face yourself in the mirror, stare into your eyes, snarl, and issue a command: "I will succeed!"

Dealing with your boss

By knowing how to respond to your boss, you can take control of your workload in the office.

It is your boss's responsibility to delegate work to you and your coworkers. He should recognize the abilities of his staff, and he should be aware of who is available for additional work. However, sometimes it can be difficult for a boss to clearly see how his staff is performing, so it is up to you to make sure he is aware of your talents and workload.

Recognizing your boss

It is easier to deal with your boss if you know what makes him tick. Try looking at his decision-making style. Does he make snap decisions (signs of a Doing type), weigh up the choices carefully (this is a Think-ing type), or make decisions based on instinct (typi-cal of a Feeling type)? Once you have narrowed down his group, it is easier to determine his Life Sign.

A Mother Hen observes and reacts to her boss's needs, making herself indispensable by doing the things he cannot do. A Boss also needs to learn what his own boss's needs are. He should let his boss know that he is an ally, not an enemy, and help with some of the workload. The Reformer thinks that her way is best, but she will not succeed with this way of think-ing as long as someone else is the boss. She should follow her boss's rules to make her own progress—she can change the rules when she gets to the top.

Something for you to do

When your boss wants you to do more work than you can handle, it can be difficult to say "no." However, there are several approaches that you can take to get the result you want. By using a few key phrases and saying them with conviction, you will have a strong defense against exploitation in the office. These phrases are designed to help you sound professional.

"I can do this project, but what is the time frame involved? I could start it by such-and-such a date, when I've completed my previous assignment. I already have an idea of what needs to be done, and these first two items should not be delayed. Perhaps we can assign them to a freelancer." (You have just told your boss how hardworking you are, how committed you are to meeting deadlines, and how efficient you are—and you have almost certainly managed to get some of your work reassigned to someone else.)

"I'm pleased that you think I can handle this project. I would enjoy tackling it, however, I am concerned that I won't have enough time to complete it to the high standards it deserves." (You have succeeded in showing your willingness to do the job while pointing out that, to the project's detriment, it will have to be rushed. This should frighten off the boss.)

"I can see that this assignment is important. I need to sit down with you and work out a schedule, so that I can get everything in place and call in some help if necessary." (In other words, you won't be able to do this on your own, and your boss will have to allow you to delegate some of it to someone else.)

Getting your boss's recognition

Different people achieve success in different ways, but one thing is certain—no one will recognize your talents if you do not make them obvious. The Artist, in particular, needs to heed this advice. If he retreats into his shell, his boss will not bother trying to pry him out, and, what is worse, he will be isolated from his colleagues. The Intellectual also needs to make more noise about her ambition. If she keeps her ideas to herself, the boss will assume she does not know her job.

The Believer is a natural team player and good at obeying orders. However, he is reluctant to accept credit, even when he deserves it. The Believer must learn to occasionally take his share of the rewards. He could take a tip from his Actor colleague. An Actor is not reticent about blowing her own trumpet, but she should be aware of taking all the credit; otherwise, her boss will mount a counterattack to win some back.

> "DO YOUR WORK WITH YOUR WHOLE HEART AND YOU WILL SUCCEED; THERE'S SO LITTLE COMPETITION."
>
> Elbert Hubbard, American author (1856–1915)

Balancing your workload

Let your boss think you can handle more work and one thing is certain—you will get more work. The Busy Bee is sure of his own ability to cope with pressure. He will finish two impossible tasks before breakfast, which results in three more assignments by lunchtime. The solution is clear—he has to hold some of his talent in reserve. He is justifiably proud of his achievements, but he should not make an ordeal of his job.

To allow everything to run smoothly, the Magician will let others walk all over her. It will make everyone's life easier, except hers. The Magician will fight back best when she feels fully justified. Self-preservation should be sufficient incentive, but it helps if she faces the fact that, by doing too much work, she is doing no one any favors in the long run. If she is constantly tired from too much work, she will only damage her health and home life—and her work will suffer, too.

Dealing with coworkers

The world of work is filled with people, each with a unique personality—some congenial and easy-going, others more of a challenge.

Work can be a distressing place if you are not able to deal effectively with a variety of personality types. It helps to remember that "difficult" is often in the eye of the beholder, and the way you refer to others may be the way that others are referring to you.

Communication

The most important factor affecting your relationships with coworkers is your ability to communicate—and that means listening as well as talking. It is the Reformer who most needs to learn when to keep her lips sealed and her ears open. She often wants to express her opinion but, even if she is right, sometimes it is better to keep quiet.

A Mother Hen's relationship with his coworkers is usually defined by supportive communication, but he must be aware that others may find his concern smothering. Because the Artist gives few clues to what she is thinking, her coworkers may be wary, even afraid, of her. Unfortunately, fear can seem like hostility. The Artist should be more communicative to her coworkers, who will then be more open to her.

Keeping negativity to a minimum

Unless you are extremely fortunate, thick-skinned, or laid-back, you are bound to experience a certain number of personality clashes at work. Do not let other people ruin your day. Some people impose themselves by creating a climate of fear, but this could have dangerous repercussions. The Boss, for

Something for you to do

Business consultant Mary J. Nestor, president of MJN Consulting in South Carolina, recommends these seven simple rules for making the workplace a happier environment:

One: the copier. Don't leave the photocopier empty. Take the time to get paper refills from the office supplies, and leave the paper trays well stocked. This rule also applies if you share a computer printer in the office.

Two: the coffee. Of course, you can take the last cup of coffee in the pot, but then make a fresh pot. Even if you are normally a slob at home, when in the office kitchen, remember to clean up after yourself—don't leave coffee stains all over the kitchen countertops.

Three: the copier again. You know how irritating it is to press the button for a single, plain original-size copy, only to realize that you've just ordered 30 thumbnail-size outputs that will take 20 minutes to copy—and you cannot cancel the job. So don't commit the same crime. Reset the copier when you have finished with it.

Four: your lunch. The smell of some foods reheated in a microwave oven can be nauseating to others not eating your leftovers for lunch. If you eat at your desk, make sure the food doesn't have a strong odor. It is a better idea to use the office cafeteria or, on a warm, sunny day, to find a park bench.

Five: your lunch again. Don't leave your desk, the floor around your chair, or the cafeteria table littered with your lunch debris. And don't leave remains of your lunch (or food that you never got around to eating) in the staff refrigerator for weeks at a time. If you do use the refrigerator to store food, remember that you are not the only one using the refrigerator—leave room for others.

Six: read your e-mail. Nothing demonstrates more clearly that you are on the ball, listening and responding, than a swift reply to your e-mail. Respect the system, too; don't abuse it by sending "spam," junk e-mails that are sent to everyone listed in your office address book.

Seven: get to work. Show your respect for your job and your coworkers' professionalism by getting straight to business when you arrive in the office. You can save the anecdotes, the questions about health, and the vacation photographs for your break.

example, is not afraid of confrontation, and he may even feel more comfortable surrounded by enemies than by friends. He needs to ask himself why enemies are better than friends.

The Believer tends to compare her skills unfavorably with others, but there is no need for her to match their abilities. She should value her own contributions and lead the way with hard work.

Sometimes, coworkers seem to exude resentment—the pay, the hours, the workload—nothing is right. The Magician must try hard not to let the negativity of others rub off onto him.

Showing respect for others

Respect and trust are essential ingredients for good working relationships. The Busy Bee must learn to conquer her impatience—it will quickly rob her colleagues of motivation and of respect for her.

The Intellectual sometimes gives an impression of superiority. He can counteract this and show some respect by paying attention to his coworkers' ideas. The Actor needs to give her colleagues the room to make up their own minds. Trying to make decisions for them is counterproductive—and it is okay if someone disagrees with her opinions.

Being part of a team

"Team spirit" is a much-used phrase, but how does
a collection of often very different individuals
develop into an effective, mutually supportive unit?

Some people are naturally team players—especially
the Magician and the Believer—but others can find it
difficult to work as part of a team. For example, the
Actor's ego might be a little too large to work comfortably alongside others; the Intellectual might
prefer to work alone; and the Reformer might struggle to do a job in someone else's style.

There are nine essential skills to effective teamwork, each of them equally important. While each
one is especially pertinent to a particular Life Sign,
they are all important to all of the Signs.

Working well together

Whether you are working on a long-term project or
a brief assignment, it is vital to show respect for your
team mates' opinions and professionalism—even if
you have misgivings about the way they approach
the job. The Reformer has strong views about everyone's attitude, but he must be careful about how he
gives voice to them. By showing respect for others,
he will have his own opinions well received; if he
shows contempt, he will get contempt in return.

Similarly, the Busy Bee often sees herself as the
only player capable of getting anything done, but
she can be sure her coworkers do not see things that
way. Everyone on a team makes a contribution, so it
is right that the credit goes to all—that way, every
team member stays motivated.

Working as part of a team can be like running a relay race.
Cooperation is essential to be able to pass the baton from
one team member to another.

Much of the strength of a team, and the satisfaction of working in one, lies in the support that its members give to each other. The Actor can be a marvelous motivator when he sets aside his ego. He wants everyone to back him up and appreciate his skills, but to accomplish this, he needs to be prepared to give as well as receive. He should make others feel that he admires their contributions, and they will be more willing to let him shine.

Everyone is capable of having great ideas, but not everyone has the talent for listening to them.

"COMING TOGETHER IS A BEGINNING, STAYING TOGETHER IS PROGRESS, AND WORKING TOGETHER IS SUCCESS."

Henry Ford, American industrialist (1863–1947)

The Boss tends to brush aside suggestions and push her own ideas impatiently ahead. This makes other team members feel frustrated and undervalued, and runs the serious risk of wasting some great insights and ideas. The Boss should listen to everyone and everything—after all, hearing out a colleague does not mean adopting everything suggested.

Team members must be prepared to help, even when that means exposing themselves to criticism. The Artist takes harsh words to heart, so he must protect himself by becoming a "different" person when he is part of a team. If he remembers that he is one of several parts, the "real" Artist can be sheltered from negative comments. He can be an active team player and still retain his privacy by opting, for example, not to reveal details about his home life.

Learning to speak up

To work well in a team everyone must sometimes be bold. The Mother Hen may lack the confidence to speak out confidently, although there is no good reason for her self-doubt. Anyone can display confidence, even when they do not feel it inside. The Mother Hen should view her ideas and opinions as her brain-children and defend them passionately.

Confrontation is anathema to the Magician, who prefers to keep everyone happy. In fact, the Magician often sacrifices his own happiness before anyone else's. He needs to learn how to be persuasive, so that he can change his coworkers' minds without directly challenging them. It is a talent that will serve him faithfully in every team situation.

The Believer is often tempted to go along with everyone else and keep quiet her private misgivings. This is not the best way to support her team. She should ask questions without being afraid of seem-

From the heart

I am often requested to help worthy causes. I'm asked to attend charity galas, to make presentations to top fund-raisers, and to visit children in hospitals. These requests always come well in advance before I'm needed. After all, it would be disrespectful to take for granted that I would be available on short notice.

I adopt the principle of "distant elephants." Elephants far away on the horizon look small and barely worth the worry, but eventually those elephants will be closer—and much bigger. Of course, I say yes when I can, but if I don't keep those distant elephants in mind, I would overbook and not be able to help anyone. This same principle applies to work situations. Make sure you allow enough time for others to fit a request into their schedules.

ing stupid. It is often the simple questions that reveal the flaws in a project.

The Intellectual also has problems with being upfront, fearing that his contribution will not be as effective in practice as it is in theory. He should set aside his fear. In a team, he is of no use if he does not participate—and his ideas just may work.

Seeking support from a mentor

Most people can identify an individual—a friend, teacher, colleague, or relative—who has had a positive impact on their lives.

Whether you realize it or not, at some point you probably have been on the receiving end of some type of informal mentoring, and you may have been a mentor to others. Mentors provide support and inspiration to help protégés recognize their natural abilities, learn new skills, establish goals, and achieve personal and professional success. Most employers realize that mentoring is a powerful tool for developing employee competency and contributes to the success of the whole organization. Sometimes a mentoring relationship between a junior employee and a supervisor grows naturally from a foundation of trust and respect. However, increasingly, organizations are setting up formal mentoring programs in which highly skilled or experienced individuals are deliberately paired with a less experienced person, or a small group, in order to impart specific skills.

Building a relationship with your mentor

When mentoring is successful, it is beneficial to both parties. A meaningful relationship is at the very heart of all successful mentoring. As the person on the recipient end, it is not enough to simply sit back and wait to be educated—you have to work hard to get the most out of the process. Whatever your Life Sign, you can benefit from having a mentor, but each Sign has specific issues that they need to address when entering a mentoring relationship.

A Reformer must learn to see his mentor as an ally instead of a competitor. He should remember that his mentor has been chosen precisely because she has the ability and the desire to help him achieve his personal best. Above all, the Reformer must strive to prove himself worthy of guidance by judging himself—before his mentor judges him.

The mentor is often older than his protégé, and where this is the case, it is easy for that person to become a parent figure—which is not a bad thing. However, the Mother Hen must try not to transfer her personal feelings about a parent onto her

---

For your information

Being a mentor

Mentoring is the best way to improve performance, motivation, and skills, for both individuals and teams. It allows people to take on more responsibility and builds their confidence. It also increases loyalty. The key mentoring skills are: asking questions, making suggestions, giving feedback, and active listening.

● The best criticism builds on what is good, rather than what is not. Feelers should keep negativity to a minimum.

● Too much advice is as bad as too little. Thinkers should strive to keep their guidance within practical limits.

● If Doers give in to impatience and do the work themselves, they will be helping no one—least of all the person they are mentoring.

mentor. As with the Actor, much of her inner motivation throughout her life has been to seek approval from her parents. Properly channeled, this longing can drive her relationship with her mentor, but both Life Sign types must be careful not to let emotions interfere with grown-up, rational judgment.

For an Intellectual, it is the personal relationship itself that is the most difficult aspect of mentoring. He naturally recoils from closeness with anyone he does not know well. He must recognize this trait in himself and work hard to create an open, trusting relationship.

Having the right attitude

All protégés need to demonstrate a willingness to learn and an ability to accept feedback. Criticism is not always negative and a good mentor will seek to be constructive. The Artist, in particular, must take advice in the spirit in which it is given. If she is too easily hurt, both she and her mentor will suffer.

Without the commitment of both parties, a mentoring relationship simply will not work. Both must invest time and be willing to focus on learning, without outside distractions. For example, the Busy Bee is bound to start off full of enthusiasm for the project, but he should beware of tiring of it too quickly. The Busy Bee will need perseverance to stay with his mentoring program.

Sometimes, younger people may be required to mentor older workers. This is especially common when new technologies are brought into the work-

place. This situation can be hard for a Boss to accept. She should resist the temptation to treat her mentor as a junior—her role as a leader is only effective when she can take advice as well as give it.

Finally, an essential part of the mentoring process is being brave enough to let go of the support. The Believer must remember that his mentor is not there to be a lifelong crutch—he must eventually stand on his own two feet.

Nine key ways to negotiate

Whatever your point of view, there will always be someone who will disagree; however, there are ways to come to an agreement.

Whether you are proposing an update to the company website, trying to arrange renovation work for your home, or suggesting a change to the annual family vacation plans, you can probably expect opposition from someone. You might want to ask yourself if this is because humans are naturally argumentative or because you are a naturally provoking person? The answer, I am afraid, is most likely to be both. Everyone loves to be right in an argument; however, most people use the wrong tactics to prove their point.

There are nine key factors that often prevent people from winning a successful argument. Each Life Sign is prone to fall into one particular trap, but, by learning all the ways of improving your negotiation skills, you will be guaranteed greater success every time. Of course, you should work on your natural areas of weakness, but do not ignore the other key factors attributed to other Life Signs. By studying them all, you will also be able to identify the skills that others possess, the skills they will use to maximize their own advantage.

The Reformer

Don't be afraid to admit when you are wrong. Concede your weak points gracefully and do not attempt to defend the indefensible. You have at times lost confrontations even when you held the stronger position, because you could not admit you might have been wrong anywhere along the line. By abandoning the battles that cannot be won, you will marshal your forces for your strongest points, and your air of calm reasonableness might be enough to disarm your opponent.

The Mother Hen

You have a tendency to argue vigorously with an intense feeling for right and wrong, but too often you are outmaneuvered by people who cleverly slip their arguments past you. While you use the force of emotion, they answer with pinpoint logic. You often feel that you have been bested by a weaker argument, but you should remember that logic can only be defeated with logic—it will always show the holes in strictly emotional arguments. Look at the facts carefully, and proceed from there. If you master logical argument, you will be invincible, because you will also have emotional force behind your points.

The Actor

The truth is a powerful weapon, and you should use it. You have a marvelously inventive mind and a sharp instinct for what others want to hear. I'm not saying that you ever tell lies, of course, but you might sometimes redesign the truth a little. And these alterations can be picked up during the course of an argument, which would only weaken your position. The truth does not need redesigning, or reshaping, or massaging. It is best served straight.

The Artist

Make sure that you state what you want, even if you have to use a little subterfuge at first. Although it is not always shrewd to reveal what you are really trying to gain in negotiations, you need to at least establish some targets to give the argument some type of direction. If no one has any idea what you are fighting for, the discussions will become confused and damaging to all involved. You may think that it is obvious what you want to win, so you don't come out and state it clearly. However, you won't get anywhere by expecting everyone else to read your mind.

The Intellectual

Resist the temptation to use sarcasm or humor when you are trying to make a point. It almost never wins an argument. The only thing you may accomplish is making your opponent feel ridiculed. Others will suspect that you do not take the issues seriously, or that you think so much of yourself that you cannot bother to show respect for anyone else. You may feel that other points of view are stupid—and perhaps you are right—but it is much stronger to reveal this calmly than destructively. You often pride yourself that you "don't suffer fools gladly," unaware that your acerbic tongue will only embitter your potential allies.

The Believer

You can improve your position by allowing your creative energy to flow during negotiations. While you are confident that you know the facts behind your argument, you must also learn to cultivate the confidence to present them well. Often the best way of presenting your case will be to tell a story. Stories engage every part of the mind—the emotions, the subconscious responses, and the imagination, as well as the cold intellect. By framing your argument in a story, you will be able to grab everyone's attention.

The Busy Bee

The best advice to give you is to be prepared. There have been many times when you have fared badly in negotiations because you have not been patient enough to prepare yourself thoroughly. Your natural inclination is to rush into an argument without taking the trouble to first study the facts. Inevitably, you will be pulled to pieces by people who know what they are talking about—once they have absorbed the initial shock of your energetic onslaught. It is always a mistake to count on your quick bursts of passionate verbiage to make up for missing facts and details.

The Boss

When in negotiations, you can usually win whatever it is you require; however, you need to learn how to make concessions to others. It is a sign of strength—not weakness—to allow your opponent to also win. When you attempt to grind your enemy into the ground, leaving no shred of consolation, you make your own task almost impossible. It is important to remember that all parties should be permitted to exit negotiations with their dignity intact, able to say that they have made some gains. This is called the "win-win" scenario—and as long as you win, why should you be so determined to see that everyone else loses?

The Magician

Your natural inclination is to be afraid of confrontation, but, instead of walking away from it, this is one area where you should face it. You will have a chance of winning only if you stand up to your opponent. If you immediately adopt a subservient position, like a young wolf lying supine to the leader of the pack, you will be walked all over. To be constantly on the defensive is to invite attack. Be bold and do the attacking yourself. Identify the weak point in your opponent's argument and hit it. This may be what he most fears. Remember that he knows the limitations of his own position better than anyone else, and his fear may be his greatest enemy. When you attack, you will be counter-attacked, but you will also have the initiative.

Health at work

It is your employer's responsibility to make sure you work in a healthy, safe environment, but it is your responsibility to follow safe work practices.

The environment in which you work can affect your health, and it is up to your employer to ensure that you are provided with adequate equipment to do your job safely. For example, employees who work with noisy equipment should be supplied with sufficient hearing protection. Computer workers should have workstations with a desk at a suitable height for the user and a chair with comfortable back support. No matter where you work, there should be adequate air ventilation, free from fumes that can cause damage to your health.

A good employer will make sure everything in the workplace is well-maintained. The Magician, for example, will look out for problems before they occur. He has fine forward-planning skills that can be vital when it comes to maintaining workplace safety. Even as an employee, the Magician will speak out if he sees that the photocopier cables are frayed or the water cooler needs cleaning.

Conversely, the Actor and the Busy Bee often see the little jobs as the bane of their working life—they never seem to have time for them, so these jobs never get resolved. However, when safety is an issue, such as a broken windowpane or a rusting step on the fire escape, the repercussions could be serious. These Life Signs need to build time into their schedule for the small nagging details.

Keeping yourself healthy

Your own personal health is your responsibility. That is true as much at work as at any other time. Whether you work for yourself or for an employer, your first duty is to take good care of yourself. Overworking is one of the most certain ways to damage your body, as well as the quality of your work. I have known many people, of all types, who have pushed themselves so hard that their minds and bodies did not have time to recuperate. The effect is cumulative over years and can lead to heart attacks and strokes.

Work overload can erode sleeping patterns. A few days of heavy workloads force you to put in

---

For your information

Getting a good night's sleep

According to one study, sleep aids memory. Subjects given a list of nonsense words to remember did better after 24 hours, with an intervening period of 8 hours sleep, than those tested just 8 sleepless hours after memorizing the list. The best sleep aids are regular physical exercise, a firm mattress, a warm, well-ventilated room, a cup of warm milk (or camomile tea if you are a vegetarian)—and sex. Too much work can make us too lethargic for sex and exercise.

- The Feelers should avoid drowning their anxieties in alcohol; it will actually make them sleep less well, not better.

- Reading a book in bed might take the Thinker's mind off work, but a surer method is to tune in to relaxing music.

- If the mind is drained but the body is full of energy, sleep will be elusive for the Doer. A relaxing bath before bedtime may help.

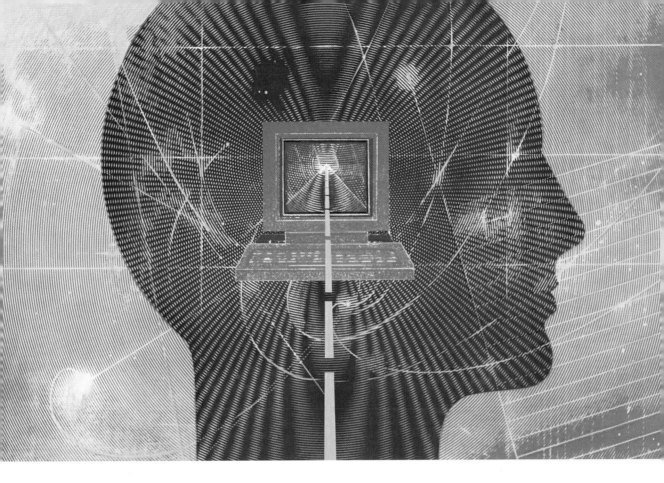

extra hours, so that you arrive home late and weary. When you drag yourself to bed, you sleep anxiously, because the certainty that you will still be tired when the alarm goes off is preying on your mind. And when you start work the next day, you are slow and your reactions are numb, so that everything takes twice as long to complete as it should. And so you stay late, again, to get more done.

The Boss has a tendency toward workaholism, which can lead to serious health issues if she does not learn to pace herself. She needs to keep a close eye on her output. If her productivity is going down, she needs to ease her foot off the gas and take more frequent breathers—and talk to her employer about reassigning some of her workload.

It is sometimes possible for the Mother Hen and the Believer, in particular, to be literally sick of work. If work tension is getting one of them down, he needs to see a doctor. Depression is better treated

early than late. There is no need for him to tell his colleagues the reason for his appointment—the common euphemism for depression is a "bad back."

The Reformer may use work to escape problems at home. For her, work can become her haven if she can avoid thinking about outside problems while in the workplace. However, she must still deal with the problems at home before they take over her life and affect her work.

> **"WHATEVER GAMES ARE PLAYED ON US, WE MUST PLAY NO GAMES WITH OURSELVES."**
>
> Ralph Waldo Emerson
> American philosopher and poet (1803–1882)

One of the most common problems in today's workplace is poor posture at a workstation and repetitive strain injury. You must learn to sit back in your chair, with shoulders upright and your feet flat on the floor. If you use a computer, your arms should form a right angle, with your wrists parallel to the keyboard. Take breaks often to avoid repetitive strain injury. The Intellectual has a natural tendency to neglect his posture at work—and if he does so, he will pay for it with chronic back pain.

Memory and concentration

The greatest aid to success in your career is the ability to concentrate, to stay focused, and to single-mindedly pursue a task until it is done.

The greatest enemy to success is the meandering mind, forever wandering off the point. Every time you break your concentration to chat, check the scores on a website, read a gossipy e-mail, or turn on the radio, you are holding back your own success.

Focusing on your concentration

Concentration requires ruthlessness. You cannot focus on your work if you are talking to others and joining in the workplace banter. The Magician must not be afraid to narrow her focus by ignoring the chatter. This is not rudeness—it is professionalism.

The Mother Hen finds it easy to allow his natural concern for others to get in the way of his work, but he must remember that, unless he is being paid to provide a shoulder to cry on, he cannot afford to be a full-time Mother Hen in the workplace.

When an Actor is focused, the result is laser-beam concentration. This intensity is hard to maintain, so she should train herself to rest and return to the task at hand when her concentration wanders.

Improving your memory

The ability to recall names and faces and to remember appointments and details of meetings is a valuable social and business skill. How often have you had an awkward moment introducing someone when you suddenly cannot remember the name? And how often do you get to the end of a funny story before you realize that you have forgotten the punch line?

Many people believe that there is nothing they can do to improve their memories. The Reformer, in particular, tends to think that people either have a good memory or they don't. He believes that if you keep forgetting things it is just the way your brain was made. However, people can boost their mind power with easy memory exercises. For example, Dominic O'Brien is the World Memory Champion, and his mental data storage powers outstrip the fastest computer 10,000 times over. He travels the world, lecturing on his techniques for memorizing. If he, a dyslexic daydreamer who failed school, can acquire megamemory, so, too, can others.

> " THE EMPIRES OF THE FUTURE ARE THE EMPIRES OF THE MIND. "
>
> **Sir Winston Churchill**
> **British Prime Minister (1874–1965)**

The Intellectual and the Believer have difficulty recalling information in its proper sequence, a common problem in dyslexia and dyspraxia, which is thought to affect 10 percent of the population (it also seems to be linked to above-average intelligence). They may find that using a series of initial letters is effective. For example, MVEMJSUNP: Mean Vultures Enjoy Making Jaguars Scared Usually Near Parks, will remind them of the sequence of planets in our solar system—Mercury, Venus, Earth, Mars, Jupiter, Saturn, Uranus, Neptune, Pluto.

Exercising your mind

Every Life Sign can learn the benefits of mnemonics, or memory techniques, although some are quicker to see the advantages. The Boss will easily recognize the potential benefits to her business profile in being able to put names to faces and instantly recall details of conversations with clients and associates. And the Busy Bee, who processes information so fast that he cannot hope to retain all of it, is always enthusiastic about anything to boost his brain capacity. These types naturally want instant results. Fortunately for them, the simplest system O'Brien uses yields instant results. It is a stimulating and fun mind workout that helps to fine-tune your memory.

Try to memorize a list of around 20 words—a shopping list, perhaps. This task is difficult for most people—much more difficult than, for example, a story. The solution is to invent a story that includes all the items on your list. Try to use vivid imagery involving all your senses—see the colors, smell the odors, taste the flavors. The more colorful and far-fetched the scenario, the easier it will be to remember. This technique works especially well for the Artist and the Magician. Their memory banks are visual instead of word-based, and they can easily weave stories involving complex image associations.

For your information

Clearing the decks

Whenever your focus flags, you'll be ready with an excuse. Instead of wasting energy on finding reasons not to concentrate, look at what is interfering with your ability to focus. Often it is the sheer clutter in a workplace that hampers you. With pieces of paper spread over every available surface, you will be distracted. Put everything you don't immediately need into a file—you can come back and organize the papers when the task at hand is done.

● Feelers can clear their desks, but without wasting their time filing—that is simply another delaying tactic.

● Thinkers should not panic. Half-finished projects won't vanish if put out of sight. The work will still be there when they are ready to do it.

● Doers may think they can juggle a dozen assignments at once, but to do a job well they need to give it their full attention.

Improving your decision-making skills

Decisions, decisions, decisions. A greater part of our waking lives is spent weighing up choices.

Some decision-making moments come and go before we consciously think about them, while others are more complex—and stressful. When faced with a difficult decision, I sometimes use a type of visualization that uses my mind's talent for precognition—an ability we all share. Here's how it works: I imagine that a decision has already been made and I picture what will happen next. As the event unfolds in my mind, I can "see" the consequences.

Novices to the Life Signs system might think there are some types who are naturally more able to act decisively—I admit that I certainly made that mistake when I began to formulate the system. Closer study has revealed, however, that anyone can make clear-cut and accurate decisions if the mind is properly trained. The most important rule is summed up in the proverb, "He who hesitates is lost." But another rule, which contradicts this wisdom, is well stated in the words of a song by the American blues maestro, B. B. King: "Never make your move too soon." Balance these two pearls of wisdom and you can learn the habit of effective decision-making.

Seeing the big picture

Both the Magician and the Believer sometimes find it hard to see the forest for the trees—or the in-tray for the reams of reports. They should be methodical when making a decision, drawing up all the pros and cons of a course of action on a sheet of paper, with the positive outcomes on one side and negatives on the other. Not all items carry equal weight, so they should score each from 1 to 10. When the list is complete, they should add up the scores on each side. This system often reveals a strange anomaly—the side that scores highest is the less popular choice. They should ask themselves what subconscious factors are influencing their analyses.

The Mother Hen may find a similar, but much simpler method works just as well for her. Flip a coin—if it comes down tails and she thinks "Oh, no," then she knows that heads is the answer she wants.

Petty decisions can sometimes mask bigger problems. Both the Reformer and the Busy Bee can be drawn into endless detail chasing and needless perfectionism. If they are calling meetings to discuss trivial issues, they should ask themselves—who is steering the company and where is it being steered?

From the heart

Many people review a decision again and again, unwilling to make a final commitment. I know I am prone to this fault. I worry about how a decision will appear to others, instead of focusing on what benefits my choice will bring. I am also inclined to be swayed by the advice of the person I last consulted, and for this reason, I make it a rule never to ask the advice of more than three well-informed people. By the time I have weighed their counsel, I have a full understanding of my own views—to keep asking for more and more advice just muddies the water and wastes time.

Considering your coworkers

Sometimes decision making boils down to serious recklessness for the Boss. But if he is advocating an extreme cost-cutting, repositioning, whole-new-ballgame decision, he needs to remember that other people's lives are involved as well as his. He needs to show consideration by listening to their views.

Once a decision has been made, it is best to stick to it. The Intellectual has a tendency to rewrite her choices according to every new snippet of data. This is admirably open-minded—and incredibly infuriating. Of course, sometimes her decisions are wrong. It happens, even to the Actor, who should remember that it is always best to be bold and admit to the mistake. He will win kudos, not lose his reputation.

The Artist loves to express her individuality at every opportunity—but sometimes it is better to follow the crowd. When she has to decide on the color of her new company car, she can demonstrate that she is part of the team by picking a popular color instead of going for something that she prefers.

Avoiding unnecessary stress

When you are under stress, all decisions become difficult. Stress saps your energy, and you cannot afford to waste precious reserves on unimportant choices. Resolve to yourself that sometimes you will "go with the flow." This laissez-faire attitude does not have to last long, but it will take some of the pressure off at an important time.

Becoming more organized

Good organization will help you make the most of the time you have available.

Balancing your time between work and home is often a struggle, but establishing good organizational skills in the office will help make your work flow more smoothly. This should allow you to leave work at a reasonable hour and have more time for your personal life.

Time management

Practice makes good time management more natural. Even a Busy Bee can start by investing in a diary or calendar. He should use it not only to note down when he has meetings and appointments, but also when he has deadlines. Referring to it often will help him to keep his work on track. He can break down a particularly large project into smaller components and assign due dates for each of them on the calendar.

Another useful method, especially for the Intellectual, is to keep reminder files—folders filled with notes and reminders of jobs to be done at a future date. Complicated projects can be better managed by setting up computer database files. If you don't know how to operate one of these yourself, ask your employer for training—it will be a worthwhile investment. The Reformer and the Believer, who have an extroverted approach to thinking, can find satisfaction in organizing their time by using multicolored stickers on their diaries and wall charts and by using creative designs in their database files.

One of the benefits of following good time management practices is that you determine early if it is possible to complete your workload on time. If not, than you have good back-up proof that some of the work needs to be reassigned. Delegation is the Boss's forte, and she should make maximum use of it. Her coworkers will probably help to keep everything running smoothly, especially if she takes the time to explain clearly what she expects of everyone.

Something to do

One of my favorite organizational techniques is to use color. I have assigned blue for everything of a legal nature, red for domestic matters, green for my appointments and schedules, and purple for parascientific information. Here are some suggestions for using this color-coded system:

- As you read a document, use color-coded highlighters to mark them, picking out important sentences or running a line down the margin of the appropriate paragraphs.

- Apply color-coded labels to your paper-base folders in your filing cabinet, and set up the folders on your computer following the same color theme.
- Establish color-matched drawers in your filing cabinet. You won't waste time filing your folders alphabetically or searching through every label.

Using this system for a legal issue, I pull out the blue folders, flick through to the one I need, then shuffle through the pages, reading the highlighted areas.

This may seem contradictory, but taking a lunch break is a good way to use time wisely. The Actor may be concerned that others will note his absence if he takes more than a few moments away from his desk, and the Mother Hen is convinced that the team will fall apart if she steps away to get a sandwich. However, the truth is that afternoons are dead zones for your brain if your lunch has been badly digested. While your stomach is processing your lunch, it diverts blood from the brain, causing sluggish thinking. You will get a lot more done before 5:00 PM if you take 20 minutes to help your body cope with lunch.

Organizational skills

Information overload is an increasing burden on everyone. Even an eight-year-old who is learning to navigate safe areas of the Internet is subject to more data every week than a 16th-century person could expect to encounter in her whole life. This overload is not going to disappear, so we have to develop new ways of assimilating the data. Junk mail, both in envelopes and via e-mail, is a great destroyer of time. Be ruthless. You did not ask for this information, so get rid of it without opening it.

In general, with every document that crosses your path, ask these four questions: "Do I need this? Where do I keep this? How long do I keep this? How will I find this again?" After you answer the first question, you will find that 90 percent of all information can be dumped. Only keep data that you will have to refer to again and which cannot be regenerated (mostly financial papers).

The other questions demand an efficient filing system. My most-used files are the temporary ones, containing documents for upcoming events. When an event is over, I empty the file. The things I use regularly are kept color-coded at the front of the cabinet. The Artist and the Magician have visual-, not word-based, memory banks. They can use visualizations to set up a filing system.

Nine key ways to speak effectively in public

Most people dread speaking publicly, and, surprisingly, the ones we think should be the best at it often fear addressing an audience.

It is not uncommon for a confident, articulate professional, who might be expected to enjoy the attention that is guaranteed when he stands up to speak, to turn into an inarticulate, nervous wreck on the podium. He mumbles and loses his train of thought, so he ends up repeating himself or leaving out important components of his speech.

Ironically, the people who most enjoy speaking in public are often the worst orators. Boring, droning, with no awareness of their audience, they are in love with their moment in the limelight and seem oblivious to their obligation to be at least a little entertaining and informative.

Effective public speaking is a skill. It requires a clear, audible tone, and the presenter must show confidence in the material he is presenting. The information must be presented in a sensible, organized manner, and sometimes visual aids may be necessary to back up the speech.

Anyone who talks well to an audience will probably have honed the talent by taking classes and practice. Some companies offer to pay for their employees to take workshops on public speaking. In fact, good speakers often start out as uncertain and nervous as you may be.

The following nine hints and tips are designed to help each Life Sign with areas of special difficulty, but any one of them may be just the snippet of advice you need to transform yourself into a highly effective orator. So read on—and when you are ready to speak in public, remember to breathe deeply, put together your thoughts, speak clearly, and project your voice to the back of the room.

The Reformer

As you make your presentation, you should establish eye contact with several members of the audience. This will put you onto a personal footing, and it will reassure your subconscious mind that you are doing nothing different from what you do every day of your life—simply talking to people. Find sympathetic faces and silently make friends across the auditorium; move from one person to another in different sections of the audience. Do not be aloof—people must feel that they can relate to you, so reach out to them.

The Mother Hen

Have some fun. Your presentation does not have to be torture for either you or your audience. Sprinkle a few jokes into the message, and try to be animated. The best way to engage your listeners is to appeal to all their senses, not only their hearing, but also their sight and their good taste—not to mention their sense of humor. So dress well, use props if you need to, and sprinkle in a few laughs. It will get you remembered.

The Actor

Prepare your material thoroughly, making sure that you know the structure of your speech well. If you are someone who performs best when your delivery is spontaneous, it is fine to leave some of the details unrehearsed, but do not allow this particular style to be an excuse for not bothering with the preparation. Failure to know your material will point you out as being lazy, ill-informed, and a lightweight—which is not the type of impression you want to create.

The Artist

Before you make your presentation, pump yourself up. Instead of keeping cool, let your emotions out and let the adrenaline flow. If you can become excited about the material you are presenting, this will transmit itself to your audience. You will project your message more powerfully, and it will stay with everyone who hears it. Remember, what you say is just as important as how you say it. If the material is boring to you, you can be certain that it will be even more boring to someone else.

The Intellectual

Make sure you pay attention to your audience. Look at them as you speak and when you use any visual aids, such as a video or overhead projector. If the audience is not fully engaged and entertained, you have more work to do. The audience matters more than the speech because, without their listening to you, the words are irrelevant. When you get it right, the audience will applaud. Although applause is a low priority for the Intellectual, it is a rare pleasure, so you might as well savor it.

The Believer

Make videotapes of your speeches and study them later. Seeing yourself for real is more valuable than watching yourself rehearse in a mirror. Make sure you listen to the whole speech, then decide whether the structure was really how you imagined it. Pay attention to the quality of your voice—squeaky, croaky, and whiney speakers can make the best material dreadful. If your voice falls into one of these categories, you might want to hire

a voice coach. Also study your posture. Are you putting all of your weight on one leg? This will seem awkward to the audience; make sure you stand as balanced as possible. Don't let your hands hang straight down your sides—use them to punctuate your speech but do not exaggerate their movements.

The Busy Bee

Pay attention to the equipment, especially any microphones and speakers. Bad sound will kill anything you are trying to say. Make sure you take the time to learn about any available presentation software and lighting; you should also take an interest in the seating arrangements. Mastering these mundane details is the sign of a pro.

The Boss

Use stories in your speeches. You want to grab your audience's interest right away, and starting with a tale will do this much better than beginning with a mediocre joke, which might send a subliminal message that you are not taking your task seriously. Stories naturally possess pattern and order, two key elements in a good speech. Strong characters in your story, people your audience knows or might want to know, will make them listen more attentively. One caveat, however—avoid telling stories about yourself. Not everyone is as interested in your life story as you are.

The Magician

Practice in front of a full-length mirror. This is not vanity—it makes good sense to watch yourself in action. Try to look at yourself through a stranger's eyes, and take careful note of your mannerisms and clothes. What immediate impression do you make on yourself. As your speech gets going, try to remain detached enough to evaluate your forcefulness and your calmness, two aspects that should be kept in balance.

CHAPTER EIGHT

Becoming fulfilled and empowered

By exploring the Life Signs, I hope to
help you understand and fulfill your
potential and to empower you to
uncover new facets to your own mind.
These last pages will help you to achieve
greater strength of character, to take joy
in everything, to become fit and healthy,
to make the most of your leisure time,
and to take control of your own dreams.

Asserting yourself

Everyone has their own mental block or barrier. By asserting yourself, you can overcome your own barrier.

Each of the Life Signs is at risk from a mental block that can cause friction in most relationships. These barriers are linked, like three walls that form a triangle. At the center of the triangle, hemmed off from all, is a unique freedom—the freedom to be yourself. By helping you to understand what these barriers are, I hope you will learn to assert yourself.

The Feeling group—the Mother Hen, the Reformer, and the Magician—often have difficulty saying "no." The Doing group—the Busy Bee, the Believer, and the Boss—can easily say "no," but they do not listen. They hear, but do not pay attention to what they are hearing. The Thinkers—the Actor, the Artist, and the Intellectual—are confident about saying "no" and are also excellent listeners, but they often fail to assert themselves strongly enough.

Learning to say no

Saying "no" can be difficult, especially if you are taken by surprise. You may not want to upset a friend or colleague who makes a sudden request, so you say "yes," and regret it immediately. One sure defense is not to make a commitment right away. Defer the question with, "Let me think about it before I give you an answer." If pressed, you can add something positive but noncommittal, "It sounds interesting." If the demand cannot wait, ask yourself why?

If, after consideration, you decide you want to say "no," there are simple ways to refuse politely without giving offense. Give one clear reason, "It sounds great, but I am too busy at the moment," or "Thanks for offering, but we already have plans for that day." You don't have to be specific. No one is interested in the details of your personal life. Do not give several excuses, even if they are all genuine; this comes across as if you want to avoid the request.

Being a good listener

Listening is an essential skill necessary for good communication. To demonstrate to myself as well as to the speaker that I have heard and understood what has been said, I repeat a summary. If a business deal is being outlined, I repeat the key points; if a

For your information

Powerful gestures

Your gestures can be assertive in many ways, demonstrating the faith you have not only in yourself but in a spiritual power. I used to be puzzled by how, in many religions, pressing the palms of the hands together in prayer or spiritual greeting became such a universal gesture. One explanation is that it comes from the Middle Ages, when the monks and nuns avoided interruption by clasping their hands under their chins to indicate that they were praying.

● The Feelers are comfortable using physical touch and gestures when communicating with others.

● The Thinkers prefer a no-touch approach, but a smile is a gesture that everyone can understand.

● The Doers may be too busy to notice their own gestures, but a friendly pat on the back can be reassuring to others.

friend is asking me to send healing energy to combat an illness, I outline the core symptoms. People may be surprised to hear their own points repeated, but it soon turns to confidence, because, it is obvious that I have been listening carefully.

Getting what you want

Whether it is an eagerness to please others, a natural shyness, or social clumsiness, the Thinkers often fail to assert their rights. To get what you want, try this three-step program: decide what you want; state what you want; and repeat what you want.

To know what you want, you have to be precise.

Even a naturally shy person can become a winner by learning how to assert herself.

How can you expect anyone to understand your needs if you cannot make them plain to yourself? Picture yourself in the situation you would like to reach, such as having more responsibility at work, and look at how it differs from your current pre-dicament. Note the things that must be in place for your wishes to be fulfilled, then write them down.

Now that you have identified what you want, tell the people who matter. When they have heard your demands, repeat them again— this makes it clear that you are serious about getting what you deserve.

Improving your physical health

Regular exercise improves your physical appearance, boosts self-esteem, reduces stress, and enhances your mood.

Leading an active life has an impact on all the systems of the body. During exercise the heart beats faster and stronger, speeding up the flow of blood throughout the body, which increases the supply of nutrients and removes waste products more rapidly. The lungs and respiratory system also become more effective, bringing in more oxygen with less work. Muscles become larger and use more energy, so fat stored in the body is metabolized, helping to reduce excess fat. These benefits help increase energy levels and stamina. Exercise also improves your ability to concentrate and your mental health. It increases your alertness, reduces tension, and triggers brain chemicals, known as endorphins, which contribute to feelings of well-being.

Good for all

All the Life Signs can benefit from exercise. The Busy Bee might think his body is fit from his daily rushing about, but he may not be getting the right type of exercise and his stressful life may put him more at risk for health problems. He needs a proper exercise routine. The Artist values spiritual virtues above physical ones, but that is a poor excuse for neglecting her body—ignoring her body insults her soul.

Physical exercise is an instant pleasure for the Actor and the Boss, who usually appreciate a quick release of the body's endorphins. Improving his physical appearance is all the incentive an Actor needs, but it is easy for the Mother Hen to let herself go when caring for others. The decline in her own health and appearance might seem to be an indicator of her selflessness, but she should fight against this illogical thinking. After all, if she does not care for herself, it will be difficult to care for others.

Getting started

The good news is that you do not need to spend hours at a time exercising. Research has shown that as little as 30 minutes of physical activity a day, five times a week, is enough to be beneficial. You can get started by changing a few everyday activities: Use stairs instead of the elevator, walk or use a bicycle for short journeys instead of taking the car, and attack housework vigorously.

Set realistic goals if you want to start an exercise plan. If you set too hard a pace, you may become discouraged or even hurt yourself. The Busy Bee, in particular, should beware of setting his sights too high in the first week. Start with short-term targets—walk 15 minutes every morning for two weeks or do five laps at the swimming pool. Achievable fitness targets are a good incentive for the Reformer, who will be proud each time she reaches a new target.

The Believer and the Magician are both social animals, and fitness can be fun for them if undertaken with others. They can find a club and exercise with a group, whether they choose badminton, yoga classes, aerobics, or one of the many forms of exercise available at their local gym. The Boss thrives on competition, and the gym is a great place to find it. A well-equipped gym will have state-of-the-art machinery that enables him to set goals for each session. He can compete with people if he enjoys company, but the machine may be his greatest opponent.

Other people prefer to exercise on their own, whether they invest in an exercise bike to use at home or go for walks. The Artist and the Intellectual will love the solitude that walking can afford. Even confirmed social animals like me, an Actor, love to get away from the throng from time to time.

Swimming is an excellent way to boost your physical health, and because the water takes your weight, even those with joint and other movement problems can enjoy this form of exercise.

Something to do

It is not necessary to invest a lot of time and energy to enjoy the benefits of exercise—even a moderate exercise routine will be beneficial. Here are a few suggestions to help you get started:

- Begin with a goal of doing moderate exercise for 30 minutes (or two 15-minute sessions) a day, five days a week.
- Start slowly and build up your routine as you gain confidence. In only a few weeks you will notice an increase in your stamina.
- Anything that raises your heartbeat, makes you feel warm, and causes you to breathe more heavily than usual can be considered moderate exercise. Brisk walking, tennis, football, aerobics, cycling, dancing, do-it-yourself activities, table tennis, gardening, housework, and playing with children all count.
- To avoid injury, do a few warm-up and cool-down stretches before and after exercising.
- If you have any medical disorders, you should always consult your doctor before starting a new exercise routine.
- For motivation and enjoyment, join a gym or exercise class with a friend, work colleague, or family member.

Stimulating your mental abilities

The brain is an incredible organ. It is constantly learning new skills and storing new memories.

Besides being responsible for controlling our body systems, the brain enables us to think, feel, and act. It constantly adapts itself according to signals from the world around us and our internal thoughts. These changes occur in many ways and over various timescales.

Building the brain

Psychologist Ian Robertson, a professor at Trinity College in Dublin, is an expert in rebuilding brains damaged by strokes and car accidents. He says, "Learning sculpts the brain. It crochets intricate new patterns in the trembling web of connections between neurones." Developing a physical skill also causes the brain to develop and grow. One example is when children learn to play a musical instrument. The planum temporale, which is in the left side of the brain, is bigger in musicians than in others. The planum temporale is vital in processing words and verbal memory, so young musicians also have a head start in verbal skills over their unmusical friends. Another factor for brain growth is starting young. Brain scans show that the students with the most developed minds were not always the best musicians, but the ones who began to learn earliest.

The guru of natural health, Dr. Andrew Weil, believes that the simplest exercise can heal our brains. He instructs patients to stimulate their healing powers by crawling like babies. Crawling sends signals to both sides of the brain—first the right hand and left knee move, then the right knee and left hand. According to Dr. Weil, "This cross-patterned type of movement generates electrical activity in the brain that has a harmonizing influence on the whole central nervous system." It is difficult for an adult to crawl without embarrassing explanations, so Dr. Weil recommends another form of cross-patterned exercise—walking. Walkers swing their left arm as the right leg steps out, then mirror the movement. Dr. Weil pares his advice for exercise to one word—walk! I would add three words—get a dog! Walking the dog gives purpose to your daily exercise. You follow patterns because the dog has to go out no matter what and is used to exercise at particular times—and you have a companion and a pacer on your walks.

Improve your mindpower

No matter your Life Sign, here are several techniques to build your mindpower. Listen to slow baroque music—Bach, Vivaldi, or Handel—especially if you are a Reformer. The body tunes in to concertos whose rhythms pulse at about 60 beats per minute (bpm) and the mind focuses as if in meditation.

Challenge yourself to read deeper books. The Mother Hen will find that an afternoon with a trashy romance will not absorb her mind or excite her emotions as much as time spent on more difficult, yet more rewarding stories.

Explore a new mental territory, such as tackling a new language. Your brain will experience a mental awakening as it absorbs hundreds of words. The Believer should join an evening class; he might enjoy learning about history or physics.

Switch off trash media. The Busy Bee is susceptible to easy sensation, but the artificial emotions of a soap opera, shock-jock radio, and knee-jerk journalism will do her brain no favors.

Try playing a mind game to enhance your visualization skills. Imagine your brain as a camera. Take mental photographs of objects in a room, then "project" those pictures in as much detail as possible on a blank wall. The Magician will enjoy this exercise.

Engage in conversation whenever you can. The Artist may avoid trivial chit-chat, but some of the most enjoyable conversations come at unexpected

moments with people he has never met and will never see again—for example, on a bus or a train.

Stimulate your brain by being a devil's advocate. Get into a debate with colleagues about a contentious issue, and argue for an opinion that is not yours. The Boss will learn from experiencing a novel viewpoint.

Avoid alcohol, even if you are an Actor. It deadens the mind, killing irreplaceable brain cells. Eat and drink healthily, and your mind will crackle into new life. The Intellectual is tempted to propel herself through the day with strong coffee. Try drinking plenty of water, and enjoy a heightened alertness.

For your information

Exercise for the brain

Dr. Rune Timerdal, of the University of Malmö in Sweden, tested 909 people in three different exercise programs. One-third of the group did aerobics, one-third did weights and muscle-building, and the last one-third did nothing. After six months, brain scans showed different exercises boosted different brain skills. Jogging, bicycling, and aerobics had an impact on left-brain activity, such as ability in mathematics, logic, and language. Weight training and body-building activated the right side of the brain, associated with more intuitive, abstract skills.

- The Feelers can benefit most from aerobic exercises, which will stimulate left-brain activity.

- The Thinkers can stimulate their intuitive skills by starting a body-building program.

- The Doers will approach any type of exercise program with enthusiasm—but they need to make sure that they stick to it.

Nine key ways to be your own coach

Having a coach can help you to supercharge your career or reach a personal goal.

A coach can provide the inspiration and guidance to show you how to achieve your target, whether it is being the employee of the month, shedding a few pounds, improving your golf game, or becoming a better bridge player. He is in a position to observe how you are doing and explain where you may be making mistakes—as well as give you positive appraisal. A good coach will make sure that his own desires don't get in the way and provide you with honest, objective, and positive criticism.

For many people, the cost of hiring a professional coach can be prohibitive. However, you can find a 24-hour coach, totally dedicated to your success and good health, who will charge you nothing—yourself. Of course, you will have to be honest with yourself to get the best results. Avoid allowing your emotions to get in the way, and be conscious of all the small details.

You can adopt the nine rules on these pages. Remember that although each lesson is targeted at a weakness that typically afflicts one particular Life Sign type, all of these rules are relevant to everyone.

The Reformer

Make sure you put your good intentions into practice. You know what you want to achieve and how you want to achieve it—but between those two there must inevitably be a degree of compromise. Never be afraid to bend your own rules. There is a lot of truth in the saying, "getting started is half done," so start taking action now. Don't wait for circumstances to be "exactly right" at some unspecified point in the future.

The Mother Hen

Your most difficult challenge will be accepting the end of a relationship. Prepare your mind for the break by cleaning out a part of your office or your home—how about that desk drawer, full of ancient files. Be ruthless, and throw away everything that no longer serves a useful purpose, no matter how useful it might once have been. When this task is done, you will be in a much better psychological frame of mind, ready to tackle anything.

The Actor

Enjoy the present moment. Things are never so bad as you think they are. If you are lamenting the fact that you are another year older or another pound heavier, remember that in 10 years' time you will look back yearningly on today. How bitter it would be if the older you had to admit, "I didn't know when I had it so good!" You are too inclined to judge yourself by your ambitions instead of your achievements, to berate yourself for the things you have yet to do instead of taking satisfaction in what you have done. Write down five things, right now, that make you proud of yourself.

The Artist

It is important that you keep in touch with others. Even if you work alongside colleagues, you might be retreating into your shell and slipping out of contact. If you are part of the trend of working from home, or if you are one of many who have been laid off or have retired, keeping in touch is even more important. It is not only a question of making sure you are aware of all the news, you also need to make sure other people don't forget and overlook you. Be pushy, and exude an air of confidence, even when you are not feeling it.

The Intellectual

 You should act as if others are watching at all times. You prefer to be on your own, untroubled by the office gossip, but this habit can lead to a weakness in self-discipline. Because you have engineered a situation where you can work in peace, you sometimes end up not working at all. Try playing this mind game with yourself. Pretend that a much disliked employer or teacher from your past has given you your current assignment. To make the point that you work best alone, you have to get it finished ahead of the deadline. Do not let that old enemy get the better of you!

The Believer

 Accept that you are an individual person, unique among the team. Their strengths are not necessarily the same as your strengths; their best days will not always be yours. But you do have your own strengths and best days. You must have the courage to be yourself, to work hardest at your best times, and to break off from the pack when you have to. For example, some people work best very early in the day, but they do not put their energy to good use because the majority of the working world are slow starters. If this is you, find out about a few personal heroes who rose very early to plunge straight into work, and make a conscious effort to imitate them.

The Busy Bee

 Keep a diary and look for the patterns that will emerge in it. At some point each day, you are losing time or money, but you are hiding this from

yourself. Your natural distaste for methodology and paperwork make you vulnerable to self-deception. Here is an example from my own experience: When the coffee-shop boom hit England a few years ago, I noticed my resting heartrate shot up six or seven beats per minute. My doctor suggested my caffeine intake might have risen, but I scorned the idea. However, I kept a log of my *grande latte* consumption for a week. It made me realize that I was drinking a lot more coffee than I had thought.

The Boss

 You need to ask yourself the right questions. A professional personal coach would ask you questions that you might prefer to sidestep, and you need to treat yourself with the same ruthlessness. You can pinpoint what others are doing wrong—now it is time for you to objectively and dispassionately apply the same skill to your own actions. Shine a light into the corners of your life that you would like others to overlook. These are the corners that urgently need clearing out—they are full of dead weight and bad memories. You would not hesitate to order a subordinate to take positive action. Now that you are your own coach, you should give yourself orders that must be obeyed.

The Magician

 Your main goal should be to make a real effort to be self-disciplined. You must constantly confront yourself and be alert to the times when your inclination is to take your foot off the accelerator. You are too fond of the easy life, but by taking too many shortcuts you will end up making life more difficult for yourself. When you make a decision, write it down and place this note in a prominent place to constantly remind you of your goal. If you are trying to lose weight, for example, find a photograph of a younger, slimmer you, and tack it to the side of the refrigerator. Every time you go for a snack, you will be confronted by your goal.

Cultivating the will to win

You can learn how to use willpower to make the most of your skills to get ahead at work or improve your talents in a recreational activity.

If you take control of yourself, anything, and everything, becomes possible. By harnessing your willpower with conviction and planning, you can achieve any goal that you set yourself. When you realize that winning is truly possible, as long as you keep your focus, your determination to succeed will soar. Whatever your Life Sign, you can learn to play to win, and work to win, and always come out of every situation on top.

Confident Bosses, introspective Artists, nurturing Mother Hens, conformist Believers—these distinct types seem very different from each other, but all nine Life Signs are united by one common factor. Everyone has a human mind in a human body, fired

Something to do

You can use a piece of paper to show you how your willpower is a state of mind that can be challenged and coaxed. Cut the paper into a square about 2½ inches (6 cm.) on each side, and fold it from top to bottom, then open it up. Fold it from side to side and open it up again. You now have a square piece of paper creased into four smaller squares. Fold it from corner to corner, open it, and fold it along the other diagonal, corner to corner. Now you have a square divided into eight triangles. Pinching it along the diagonals, make it into a star shape.

Take a needle and a small ball of putty. Stick the eye of the needle into the putty, with the sharp tip pointing straight up, and balance the paper star on it. The needle's point should be at the center of the paper where the creases meet, but without piercing it. A light breath or a touch of the finger should set the star spinning smoothly.

Without touching the star or breathing on it, you can make it spin simply by cupping your hand around it or just staring at it. Put your paper spinner on a table and sit in front of it. Rest your elbow comfortably on the surface and bring your open right palm toward the star. Without touching it, curl your fingers around the spinner. Stare at it and breathe evenly and lightly; convince yourself that when the paper starts to turn it will not have anything to do with your breathing.

Focus on the star and urge it silently in your mind to spin. For 30 seconds or so it is likely that nothing will happen. Then the star may start on its axis, very slowly, probably in a counterclockwise direction, and gently spin. A change of hand will bring a reversal of spin.

This is not air currents or body heat, but psychokinesis, a psychic power that most people refuse to accept exists. About 60 percent of Life Signs readers will be able to perform this feat of psychokinesis. It is not anything occult or magical. It is just science that nobody knows how to explain yet. Many readers will find they do not get a result immediately, but success comes after two or three days of increasingly skeptical attempts.

by a human spirit. You try to balance these factors, but in most people the body is dominant, even if they have deep spirituality and intelligence. To gain the willpower to be your best, you have to forget your body and focus your mind on the task. It does not have to be a difficult or unpleasant task—in fact, focus comes more easily when the task is enjoyable.

Achieving focus

A person leading a busy or stressful life will have difficulty focusing on a particular goal. He must learn to put other issues aside, and to have confidence in his ability and a positive attitude before he can completely focus on a specific goal. For example, each time a Mother Hen catches herself about to say "I can't…," she should rephrase the idea without the negative concept. Optimism comes easily to the Actor, and he is not one to be held back by self-doubt. However, sometimes he feels frustrated that other people do not act with his own enthusiasm. He needs to put these thoughts aside and concentrate on his own agenda.

Repeated setbacks can make the Reformer resentful, but if she remains strong, she can put every disappointment aside and focus on new challenges ahead. The Artist should give himself pep talks. By starting an internal monologue, imagining the voice of an energetic, can-do personal coach, he will soon have the confidence to focus on his next goal.

When bad morale is afflicting colleagues and friends, the Believer is susceptible to this negativity and takes on the moods of those around her. By being conscious of this trait, she can guard against it. A positive approach will always go further toward focusing on her target.

With so much to say and too many things in his schedule, the Busy Bee is often tempted to take the easy route and abandon a task to someone less brilliant but

more patient. This is a betrayal of the Busy Bee's talents. He must learn to be focused and finish the job.

Speaking out is sometimes necessary to take control, but this can be tough for the Intellectual and the Magician. By the time they find the courage to speak, the moment has passed. They need to build up their courage by repeating positive affirmations inwardly, "I will be outspoken. I will say what I mean without hesitation." When the time comes for instant courage, they will quickly focus on it.

The Boss often idealizes a period in her past when everything seemed to be easier. But the world changes and the old times will not come back. Instead, the Boss should focus on building a new "golden era" in which she can reign.

Controlling anger

Everyone gets angry at one time or another, but we must all learn how to cope with this raw emotion in a controlled way.

Contrary to popular perception, anger is not just a masculine trait—an equal number of women get just as angry as men. In some situations anger is an appropriate response, but frequent fits of anger benefit no one. It can drive away those you love, and it can trigger others to react violently toward you.

In today's fast-paced society, where there seem to be too few hours in the day to take care of both work and family needs, stress often builds up until it is released in angry outbursts. These can take the form of yelling at a partner or child, who may have done nothing wrong. However, it is now more common for people to turn their outbursts of anger onto strangers, whether it is in the form of verbal abuse while competing to get a seat on a crowded commuter train or a road rage incident, where verbal threats can lead to physical violence and unsafe driving practices can put lives in danger. In fact, road rage has become one of the most common outlets for uncontrolled temper tantrums.

Taking control

There are several techniques to calm a potentially explosive argument. In any situation where anger starts to appear, you should never resort to threats, either verbal or physical. If you threaten to punch someone or raise your fist, you will only stir up more anger—in both yourself and your antagonist. By the same token, stay away from foul language, insults, and abusive name-calling. Another rule is to stick to the argument. Do not drag in new areas of conflict and old grievances. You will simply provoke anger and tap into your own unresolved aggression.

Another efficient technique is to substitute "I" for "you." Do not tell your opponent how she is feeling and what she is doing wrong—that is guaranteed to make anyone mad. State instead how you feel, and what you want. "You've done this all wrong" is an aggressive, counter-productive attack; "I wanted the job done differently, like this," is more likely to achieve a positive result. Talk about yourself and your needs, not the failings of others.

Beware of other people's outbursts. If you are the victim of road rage or verbal attack in a supermarket, for example, step away and keep moving. The Artist should let angry people stew in their own juices and not get drawn in.

Search out the roots of your anger. The Magician in the grip of aggression is usually motivated by a specific event or injustice. She should focus on the source and, if she cannot change it, she should make

From the heart

My favorite phrase when angry is "Let's sleep on it." I am not afraid of confrontation, and I know that many issues need to be faced and talked through—but many more are heated issues of the moment that dissolve overnight. What seems important at first can often be resolved, as long as the mind is operating calmly. "Let's sleep on it," is the perfect cooling-off phrase. It suggests that everyone concerned has a valid point of view; that we are all getting a little heated; that this is an important subject that deserves mature, rational treatment.

a decision to live with it. She should stop seething and carrying around a harmful emotion. If the Reformer is angry on the inside, that anger will build until it has to burst out, often venting itself on an inappropriate and innocent target. He can vent his anger safely, during sport and exercise. By channeling aggression into the gym or onto the pitch, the Believer can enhance his performance.

Small issues can get to people. The Busy Bee should look at life with the proper perspective. It is all small stuff, here today and gone—the same day, very often, within an hour or two. She should let her anger go with it. The Intellectual can practice forgiveness by taking a conscious vow to stop holding grudges. It is a difficult stance to maintain, but all the more rewarding for it. The Actor is naturally successful, capable of grand gestures that others envy. He can avoid dragging himself down to a level of pettiness by being big and turning the other cheek.

The Mother Hen should avoid watching television programs or films that show gratuitous violence—they only serve to teach bad lessons that can creep into her own life. A Boss should avoid alcohol if it provokes him to anger. Alcohol is a depressant, and his usual energy levels will be sapped by excessive drinking.

Becoming better organized

Time is often a commodity in short supply, but by learning how to be more organized, you can make better use of every minute for a happier home life.

Balancing your family, home, and finances is often a juggling act, especially if there is also a job in the equation. All too often, trying to do too much can lead to unproductive stress. By learning how to become better organized, you can reduce stress and make more time for your family and yourself.

The first steps

It is common to lose sleep when worried about how you can manage everything, which only exacerbates the situation. However, the tasks that seem impossi-

ble during the small, dark hours are often perceived as being quite manageable when the mind is rested. The Reformer is susceptible to sleepless nights. He should learn relaxation techniques (see p. 154) to help himself doze off.

Even the Busy Bee cannot do everything at once, so she and others like her need to set priorities. Clear planning can halve the time spent on chores. Start by making a list of everything that needs to be done. To establish the importance of each task, ask how disastrous it would be if a job went undone

until tomorrow. Then set to work on the urgent items first, assigning what needs to be done a day at a time. The Magician often procrastinates; he will have to put aside distractions before he can successfully plan his tasks.

Making time for the needs of your partner and children is important to the stability of any family—it will also be rewarding. Establish a schedule for school runs and activities with your children. Strive to have all your family have their meals together, especially if you are a Believer. Nothing bonds a family so closely as sharing food. The emotional rewards will easily repay the extra effort.

Home care

Establishing routines for repetitive chores, such as doing laundry on Mondays or vacuuming on Tuesdays, is often the best way to organize your household tasks. In this way, they will not pile up. Chores have a rhythm that can be relaxing and even enjoyable. The Boss, for example, often resents the time spent pushing a lawnmower; if he simply gives in to the task, he may enjoy the pattern of it—as well as the sense of achievement that follows.

Getting help is permissible, and encouraged. The Mother Hen does not have to do everything herself. If she finds the ironing or the cleaning or mowing the lawn onerous, she should consider paying someone else to do the job for her, which will allow free time and energy for herself.

Some jobs are best done as you come across them. The Artist's instinct is to leave dropped food on the kitchen floor. However, cleaning it up will take more energy later on than it will at the present time. The Intellectual has a talent for making distasteful jobs become invisible. A visitor would see her living room as a disaster zone. When it comes to cleaning and tidying up, the Intellectual will have to imagine herself as a visitor to her home.

Get rid of clutter, especially if you have a home office—clear your desk of every possible item. Clutter only attracts dust and makes it impossible to find important papers quickly.

Keeping on top of your finances

If you are struggling to pay your bills, work out where your money has gone over the past two months, and what you will need to meet all your essential expenses in the coming month (see pp. 156–157). This includes making credit card payments on time and ensuring that you do not overdraw your checking account even for one day. This may be boring for the lavish Actor, who enjoys spending, but budgeting is important. The cost of interest charges, penalties, and bounced checks can raise monthly expenses by 10 percent—making it inevitable that there will be another financial crisis next month.

For your information

Focusing through prayer

The U.S. Attorney General John Ashcroft begins each morning meeting with prayers. Prayer can bring calm and purpose to any enterprise, including running your home. It helps to focus the mind on the task at hand and to remind our egos that there are greater issues in life than those we are about to face. I often pray for strength and guidance, and, when I am in earnest, my prayers are always answered. Prayer gives me the inner resolve that lets me make changes myself.

 The Feelers are more likely to accept prayer as a way to focus on their homes and families.

 The Thinkers can use prayer to help focus on the best way to become more organized.

 The practical, organized nature of the Doers helps them in every aspect of home life, including daily prayer.

Planning ahead by dreaming ahead

We all have dreams about how we would like our lives to be. By planning ahead, you can take the first steps toward realizing your dreams.

The one thing that remains the same for all the Life Signs is that the future is not preordained. There is one key figure in the creation of your future, and that is you. Even the Believer, if she has faith in herself, can change things if she really wants to.

Taking the first steps

You can start planning ahead by taking a look at your life as it is now and deciding what you like about it—and what needs changing. Perhaps you are a Mother Hen, raising a loving family, but you realize that when the children leave home you will need something else to devote your energy to and occupy your time. Now is the time to think about what you would want to do—for example, become involved with a local volunteer group, take up an interesting new hobby, or open up a small flower shop. Or are you stuck in a boring job, with little chance of change or promotion? Maybe you want to change your career to find fulfillment. If that is the case, then you should start thinking about what that new career will be and whether you will need training or some type of educational degree.

The Busy Bee is forever plunging frenetically into new projects, but the headlong rush of the present should not be allowed to banish all thought of the future. At the pace a Busy Bee seems to live his life, tomorrow will come around too quickly. He needs to prepare his mind for it now.

The second consideration is that without your planning for it, the future will bring its own changes. One of the most certain changes for most people will be your professional position. You may grow in status, or you may be overtaken by others. Particu-

Something to think about

We need to dream. Dreams cleanse the mind. We all dream every night, but some people cannot recall their nocturnal adventures. How wonderful it would be if you not only remembered your dreams, but if you could control them, too—you could meet old friends or visit far-off places. You can do this, through a practice called lucid dreaming.

Start by keeping a journal, a bedside dream book. Whenever you wake, try to remember what your dreamed. If it is still the middle of the night, do not force yourself awake to make your notes—a few simple words are adequate. Later, they may be enough to bring the whole dream back. Practice helps, and the more you experiment with keeping a dream journal, the clearer your memories will become, and the longer they will be retained.

The next step, before you fall asleep, is to use the same spoken formula, "I give myself permission to take control of my dreams, and to stay asleep as I do this." Soon you will be controlling your dreams.

larly in the latter case, the Boss needs to keep her mind flexible and open to challenges.

Once you have established what your dreams are, you need to plan for them, and sometimes they will require financing. For example, a second home or a year-long trip around the world to celebrate your retirement will be expensive. You should study your finances now to determine what your monetary needs will be in the future. Some people will need to force themselves to save. This can be tough for the Actor, who has a tendency to spend money as quickly as he can earn it.

Even if your mind remains constant, your body will change in the future. You can prepare for your future plans by keeping your physique as elastic as your brain. Make commitments to a sensible schedule of exercise now. The Intellectual needs to guard against putting off exercise until some unknown time in the future—in reality, this will mean never.

People grow as time passes, and relationships change. The people you know and love will alter in ways subtle and not-so-subtle. If the Magician grows with the times, she will keep her friends.

Coping with setbacks

When things do not go according to plan, your priority should be to adjust to the new reality. Clinging to old hopes will slow you down and could lead to unhealthy resentment. The Reformer, for example, should remember that there is a new future shaping up, and he should get ready to embrace it.

Some people have a fear of the future based on past experiences. The worst thing about fears is that they prevent you from trying new experiences—as well as their alarming capacity to create whatever is most dreaded. The Artist, in particular, should learn to put aside the past and to engage her mind in some enjoyable dreams to generate a better future.

Every life features its fair share of afflictions, but some people seem to have more bad luck than others. They need to teach themselves to be tough and to endure the difficulties—but remember, better times will always follow.

Realizing your dreams

By being persistent and remaining strong in your self-belief, you can make your dreams come true.

As you use the Life Signs patterns to reach for your own dreams, always be aware that some things are invisible or unknown to you. You might find that achieving your dreams will come easier than you expect but, more likely, unexpected circumstances will get in the way. The most important thing is to never give up hope—you must believe in yourself and your dreams if they are to be reached.

> **"FOR TRUE SUCCESS ASK YOURSELF THESE FOUR QUESTIONS: WHY? WHY NOT? WHY NOT ME? WHY NOT NOW?"**
>
> James Allen, American essayist (1849–1925)

Reaching for your goals

To see what is possible, look around you at what others have and how they have achieved them. If others can do it, so can you. The Intellectual is the least envious of people—he will find it easy to be happy for others for their own sake. Now he should take those achievers for his role models, and make it happen for himself. Whatever you desire to achieve, go for it and do not hold back. You can do it if you maintain the highest level of self-belief. This is where the Actor's talents are most valuable—she can energize herself with her own visions.

Set aside feelings of guilt when you want to make your life more fun. Perhaps you would like to learn salsa—go to the class and do not listen to that small voice saying that you should be doing something for others. The Mother Hen should remember that self-neglect is the worst neglect of all.

Always believe in yourself. For example, if you would like to learn to draw, but have held back from joining a drawing class because you fear you lack the talent, walk away from the negativity that is holding you back. The Magician should remember that we are all multi-talented beings. How does he know what he can do until he tries?

Meeting the challenge

Complete what you set out to do. By leaving work unfinished, you establish a record of failure that your subconscious will emulate in the future. Set up a pattern of achievement instead. The Reformer should learn that it is better to finish an imperfect project than to leave a perfect one unfinished.

As you pursue your dreams, the path ahead can become dark and twisting. Within reason, you should stick to your decisions about where you want to be and what you desire to achieve, but be prepared to make changes if your original plans are not

---

From the heart

I believe that, where some skills and talents are concerned, there will always be others who are able to progress more quickly than I can. For example, I am slow in math. Although others are going forward at a great rate, that does not mean that I am going backward. I am making progress at my own speed, heading toward the goal, the ambition, the dream. I will get there, and when I acquire confidence, when I understand the problem, I might accelerate suddenly. So watch out if I'm behind you—this can only mean that I'm in position to overtake you.

possible. The Artist should not be afraid to continue along a diverted path. People need to know when to take small steps and when to leap. If a choice is difficult, remember the words of the British Prime Minister David Lloyd George, who said that small steps would not carry you over a chasm—only a great leap would do. The Believer must learn when to risk it and take that great leap.

Celebrate your victories. By marking each success, you will instill a sense of achievement in your spirit that your subconscious mind will be eager to emulate. The Boss will find that he is living with a greater sense of enjoyment and fulfillment.

A word of caution: Get-rich-quick plans are inviting illusions, especially the so-called "pyramid schemes," which require you to give someone your own money before you see a promised return. What better way to open the way to a more rewarding life? Sadly, if it were possible to get rich through these schemes, we would all have done it long ago. If you are a Busy Bee, it is time to stop longing for a lottery win and take command of your life.

Nine key ways to attract wealth

Although it is unlikely that you will become a millionaire, you can increase your wealth, as well as make the most of what you already have.

I have always believed it would be wrong to use my psychic abilities to gamble for wealth. As a young man, I once won a great deal of money at the roulette table. But on my way home, I felt guilty, as if I had betrayed myself and my gift. I struggled out of the car and hurled the cash away from me. I have always hoped that the money found its way to someone who truly needed it.

To pray for money is not wrong, if your need is real. George Muller, who ran children's charities in England for over 30 years, raised funds by prayer alone. He never asked anyone for aid, yet it was always given. Your own needs are not likely to be as great, but they will be important to you.

Increasing your wealth does not necessarily mean becoming rich. Many families can benefit from just a little extra cash to help make ends meet. Or there might be something special that you are saving for—a wedding anniversary celebration or your child's college education. This might mean bringing in some extra income. However, you might already be earning enough money to meet your goals, but you are not spending your money wisely. You can try the following nine techniques for attracting wealth to your wallet and your home. Although each technique is especially suited to a particular Life Sign type, any of the types can benefit from it.

The Reformer

You should identify the areas of work where you spend a lot of time but make little money. Some business analysts have found that many firms typically spend 80 percent of their time dealing with only 20 percent of their clients—and these clients are often not the most profitable ones. You should keep a record of how you spend your time the next month, and compare your workload to your best sources of income. Then refocus, concentrating on your best clients—or on finding more like them. Even if you do not own your own business, an employer who is making more money because of your actions may show his gratitude through a bonus or pay increase.

The Mother Hen

You can save money by analyzing your household and personal spendings. Keep a record of your expenses for a few months. You can enter every bill into a spreadsheet if you have a computer. Even if you simply make a list of what you spend, you will soon see where the money is going. Identify every payment that, with hindsight, was less than strictly necessary. Count up these figures and you will be shocked at the money you are wasting. You could be saving that cash. Do something about it.

The Actor

Before you can save money, you need to deal with your debts. No one can be wealthy while they have unpaid credit card bills mounting up. The catastrophic compound rates of interest charged by some card companies—up to 30 percent—do more than drain your bank account. Paying off a large monthly interest can make it difficult to pay off the original amount borrowed, so you do not make any gain toward lowering your debt. This cycle can sap your will to make money. You need to make sure that you pay off more than the interest each month until you eventually wipe away the debt. When you have clawed your way out of the red, make a deal with yourself to save a set percentage of each month's income. It is staggering how quickly your money will grow if you invest 10 percent of your earnings at a compound rate of interest.

The Artist

Any past failures are irrelevant. You had debts, but that does not mean you have an excuse to run them up again. You are vulnerable to allowing your credit cards bills to mount up but, now that you have the benefit of greater maturity and experience, you can exert more control. You may also have made bad investments or been bamboozled by clever salesmen in the past, but you have learned your lessons. Now it is time to believe in your capacity for success—it is real and it exists.

The Intellectual

Why try to achieve wealth on your own, when there are people who can help you? Find a mentor and emulate his experience. However, this is not only about investment opportunities and accounting practices, perhaps recommended by a financial advisor. Take a look at your personal appearance, telephone technique, time management skills, and public speaking ability. All these elements affect how you impress other people, and a better impression will make others more likely to invest in you.

The Believer

Embrace any new technology available to you. To maximize the present, you have to adapt to the future. If you are living in a state of willingness and readiness, you will feel more confident and appear more able. New technology is a tool, not the whole of the future, and by gaining new skills as quickly as possible, you are making a serious investment in yourself. Beware of colleagues with negative attitudes to new technology—negativity is contagious, and it can infect every part of the corporation.

The Busy Bee

You need to take time to recuperate. Working long hours during the week and weekends will run you down. After a vacation, make a mental note of how much your energy levels have risen. Your life would be more successful if you could sustain those levels—and you can, if you permit yourself more time off. A day off, or a long weekend can massively recharge your morale and will to win, paying major dividends on the time invested in rest.

The Boss

Invest in your mind. It is your greatest asset, so build it up and make it pay. If you watch television, make sure there is some value in the programs you choose—documentaries can be as entertaining as soap operas, and you will be increasing your understanding of the world, laying down riches in your subconscious, which could emerge as riches in your pocket. Radio shows and current affairs journals may be more rewarding than television.

The Magician

Instead of sitting back and waiting for it to happen, make a plan for wealth. Imagine your life with money. Confront your current living standards and visualize an improvement in income and savings. Spend money in your mind—believe that you can be more wealthy. Do not keep this plan locked away in your mind—write it down and think big. Drive vagueness out of the picture. You have got to know exactly what you want before you can go for it.

Making more of your leisure time

For adults in today's fast-paced lifestyle, finding time to unwind can seem like another demand, another item to add to an already busy schedule.

Learning how to relax and enjoy your leisure time is an essential ingredient for an active life—not a luxury. All work and no play makes a person increasingly ineffective in all areas of her life. Fatigue saps performance, with tasks taking longer and more mistakes being made. Constant tension also affects your body, causing aches and pains, digestive problems, and raising blood pressure. Even your appetite can be affected, and missed or rushed meals only add to tiredness. The good news is that all of these effects can be countered with relaxation.

Learning to relax

You need to learn how to relax before you can truly enjoy your leisure time. There are quick fixes that can give instant relaxation, such as sports, yoga, and meditation (see p. 154). Some people are inclined to be skeptical of spiritual development, especially the Boss, unless there is an element of physical activity. He can find out about yoga classes close to his home, or learn an Eastern art of self-defense, such as tai chi chu'an—these disciplines hone the body as well as the mind. The Mother Hen must remember that she needs time for herself, so she should not feel guilty about taking these classes. These activities often involve spiritual discipline, and the Actor can be tempted to look for a shortcut that involves no discipline. He needs to avoid falling into the trap of using alcohol—in the long run it may only increase his stress.

Whether you have reached retirement age or are just starting your adult years, you will benefit from taking a break to relax and enjoy yourself.

Something to do

Here are some tips for relaxing that don't require you to invest much time or energy to enjoy them.

- Take a break each day to spend at least 5 to 10 minutes outdoors in fresh air.
- Spend about 10 to 15 minutes each day on a body-mind relaxation technique, such as meditation (see p. 154).

- Do something that is completely unconnected with your work two or three times a week.
- If you are feeling awake at bedtime, relax in a warm bath or enjoy a cup of warm milk.
- Do not neglect your friends and family. Find a few minutes to make a phone call, and turn to them when you need support—but don't forget to return the favor in their times of need.

Take a vacation, especially when you feel you should keep working. No one can be at their best when they are denied proper rest. Even the Busy Bee needs, and deserves, a break. If you cannot wait until you can take time off from work, send your mind on vacation with a few minutes of visualization. Imagine a room in a city or town that you would like to visit. Picture it, explore it, furnish it. Let the sun shine in the windows and imagine yourself relaxing in this secret place. This visualization will always be helpful to the Artist.

Allow some time for physical enjoyment. If you are in a loving relationship, sexual and nonsexual contact is a wonderful blessing. If you are alone, pamper your body with a massage and a pedicure at a health spa—even if you are an Intellectual.

The best antidotes to daily strain are your family and friends. A Believer who is surrounded by children and grandchildren, or who discovers a different type of family by joining a social activity, such as a choir or drama group, is sure to find relaxation.

Enjoying your leisure time

If you feel you never have enough leisure time, there may be a simple, one-word explanation: television. For many people, television is a time glutton, sucking away your spare moments into its screen. I am not talking about an hour spent watching a favorite show—I am warning against TV drift, where you spend endless time watching programs that you did not need or want to see. It is a few seconds spent staring at a chat show or the news that somehow stretches to claim 15 or 20 minutes. And yet it seems so innocuous; how could it be responsible for taking over all of your leisure time? Do not take my word for it—try keeping a journal. Each time you turn on the television, make a note of how long you have been watching it. At the end of the week, count up the hours—time that could have been spent doing something more enjoyable and rewarding.

Instead of watching television, spend time with family or friends, perhaps going for a walk or attending a sports activity. Alternatively, take up a hobby. At first, you might make excuses that you are too tired, but if you follow my advice for becoming relaxed, you will soon have energy for your leisure time. Your choices are endless—you could sing, dance, read, write, garden, draw, or learn to play a guitar. It is up to you to decide what you want to do with your time.

Hobbies are for fun and should be kept lighthearted. The Reformer must remember that if she becomes obsessed with her hobby, it will cease to be fun for anyone, including her family. Music is one hobby that has the power to transport you to realms of peace and mental freedom. Indulge this aspect if you have the Magician's mind, especially by enjoying live concerts instead of being content with second-hand recorded music.

Taking joy in everything

Joy is not an elusive emotion. As long as we know how to recognize it, joy can be discovered at any time and anywhere.

Happiness, which is the long-term endurance of joy, is rare indeed, but the absence of happiness does not mean there must be sadness. Even when life is giving you few chances at happiness, you can take joy in something. The banal, the commonplace, the insignificant, the petty, the everyday—all these are sources of joy. We can all feel a little happiness by learning how to appreciate the simple things in life.

University of Michigan psychologist Norbert Schwarz has shown that the most trivial things can make us surprisingly happy. He asked two groups of students to do photocopying for him. When each student from the first group went to the photo-copier machine, he found a dime on the lid. For the second group, there was no dime. When each student had completed the copying, Schwarz asked, "Taking all things together, how happy are you with your life as a whole?" The students who were a dime

From the heart

I was rushing to catch a train, and at the train station I glanced up at a clock and saw I had only a few minutes before the train was due to leave. I was in Busy Bee mode, which emerges when I am under stress. It suddenly occurred to me that there were no numerals on the clock. I stared at it for 20 seconds, and I was struck with the beauty of this timepiece, with its long dark hands against a marble face and bright bulbs set on each hour. As I took joy in the clock, the Busy-ness ebbed away. I turned slowly away and strolled to catch my train.

richer were also significantly happier! One tiny piece of "luck" had lifted their whole outlook.

Learning to slow down

Physically slowing down is counterintuitive for the Doers, but they should try it anyway and learn from the experience. By spending a weekend without the news, the Busy Bee will discover some leisure in which he can find more enjoyable ways to spend his time. The Believer will learn by leaving her car at home for the day. If she travels by foot or bicycle, she will have time to observe all that is around her. The Boss may think that he needs to work non-stop to show how important he is in the office. However, taking a few minutes to relax will refresh his mind and make him more productive in the long run.

Slowing down will maximize your emotions, a benefit for the Feelers. The Mother Hen is prone to doing too much for others. If she stops to relax, she might learn to appreciate her family and friends simply for their company. She does not have to be constantly doing something for them. The Reformer is full of opinions, but sometimes he rushes to get his ideas out. By keeping quiet and listening to other people, he may discover new thoughts that will intrigue him. The world is a brilliant canvas of vibrant colors. The Magician has the ability to see its wonder by taking a look at the sky or a tree in the same way as she would look at a painting.

Your mind needs to slow down, too, so the Thinkers need to find ways to slow down the rush of their thoughts. Fun for fun's sake is okay, especially when you are young. However, fun is okay at any

For your information

Money isn't everything

Money will not make you happy. This old adage was recently proven by researcher Philip Brickman at Northwestern University, who studied lottery winners. He noted that, once the winners' initial euphoria subsided, happiness levels quickly reverted to normal. Another academic, University of Virginia psychologist Timothy Wilson explains the phenomena by theorizing that our minds have an immune system like our bodies, which enables us to adjust to shocks without suffering full-scale personality changes.

● The Feelers, who care more for emotions than material items, are less likely to worry about money.

● The deep thoughts of the Thinkers will reveal to them that joy does not depend on money.

● The Doers might think that money will help them achieve their goals. They can learn to turn to the simple things for happiness.

age. The Intellectual can learn that life is not all education—kicking a ball about can be a great release. Ambition has brought the Actor a long way, and it will carry him further yet. But the Actor sometimes forgets to savor what he has right now. He should occasionally set aside his ambition for a while and enjoy the moment. On the other hand, the Artist can find it easy to waste the evening away, simply staring into space. She will find it more rewarding to call a friend or pick up a hobby. The simple pleasure of finishing a jigsaw puzzle or putting the final touches on a painting will be far more rewarding.

What's next?

Now that you have learned the basics about the Life Signs, you can apply them to yourself—and to others—to make the most of your life.

"What's next?" I thought. Anything can be next! Human beings are truly limitless creatures. We are limited only by our imaginations and our determination. As our minds grow, so does our potential—and there are no known boundaries to what the human mind can achieve. There are mysteries we have not solved, challenges we have not conquered—but I emphatically believe that they will be overcome in time. What's next? Everything, if you put your mind to it.

Final thoughts

All of the strongest qualities in each of the Life Signs are open to you. You do not have to be a Boss to learn inspirational modes of behavior, dynamic decision-making, energizing ways of speaking, and galvanizing patterns of achievement. You do not have to be a Magician to learn the arts of making peace and winning friends, matching compromise with assertiveness, and loving the present moment. You do not have to be an Artist to acquire deep self-knowledge, to face your weaknesses, to find original and compelling ways of self-expression, and to inspire others to explore their own creativity. Many of these paths may have appeared to be barred to you before you discovered Life Signs. Now, by understanding how certain skills come more easily to certain personality types, you can pursue your goals without blaming or doubting yourself when some virtues are harder to achieve than others. Here are some final thoughts for each of the Life Signs, and, as always, they apply to all the types:

By accepting her Life Sign and trying to understand the other Signs, the Reformer will be able to set aside her perfectionism. It has driven her to great achievements, but it sometimes holds her back.

The greatest lesson for the Mother Hen is to be as generous to himself as he is to others. This means finding time for his own needs, because someone who neglects himself cannot truly care for others.

Life Signs will help the Actor turn the focus away from her own personality and ego and enable her to understand the needs of others. From here, it is a short step to offering help and guidance.

Great talents are locked inside every person. In the Artist they are locked more securely, because the talent is so much greater. By finding the key to express himself, his heart and soul will pour forth.

To reach out to other human beings is the most vital thing the Intellectual can do. She often prefers to remain alone, and she may even fear contact, but the rewards she will experience when she connects with others will outweigh any doubts and fears.

The Believer is a tribal personality, intensely loyal to those who are like him. He is learning to trust others who are not like him, not part of his society. When his tribe is all of humanity, he will be a consummate and contented Believer.

The Busy Bee's wonderful talents require discipline and self-control, and it is this that she can learn with the aid of Life Signs. Whenever her spirit runs riot, she needs to recognize the risk and rein it in.

The Boss devotes great energy to outward success and earns admiration. With Life Signs, he can turn that energy inward to a spiritual realm that in the past he did not understand.

The Magician's life is a journey of development and learning, whose goal is to understand the head, heart, and soul. The wisdom she gains through the Life Signs is taking her much farther on that journey.

For your information

A story of inspiration

Ruth Steward was recovering from a near-fatal accident when she asked for my help to compete in the London Marathon to raise funds for a charity. Still convalescing, she lacked fitness and practice, but Ruth was determined to compete—what she needed from me was an energy boost.

I taught Ruth mantras, mental refrains to energize her mind. I empowered an amethyst for her. "That's the energy," I told her, "which will be released into your body as you run." Ruth's Life Sign is the Believer, and she needed belief in herself to propel her through the race. She crossed the finish line in only 4 hours, 10 minutes.

- Fear is a powerful force that can drive the Feelers to their goal. Brave souls feel and welcome fear.

- The higher the Thinkers aim, the higher they fly; they have no need for doubt and cynicism.

- There is no limit to what the Doers can do with determination and stamina. They should unleash their strong willpower.

Reformer, Mother Hen, Actor, or Artist; Believer, Intellectual, or Busy Bee; Boss, or Magician—whatever your personality type, your mind is unique. I hope this book has enabled you to acquire a formidable set of mental tools to stretch your mind and access new strengths of purpose and self-confidence. I hope you have enjoyed the journey as much as I have. Most of all, I hope that you are electrified with determination and buoyed with energy to keep your mind, body, and spirit filled with joy and love every step of the way through the journey of your life.

About Uri Geller

Many of us are aware of Uri's spoon-bending powers, but he has many other talents.

Uri Geller has been studied by many scientists. One of the world's most prestigious scientific magazines, *Nature,* published a paper on Uri Geller's work at the Stanford Research Institute in the United States—a unique endorsement and an irrefutable proof that his powers are genuine. His work with the FBI and CIA has ranged from using mind power to wipe KGB computer files and tracking serial killers to attending nuclear disarmament negotiations to bombard and influence delegates with positive thought waves to sign the Nuclear Arms Reduction Treaty. For decades this aspect of his career was too confidential and controversial to discuss.

To provide himself the financial freedom to help others, Uri has used his psychic gifts to detect oil and precious metals. Uri's tireless dedication to charitable work led to his appointment as Honorary Vice-President of the Royal Hospital for Children in Bristol and the Royal Berkshire Hospital, both in England.

Uri's drawings, paintings, and artworks have been exhibited in major galleries and museums in the United States, Europe, Japan, and Israel. His pottery, crystals, glass, and natural rock crystal jewelry creations are in great demand worldwide.

Quotes about Uri Geller

The following is a small sampling of the many people who have observed and commented on Uri's psychic abilities. You can learn more about Uri and discover more quotes by visiting his website—uri-geller.com.

"I was in scientific laboratories at Stanford Research Institute investigating a rather amazing individual Uri Geller. Uri's ability to perform amazing feats of mental wizardry is known the world over. We in science are just now catching up and understanding what you can do with exercise and proper practice.

Uri is *not* a magician. He is using capabilities that we all have and can develop with exercise and practice." Dr. Edgar D. Mitchell D. S. C., Apollo 14 Astronaut and the sixth man to walk on the moon.

"Geller has bent my ring in the palm of my hand without ever touching it. Personally, I have no scientific explanation for the phenomena." Dr. Wernher von Braun, NASA scientist.

"Geller altered the lattice structure of a metal alloy in a way that cannot be duplicated. There is no present scientific explanation as to how he did this." Eldon Byrd, U.S. Naval Surface Weapons Center, Maryland.

"I think Uri is a magician, but I don't particularly believe that he is using trickery. I believe there are psychic abilities. They don't accord with any science we have at the moment, but maybe some future science will back them up with theories." Brian Josephson, Professor of Physics, University of Cambridge and winner of the Nobel Prize for Physics, 1973.

Books by Uri Geller

Uri has been involved in the creation of a number of books, both factual and fiction. Below is a list of other books by Uri:

Confessions of a Rabbi and a Psychic
Robson/Source, Chicago, 2001

Mind Medicine
Chrysalis, London, 2001, Barnes & Noble, 2002

Unorthodox Encounters
Robson, London, 2001

Uri Geller's ParaScience Pack
van der Meer, Great Britain, 2000

Dead Cold
Headline Feature, London, 1999

Ella
Headline Feature, London, 1998

Uri Geller's Little Book of Mind Power
Robson, London, 1998

Uri Geller's Mind-Power Kit
Penguin, New York/Virgin, London, 1996

Change Your Life in One Day
Marshall Cavendish, London, 1990

Shawn
Goodyear Associates, Great Britain, 1990

The Geller Effect
Henry Holt/Jonathan Cape/Grafton, 1986

Uri Geller's Fortune Secrets
Sphere, London, 1987

My Story
Praeger, New York/Robson, London/Warner,
New York, 1975

Recommended reading

In researching the many issues that have appeared in *Uri Geller's Life Signs,* Uri has found the following books helpful:

Butler, Gillian and Tony Hope *Manage Your Mind*
Oxford University, England, 1995

Eysenck, Hans and Carl Sargent *Explaining the Unexplained*
Multimedia Books, London, 1982

Fordham, Frieda *An Introduction to Jung's Psychology*
Penguin Books, London, 1953

Godwin, Malcolm *The Lucid Dreamer*
Element Books, Shaftesbury, Dorset, England, 1995

Gracian, Baltasar, translated by Christopher Maurer
The Art of Worldly Wisdom
William Heinemann, London, 1993

Gregory, Richard (ed) *The Oxford Companion to the Mind*
Oxford University, England, 1987

Handy, Charles *The Hungry Spirit: Beyond Capitalism, a Quest for Purpose in the Modern World*
Broadway Books, New York, 1999

Mitchell, Edgar *Psychic Exploration*
GP Putnam's Sons, New York, 1974

Moir, Anne and David Jessel *BrainSex: The Real Difference Between Men and Women*
Dell Books, New York, 1993

Ostrander, Sheila and Lynn Schroeder *SuperLearning*
Souvenir Press, London, 1979

Riso, Don Richard *Discovering Your Personality Type*
Houghton Mifflin Co, New York, 1995

Schwarz, Berthold Eric *Parent-Child Telepathy*
Garrett Publications, New York, 1971

Watson, Lyall *Jacobson's Organ and the Remarkable Nature of Smell*
W. W. Norton and Co., New York, 2000

Wilson, Glenn and Chris McLaughlin *Winning With Body Language*
Bloomsbury Publishing, London, 1996

Zohar, Danah and Ian Marshall *Spiritual Intelligence*
Bloomsbury Publishing, London, 2000

Index

Note:

Main references are in **bold**. Page numbers in *italic* refer to captions for illustrations.

Acknowledgments

Illustration credits

Nine Life Signs artwork by Patrick Mulrey.

Life Signs symbols
Artist, Believer, Boss, Busy Bee, Doer, Intellectual, Magician, Mother Hen, Thinker: Digital Vision
Actor: Randy Faris/CORBIS
Reformer: William James Warren/CORBIS
Feelers Heart taken from plate designed by Uri Geller

Portrait of Uri Geller provided by Carlton TV

All other images provided by Digital Vision except:

t = top; **b** = bottom; **l** = left; **r** = right

2/3 Vicky Emptage/Illustration Works; **6t** Getty Images/Keith Brofsky; **6tc** Getty Images/Robin Lynne Gibson; **6cb** Getty Images/Kellie Walsh; **6b** Getty Images/Conny Kalfus;**7t** Getty Images/White.Packert; **7tc** Getty Images/Piecework Productions; **7cb** Getty Images/Bruce Ayres; **7b** Getty Images/Paul Simcock; **10/11** Getty Images; **12** theartarchive; **14/15** Getty Images/Ken Fisher; **19** AKG; **21r** Digital Art/CORBIS; **28** Laura Wickenden; **29** Camargue PLC; **35** Laura Wickenden; **37** Laura Wickenden; **40t** Matthew Ward; **40b** Bruce Wolf; **41b** Clive Corless; **42** Reed Kaestner/CORBIS; **44** Michael Lewis/CORBIS; **46** Craig Aurness/CORBIS; **48** Laura Wickenden; **49t** Jay Syverson/CORBIS; **49b** Dave G. Houser/CORBIS; **54** Larry Lee Photography/CORBIS; **58** Steve Raymer/CORBIS; **59** Lennan Ward/CORBIS; **60** Brigitte Bruyes/CORBIS; **62/63** Getty Images/Robin Lynne Gibson; **68/69** Joe McDonald/CORBIS; **79** Eric Crichton/CORBIS; **83** Getty Images/Malcolm Piers; **87** Michael Boys/CORBIS; **88/89** Getty Images/Kellie Walsh; **91** Vicky Emptage/Illustration Works; **94** Getty Images/Jerome Tisne;**110/1** Getty Images/Conny Kalfus;**114b** Claudia Dulac ; **114/5** Claudia Dulac; **116** Ronnie Kaufman/CorbisStockmarket; **119** Superstock; **123** Getty Images; **125** Getty Images/Ghislain and Marie David de Lossy; **128** Getty Images/Ron Chapple; **132** Ronnie Kaufman/CorbisStockmarket; **136/7** Getty Images/White.Packert; **139** Vicky Emptage/Illustration Works; **142/3** Getty Images/David McGlynn; **145** Walter Hodges/CORBIS; **146/7** Michele Warner/Illustration Works; **148** Getty Images/Dennis Galante; **150** Getty Images/Charles Thatcher; **153** Getty Images/ Ron chapple; **154** Tom Stewart/Corbis Stockmarket; **157** Getty Images/Christian Michaels; **158** Getty Images/Chris Lomas; **161** Laura Wickenden; **162/3** Getty Images/ Piecework Productions; **164** Getty Images/Roy Ooms; **166/7** Getty Images/Mark Wright; **168** Getty Images/Andrew Judd; **172** Getty Images/Nicholas Rigg; **175** Getty Images/Klauss;**179** Getty Images/Michael Llewellyn; **180/1** Getty Images/Bruce Ayres; **182** Superstock; **186** Getty Images/Ray-Mel Cornelius; **188** Getty Images/Alberto Ruggieri; **190** Robert Harding Picture Library; **193** Getty Images/John Labbe; **197** Getty Images/Gary Kaemmer; **200** Digital Art/CORBIS; **203** Getty Images/Alberto Ruggieri; **206/7** Getty Images/Paul Simcock; **208/9** Getty Images/Philip Lee Harvey; **210** Getty Images/Spencer Rowell; **212** Getty Images/Gary Kaemmer; **217** Getty Images/John Labbe; **220** Images Colour Library; **222&224** Getty Images/Steven Hunt; **228** Robert Harding Picture Library; **230/1** Getty Images/Peter Sherrard; **232** Getty Images/John Labbe.

Every effort has been made to trace the copyright holders. Marshall Editions apologizes for any unintentional omissions and, if informed of any such cases, would be pleased to update future editions.